Nourishing Desire

Nourishing Desire

A Guide to Sexual Recovery and Discovery for People with Eating Disorders

Jessica Singh, PhD, LCSW, CST

Jessica Kingsley Publishers
London and Philadelphia

First published in Great Britain in 2026 by Jessica Kingsley Publishers
An imprint of John Murray Press

I

Copyright © Jessica Singh 2026

The right of Jessica Singh to be identified as the Author of the Work has been
asserted by her in accordance with the Copyright, Designs and Patents Act 1988.

The information contained in this book is not intended to replace the services
of trained medical professionals or to be a substitute for medical advice. You
are advised to consult a doctor on any matters relating to your health, and in
particular on any matters that may require diagnosis or medical attention.

A CIP catalogue record for this title is available from the
British Library and the Library of Congress

ISBN 978 1 80501 954 1
eISBN 978 1 80501 953 4

Printed and bound in the United States by Integrated Books International

Jessica Kingsley Publishers' policy is to use papers that are natural, renewable
and recyclable products and made from wood grown in sustainable
forests. The logging and manufacturing processes are expected to conform
to the environmental regulations of the country of origin.

Jessica Kingsley Publishers
Carmelite House
50 Victoria Embankment
London EC4Y 0DZ

www.jkp.com

John Murray Press
Part of Hodder & Stoughton Ltd
An Hachette Company

The authorised representative in the EEA is Hachette Ireland,
8 Castlecourt Centre, Dublin 15, D15 XTP3, Ireland (email: info@hbgi.ie)

To my dear mother-in-law, Somi

Your unwavering support, boundless kindness, and gentle spirit have shaped me in ways that words cannot fully express. Though you are no longer with us, your love and wisdom continue to guide me every day. Thank you for always believing in me, for your encouragement, and for being a constant source of light.

Contents

Acknowledgments

I would like to express my heartfelt gratitude to all those who have made this book possible. While the list is too long to fully capture, I must take a moment to thank my wonderful husband, Roy, my amazing children, Isis and Rami, my loving mother, Zoraida Rosario, and my dear friends and sisters, Amanda Kingsley and Candy Gabriente, for their unwavering support, encouragement, patience, and all the little things that made this journey possible.

A special thank you goes to Dr. Marsha Linehan, Dr. Thomas R. Lynch, Dr. Andréa Poyastro Pinheiro, Dr. Kamryn T. Eddy, Dr. Cara Dunkley, and all the brilliant clinicians and researchers whose work laid the foundation for this workbook. Their dedication to their craft continues to inspire me. I am also deeply grateful to Dr. Judy Scheel and Dr. Rachel Needle for their guidance and support during my doctoral journey, which shaped much of the research behind this workbook.

Finally, I want to thank my clients, whose lessons and insights have been invaluable in shaping this work. Your experiences have made this possible, and I am grateful for all that I've learned from you.

Preface

As someone who has lived through the struggles of an eating disorder, I have a deep understanding of the complexities involved in recovery. For 15 years, I battled with my own relationship with food, my body, and intimacy. During that time, I became acutely aware of how these struggles permeated all aspects of my life—including my ability to connect emotionally and physically with others. It was only through the challenging and often painful process of recovery that I learned the importance of cultivating a healthy relationship with my body and, subsequently, with intimacy and connection.

I am Dr. Jessica Singh, a certified sex therapist and clinical sexologist with over a decade of experience working with individuals and couples. I hold advanced degrees in clinical social work and clinical sexology, and I am a trained specialist in eating disorder recovery, with a focus on the complex intersections between body image, sexual health, and emotional well-being. My journey from struggling with an eating disorder to becoming a psychotherapist has been both transformative and humbling.

In my work as a psychotherapist, I support individuals from all walks of life—of various genders, ages, and backgrounds—who are navigating their own paths to healing from eating disorders. Over the years, one common theme has emerged in my practice: even after progress in recovery, many individuals find that their relationship to intimacy remains fractured. They may experience feelings of isolation, anxiety, or even shame when it comes to sex and connection. As I witnessed this struggle time and time again, I felt compelled to create a resource that could help individuals reclaim their intimacy and explore their sexuality with confidence and compassion.

This workbook is the result of that desire. It is a tool for anyone who has ever felt disconnected from their body, their desires, or their ability to experience intimacy. Whether you're in the early stages of recovery or have been working on healing for years, this workbook provides practical exercises, reflections, and insights designed to help you understand and navigate the complex interplay between eating disorders, body image, and sexuality.

Throughout this journey, I invite you to approach this work with curiosity and compassion. As you move through the material, be gentle with yourself. Some of the topics may be uncomfortable or challenging, but remember that discomfort is often a part of the healing process. Each step forward—no matter how small—is a victory in reclaiming your capacity for connection, joy, and pleasure.

This workbook was created with the understanding that there is no one-size-fits-all approach to healing. Each person's path is unique, and recovery involves embracing your individuality. Whether you are struggling with anorexia, bulimia, or any form of disordered eating, you will find tools here that can be adapted to your needs. My hope is that as you work through this material, you will find a path that feels authentic to you and your journey.

Please remember that you are not alone in this process. I know what it feels like to be trapped in isolation, to feel disconnected from your body and from others. But I also know that it is possible to heal and reclaim a life filled with intimacy and connection. As you embark on this journey, I am here with you, offering support and encouragement every step of the way.

This is your journey. It is one of healing, transformation, and ultimately, rediscovery of the person you truly are. Welcome.

Name It

— CHAPTER 1 —

Introduction

Recovering from an eating disorder is a deeply challenging journey that demands immense courage, resilience, and patience. It often involves not only changing behaviors around food but also confronting deeply held beliefs about yourself and your body. Exploring sex, sexuality, and intimacy during recovery can feel especially difficult, as these areas are often entangled with shame, vulnerability, and fear of rejection. Yet, facing these challenges is crucial for cultivating a fulfilling and healthy relationship with yourself and others, and for reclaiming the ability to experience genuine intimacy and connection.

For 15 years, I struggled with my own eating disorder, and during that time, I experienced firsthand how profoundly it impacted every aspect of my ability to connect intimately with others. Recovery has been a long and demanding journey, but it led me to my work as a psychotherapist, supporting people of all ages, genders, and walks of life who are dealing with eating disorders. When new clients come into my office, I often start by asking them what brings them to therapy. Over the years, I've noticed a common thread: many of you have been through years of therapy, and while some of the eating disorder behaviors have improved, there's still something missing. You might feel as if you're on the outside looking in, trying so hard to fit in but still feeling different. You may struggle with feelings of anxiety or depression, putting on a brave face while deep down you're hurting. No matter how many people you surround yourself with, true connection seems out of reach— you may have many friends but still feel emotionally lonely. Despite your best efforts, forming meaningful relationships can feel impossible because trusting others enough to be vulnerable is just too hard. And when it comes to sex, you may find yourself feeling disconnected, either with no desire or a lack of connection to your body or your partner(s).

In my practice, I also began to notice that even after significant progress in their recovery, many of my clients continued to struggle with issues around sexual intimacy. This realization inspired me to create this workbook, with the hope of helping others to navigate the complex interplay between eating disorders, body image, and the ability to experience intimacy and connection. This workbook is here to help you navigate these inter-sections—your body, intimacy, and recovery—so you can build a healthier, more connected life.

So welcome! It takes tremendous courage to be here and to choose to work on such an important and too-often stigmatized part of your life. I want you to know that I am here to support you throughout this journey. As you move forward, be prepared to reflect deeply and face some topics that may cause discomfort, but remember that this is all part of the healing process. Please know that it's okay to take a deep breath and tackle this material bit by bit, at your own pace. Remember to be gentle with yourself—you are not alone, and you are capable of this work.

INTIMACY AND RELATIONSHIPS IN RECOVERY

Recovery touches every part of our lives and goes far beyond just changing our relationship with food. The way we inhabit our bodies shapes our con-nections with the world, especially socially. When we're disconnected from or even hating our bodies, it can lead to feelings of shame and make it really hard to connect with others.

When I struggled with anorexia, I shut myself off from so much, includ-ing the joy of embracing my physical form instead of constantly fighting it. Eating disorders don't just affect eating; they impact our ability to be part of social and family life, like sharing meals or making commitments. And they certainly make intimacy difficult, as intimacy means sharing your true self with another person—something that can feel risky, especially when your eating disorder wants to stay hidden and unchallenged. Eating disorders thrive in isolation, making intimacy feel risky. I, too, pushed people away out of shame, only to realize that the walls I'd built became harder to break down. As I distanced myself more and more, I found it harder to engage fully in life and form meaningful connections.

Eating disorders often create a distorted lens through which we see the world. The isolation that comes with them can feel like a refuge—a way to feel secure and in control. This self-isolation may have been a way to cope when the world felt unsafe or overwhelming. Whether it was too much stress, too much loss, or feelings of neglect or rejection, an eating disorder can seem like a way to regain control. But while it might have once helped you survive, it's no longer serving you. The eating disorder isn't a safe haven anymore—it's keeping you from living your fullest life.

Recovery is about being open and honest with yourself and others. It's about daring to dream of a more fulfilling life, one where intimacy and deep connections are possible. I've learned that without the eating disorder, I am my true self, and I can communicate my growing self-acceptance to others. This has led to richer, more authentic relationships. At first, the idea of having a healthy, "normal" body scared me, but as I grew into my adult body, I realized I didn't need to be ashamed of it. Now, I feel comfortable in my skin—I can be sensual, and I can give and receive love freely.

EATING DISORDERS AFFECT INTIMACY OF ALL KINDS

Eating disorders often feel as if they take on a life of their own, constantly feeding the person lies about what's happening in their body and their world. There is a lot of pressure from the eating disorder to meet imagined expectations from others, and it can feel overwhelming. Many times, people struggling with eating disorders place far higher expectations on themselves than they do on anyone else, especially when it comes to their eating habits, their appearance, and their body size.

These disorders can take over someone's identity, creating what is often called a "false self." This is the version of themselves they show to the world—the image they feel they need to project. But it's not the real them, and it often stands in the way of genuine connection. Eating disorders tend to shape how someone sees themselves and the world around them, which can have a big impact on all areas of intimacy.

While researchers have been exploring how eating disorders affect families for a long time, most of that research has focused on parents and children. But eating disorders don't only start in childhood, and they definitely don't disappear when someone becomes an adult. It's also important to look at how these disorders impact romantic relationships and friendships. Intimacy—whether emotional or physical—is an important part of healthy relationships. But when someone is struggling with an eating disorder, their loved ones often feel a sense of distance. For the person with the eating disorder, the closeness of intimacy can feel scary, and sometimes they end up withdrawing even more from their friends or partner(s). Eating disorders can make connection hard, but understanding what's happening is the first step toward bridging that gap.

AN OBVIOUS PAIRING

As we explore the intersection of eating disorders and intimacy, it's important to recognize another key connection—our relationship with food and sexuality. Talking about sex can stir up all kinds of emotions—everything from desire and excitement to nervousness, discomfort, or even fear. Though it's still often seen as taboo to discuss sexuality openly, it's woven into almost every part of our lives—from the media we watch to the conversations we have and even the information we search for. Since sex is such a fundamental part of being human, it's only natural that our mental and emotional well-being influences our relationship with it.

When we think about food and sexuality, it's easy to see how connected they are, especially since both revolve around the human body—an intricate, wonderful system that allows us to feel emotions and express them in so many ways, both verbally and physically. Food and sex have always been intertwined, likely because both are basic needs for human survival. Just think about how much sexual imagery is used in food ads—like the iconic "sexy green M&M"—to see the depth of this connection. Throughout history, many foods have been used to enhance sexual experiences, either for their supposed libido-boosting properties or by incorporating them into intimate moments. Both eating and sex offer earthy, physical experiences that awaken our senses and engage our bodies. Just as we need food to nourish us, there's a physiological drive for sex that gives us the opportunity to connect with others on an emotional and vulnerable level.

However, for someone struggling with an eating disorder, both food and sex can become sources of stress. Our sense of sexuality is deeply connected to how we feel about ourselves—emotionally, physically, and psychologically—and an eating disorder can distort all of that. The way we see our bodies, how we feel about ourselves, and how satisfied we are with our appearance all play a big role in our sexuality. When an eating disorder is present, it takes control of these aspects, often causing significant disruptions. It makes sense that when someone uses food to manage, suppress, or ignore their primal needs, their relationship with sex is also affected.

How we feel about our bodies impacts how we connect with others, and vice versa. Whether or not someone has an eating disorder, defining a healthy and balanced sexuality can be challenging. Body image issues, low self-esteem, perfectionism, and shame are struggles that many people face, regardless of gender or whether they have an eating disorder, and these struggles can also stand in the way of enjoying a fulfilling sexual relationship. You can't talk about sexuality or eating disorders without talking about the body. So, how do we experience, perceive, and process sexuality when it comes to the minds and bodies of those struggling with an eating disorder? While every person's journey is unique, and each individual experiences things differently, certain sexual and relationship challenges are often universal among those with eating disorders.

I've always found it surprising that sex and intimacy—so often deeply affected by eating disorders—are rarely talked about in therapy. So, it's no surprise that many people with eating disorders carry negative feelings about sex long after they've completed treatment. Some people do notice an improvement in their sex drive once they've stopped disordered eating behaviors and strengthened their bodies. But even with progress in recovery, ongoing challenges in relationships and sexual functioning can persist. Issues like shame, interpersonal struggles, negative attitudes toward sex, and body dissatisfaction often linger well beyond the more obvious symptoms of an eating disorder. Addressing sexuality as part of the treatment process for eating disorders is incredibly important. Discovering who you are apart from the eating disorder is a crucial part of recovery.

Sexuality is a fundamental part of who we are as human beings, and it's a cornerstone of many close romantic relationships—but it can also be a really tough topic to navigate. Because of that, it can be challenging to learn about your sexual identity and understand how you express it. It's often helpful for people with eating disorders to work on shifting their thoughts, breaking down barriers they've built up to intimacy, and developing their social skills in non sexual settings—while also maintaining strong boundaries.

Rebuilding positive sexual relationships starts with feeling secure in non-sexual relationships. Getting comfortable in social situations can be tough, but with practice, it gets easier. From there, you can gradually work your way to deeper intimacy. The main hurdle is that intimacy takes time and vulnerability, and initiating it can be difficult. But sex is a basic human need that lets us form meaningful emotional connections with others. If you want to prevent your eating disorder from continuing to negatively affect your sex life, now is the time to start making changes and getting the support you need.

Understanding what led to the eating disorder, how it affects your mind and body, and how it impacts your sexuality gives you more power in your recovery. When you know what's happening, it's easier to think things through and make different choices. Instead of falling into self-destructive habits, you can make decisions that lead to empowerment. By becoming aware of your power, you can reclaim your body and your relationship with pleasure.

THIS WORKBOOK

This workbook is here to help you understand and address the psychosexual effects of either having too much or not enough control over your emotions, thoughts, and relationships. Everyone copes differently, and your unique coping style can play a huge role in how eating disorders develop and how they can be treated. Knowing these differences helps us tailor treatment in a way that works for you, because there's no one-size-fits-all approach to recovery. Some of us may be more introverted and restrained, which can be linked to restricting behaviors, while others may struggle with impulsiveness, which can lead to binging or purging. But these are just tendencies, not strict categories, and everyone's experience is different. That's why it's important to look beyond labels and truly understand your individual style and needs. Throughout the workbook, you'll find reflection questions designed to help you process your thoughts and experiences. I encourage you to keep a notebook and pen handy to jot down your insights as you work through each section.

This workbook draws on two approaches: Dialectical Behavior Therapy (DBT) and Radically Open Dialectical Behavior Therapy (RO-DBT). DBT helps with emotional regulation and mindfulness—being aware of your feelings without judgment—while RO-DBT focuses on opening up, letting go of extreme emotional control, and learning to connect with others. Together, these methods are designed to help you move beyond unsuccessful attempts to micro-manage emotions or situations and transition from a place of isolation to one where you can be open, flexible, and truly yourself.

Overview of the workbook chapters

This workbook is designed to guide you through a transformative journey of self-exploration, healing, and growth. By addressing the connections between body image, sexuality, and attachment, it provides practical tools and insights to help you overcome challenges, nurture healthier relationships, and reclaim your sense of self. Divided into three comprehensive parts—*Name It*, *Tame It*, and *Reclaim It*—each section builds on the last, empowering you to better understand your experiences, develop essential skills, and embrace a more fulfilling, connected life.

Part 1, Name It: This part introduces foundational concepts and helps you begin exploring your own experiences with body image, sexuality, and attachment. It covers the basics of eating disorders, concerns about sexual functioning, and the impact of attachment patterns on intimacy and eating behaviors.

Part 2, Tame It: This part teaches you how to challenge unhelpful thinking patterns, improve body image, and develop emotion regulation skills. Topics include radical openness and radical acceptance, cognitive distortions, body satisfaction, mindfulness, and building intimate connections.

Part 3, Reclaim It: The final part emphasizes reclaiming sexual health and pleasure. It focuses on improving communication with sexual partners, recognizing boundaries, and integrating the skills learned throughout the workbook for enhanced intimacy and connection. It also includes a list of references and resources for further support.

Throughout this book, you'll find case examples that illustrate the concepts and experiences we explore. While these stories are fictionalized to protect privacy, they are inspired by real individuals and clinical experiences, reflecting the authentic challenges and triumphs many face.

A gentle reminder

Throughout this workbook, you'll be encouraged to reflect on and work through some challenging life events. I encourage you to consider working with a psychotherapist or counselor to help you process and navigate any distressing emotions or roadblocks that may arise. You might face feelings you've tried to avoid, and there may be moments when you think, "I can't do this." But I want you to know that you absolutely can. My goal is to support you every step of the way with empathy and care. You're not alone in this journey. I'll be here to help you learn practical skills that you can use in your daily life, giving you the security and confidence to keep moving forward. With each challenge you overcome, you'll feel a growing sense of confidence in your ability to persevere, and that feeling of progress can be incredibly empowering.

Language used

Relationships, gender, and sexual norms are more flexible now than ever before. In this workbook, you'll find discussions presented in gender-neutral language that are inclusive of all sexual orientations and relationship structures—whether you're casually dating, in a traditional monogamous relationship, navigating modern monogamy, being "monogamish," in an open relationship, swinging, or exploring polyamory. The inclusion of "partner(s)" is intentional, to honor all the different ways people connect and love.

There is a big emphasis on intimacy of all kinds, but you get to decide the type and level of intimacy that feels right for you and your relationships. I'm not here to judge the many forms of sexual intimacy that exist beyond traditional dating and marriage. Instead, I've worked hard to present this material with sensitivity to diversity, and with empathy, compassion, and encouragement for you.

While this workbook discusses different classifications, eating disorders (EDs) are generally referred to in broad terms, such as "eating disorders," "disordered eating behaviors," and "disordered eating patterns." I conceptualize eating behaviors as existing on a spectrum, which isn't always clearly defined. This framework helps to include anyone who might not have a formal diagnosis but still meets some criteria, and it aims to avoid the minimization of behaviors that don't fit neatly into a category. My focus here is on symptoms, presentation, causes, and specific complications, rather than diagnoses.

FINAL THOUGHTS

This workbook's main goal is to give you useful, evidence-based tools to improve your own sexual health. You can explore your sexuality with confidence by using the exercises, information, and tools provided in these pages to learn more about yourself and your sexual health, and to have more open and honest conversations about sex with your partner(s). Strengthening your own eating disorder recovery is necessary to reach that stage of reclaimed sexual well-being. That's why you'll also find exercises, information, and tools here that can help you better understand your eating disorder, coping mechanisms, relationship with yourself, and relationships with others.

If you want to improve your relationship with your body, your sexuality, and yourself, you've come to the right place. If you want to decrease sexual frustration or anxiety, or increase your access to sexual pleasure, you're in the right place. You're also in the right place if you want to learn more about your sexual identity, understand the reasons behind your arousal, desire, and pleasure, and start breaking down the barriers that prevent you from having great sex. Welcome!

CASE EXAMPLE: Emma

Meet Emma. At 25, she had been struggling with an eating disorder for over a decade. For Emma, restricting her food was all about trying to feel in control, but it left her feeling disconnected from her body. Although she'd been in recovery for two years, intimacy with her partner, Jules, was still difficult. Emma often felt uncomfortable with physical closeness, overwhelmed by shame and dissatisfaction with her body.

Emma knew something had to change. She started therapy and worked through the exercises in this workbook, slowly beginning to reconnect with her body and sexuality. One of her first steps was to be kinder to herself, recognizing that her body wasn't just something to control but something that could feel pleasure and connection. Emma worked on building her self-esteem by challenging negative thoughts and practicing self-compassion.

Emma and Jules also began having more open conversations about intimacy. They practiced setting boundaries and expressing their needs without judgment. As Emma grew more comfortable with her body, she started enjoying physical touch without all the self-criticism. They began by focusing on nonsexual forms of intimacy—like cuddling, holding hands, and just spending quality time together—to rebuild that sense of closeness and trust.

Over time, Emma noticed positive changes in her relationship with Jules. She felt more confident in being vulnerable and experienced intimacy in a way that felt safe and fulfilling. Emma's journey wasn't always smooth—there were setbacks along the way—but every small victory helped her regain flexible control over her sexuality. By working through her fears and embracing her body, Emma started to reclaim the pleasure and connection she had long denied herself.

— CHAPTER 2 —

A (Dys)functional Sexuality

GOALS

▶ Understand what might be causing sexual challenges related to eating disorders.
▶ Recognize if your eating disorder has impacted your sexual well-being.

AN EXTRAORDINARY MACHINE

Let's begin by grounding ourselves in the reality of our bodies—wonderful, vulnerable, and complex. From this perspective, our bodies are not enemies to conquer, but treasures to love and celebrate. Their natural functions and needs are not dirty or shameful, nor do they need to be hidden or controlled. Just like each of us, our bodies are strange, fascinating, beautiful, chaotic, and ever-changing. They require care, nourishment, and touch—not because these things are good or bad, but simply because they are essential human truths.

Our bodies make us vulnerable, and that vulnerability is a universal part of being human. We may try to hide it, but we all share it. We get sick, we get hurt, we grow older. When our hearts ache—whether it's physical or emotional—it hurts all the same. And while pain may manifest in one area, it affects our entire being, influencing our self-perception and sense of worth. But healing, in all its forms, brings comfort and connection. Sexual intimacy, with all its tenderness, awkwardness, and beauty, can play a role in that healing by bridging the gap between mind, body, and heart. Many of us are trying to reconcile our deep need for each other with our desire for autonomy, while also holding on to hope that we can grow and change through these connections.

There are many ways to cultivate authentic sexual well-being. If you wish to enhance your sexual connection, start by deepening your awareness of your own body and desires. But remember—growth takes time. By strengthening your relationship with yourself, you lay the foundation for richer, more fulfilling intimacy with others. Give yourself the space to explore your sexuality at your own pace—to try new things, to discover what feels right. Allow your sexuality to unfold naturally, without force or pressure.

My advice? Embrace the freedom to experiment with your sexuality and self-expression. The world is already full of expectations and pressures to conform to standards that may not honor who you truly are. Imagine what could happen if you allowed yourself to follow your desires, speak your truth, and move in ways that feel right for you. Expand your understanding of who you are, savor your own company, and above all, be generous with your self-love.

EATING DISORDERS AND SEX

Sex is one of the many things that can feel absent during an eating disorder and can become part of the recovery process. It's not uncommon for people with eating disorders to also experience sexual difficulties. People with eating disorders often separate their sexual desire from actually engaging in sexual activity, much like we dissociate hunger from eating. Sexual insecurities, fears, and desires often find expression in eating disorder behaviors and rituals. Sex can become a tool, used to meet needs, gain control, or even as a way to manipulate, but understanding our motivations allows for open, honest communication with ourselves and our partners. There is no shame in wanting sexual fulfillment, emotional closeness, or anything else we may need.

Eating disorders are complex and go beyond issues of food and eating. They reflect a deeper struggle with embodiment—our sense of being in and experiencing life through our bodies. Embodiment means experiencing the internal, external, and existential aspects of life through our physical selves. In many ways, eating disorders represent an attempt to avoid this experience. They seek the very things they destroy: well-being, connection, joy, and peace. No amount of control over food or the body can truly make us feel safe or at peace—eating disorders have shown us that.

That's why it's so important to talk about eating disorders and sexuality. Rarely do those of us with eating disorders make time to reflect on our attitudes toward sex—often, it only happens after something has gone wrong. But by being curious and open about our experiences and beliefs around sexuality, we can start to discover what feels right for us. An essential part of eating disorder recovery is rediscovering who we are outside the disorder.

Only by exploring our sexuality can we fully embody who we are and build intimate relationships that are true to ourselves. As we begin this conversation about eating disorders and sexuality, I invite you to bring your curiosity along for the journey.

EXERCISE: Reflection

Grab a notebook and get comfy. Start by asking yourself the following questions, with compassion and genuine curiosity:

- What words best describe how I feel and what I think about sex?
- Am I aware of and comfortable with my own sexuality?
- How might my eating disorder be impacting my sexuality?
- What may be keeping me from being fully intimate with another person?

WHAT IS SEXUALITY?

Sexuality is all about how we connect with ourselves, our bodies, and other people. From the moment we're born, we are all sexual beings—it's simply part of being human. Sexuality motivates us to seek love, intimacy, and happiness. Sexuality can be expressed in many ways—through our thoughts, beliefs, fantasies, values, relationships, roles, and attitudes—not just through actions. It's a deeper experience that touches everything, including how we see ourselves. It's a part of our identity that can be incredibly powerful and positive, but it can also bring up feelings of fear and anxiety. Everyone's understanding of their own sexuality is unique and constantly evolving. Because it's made up of so many different pieces, it's normal for it to feel a bit confusing sometimes, or to discover that different parts of our lives interact in surprising ways. That's okay—it's all part of learning and growing. Exploring and understanding our sexuality is a crucial part of our health and well-being, and it's important to do this in a way that feels right for us and is rooted in consent and respect for our own values.

WHY DO WE HAVE SEX?

People have sex for all sorts of reasons, and not all of them are obvious. Some of the more common reasons include showing love and trust, wanting to have children, or simply because it feels good—physically, emotionally, or both. In a new or short-term relationship, the focus often centers around sharing pleasure and creating a bond. Over time, in a long-term relationship, our reasons for having sex can shift and change as we grow together.

While physical attraction and gratification are common reasons, they're not the only ones. People are motivated by a wide range of feelings when it comes to sex. Sometimes, motivations can be positive—like a desire for closeness, affection, or pleasure—and these are known as "approach motivations." But not all motivations are positive. Sometimes, people have sex to avoid negative outcomes or feelings, like trying to keep a partner from leaving or to escape feelings of rejection. These are called "avoidance motivations" (Elliot, 2008).

Our reasons for having sex can significantly affect our emotional well-being and relationships. Approach motivations tend to lead to more fulfilling and satisfying experiences—in both the sexual and relationship sense—while avoidance motivations are often linked with lower satisfaction and more challenges. Understanding why we have sex can help us make more conscious choices that benefit our emotional health and relationships.

COMMON APPROACH AND AVOIDANCE MOTIVATIONS FOR SEX

Approach:

- To feel pleasure for self or partner(s)
- To satisfy a partner's needs
- To deepen intimate connection with partner(s)
- To express your love for partner(s)
- To procreate
- To feel powerful and sexy
- To reduce stress

Avoidance:

- To avoid tension within relationship
- To stop partner(s) from leaving
- To prevent partner(s) from losing interest
- To avoid feeling bad about self
- To avoid upsetting partner(s)
- To avoid an argument/fight

IS SEX NECESSARY IN A RELATIONSHIP?

Not necessarily! It really depends on the people involved. While sex can definitely play a big role in creating happy, fulfilling relationships, it's not always a must. Every relationship is different, and what matters most is what feels right for you and your partner(s). For some, having a sexual connection is a key part of their bond. For others, the focus is more on emotional intimacy or other forms of connection. Sex doesn't have to be part of a romantic relationship. It's also totally normal for the sexual side of a relationship to change as it progresses. What's most important is that any sexual experience you do share is filled with pleasure, satisfaction, and mutual consent.

Just as there isn't a one-size-fits-all reason for having sex, there are endless ways people identify and express their sexuality. The number of partners, the frequency of sexual activity, and even the intensity of sexual desire can be different for everyone. You might choose not to engage in certain sexual activities or even to abstain from sex entirely. And your feelings about sex might evolve over time. There's no right or wrong way to experience your sexuality—whether that means having sex, not having sex, or defining your sexual self in any way that feels true to you.

EXERCISE: Reflection

- How important is sex to me?
- What are my reasons for having sex?

UNDERSTANDING SEXUAL DYSFUNCTIONS

Whatever the reason, many individuals and couples place a high value on their sexual relationships. It's completely normal to feel disappointed, frustrated, worried, or dissatisfied when things don't go as planned in the bedroom. The term "sexual dysfunction" is used to describe ongoing sexual challenges, but it's important to remember that almost everyone who has sex will experience some hiccups now and then. Since many people aren't comfortable talking about their sex lives openly, it can be easy to feel isolated or think that you're the only one going through these challenges. Sexual dysfunction can be temporary, showing up in specific situations or with a particular partner, or it can be something that sticks around longer and involves multiple partners or different circumstances. The good news is that, in nearly every case, there is help available, and treatment can make a big difference, no matter what you're facing.

Common sexual dysfunctions can vary depending on the anatomy involved, but here are some prevalent issues (American Psychiatric Association, 2013):

- *Low sexual desire:* Reduced interest in sexual activity or lack of sexual desire.
- *Performance anxiety:* Anxiety related to sexual performance, which can interfere with arousal and enjoyment.
- *Vaginismus:* Involuntary tightening of the vaginal muscles, making penetration painful or impossible.
- *Dyspareunia:* Persistent or recurrent pain during intercourse or penetration.
- *Arousal disorder:* Difficulty in becoming aroused, which can include reduced lubrication or lack of physical excitement.
- *Anorgasmia:* Inability to achieve orgasm despite adequate stimulation.
- *Erectile dysfunction:* Difficulty in getting or maintaining an erection firm enough for sex.
- *Premature ejaculation:* Ejaculation that happens sooner than desired during sexual activity.
- *Delayed ejaculation:* Difficulty in or inability to ejaculate despite adequate stimulation.

Factors affecting sexual functioning

Understanding what's behind a sexual issue can be a lot more complex than it seems at first. It often means looking at many different factors that might be affecting sexual satisfaction. Sexual challenges can come from biological, psychological, or social causes—or sometimes a mix of all three. It's important not to point the finger at just one factor because, in many cases, it's much more layered than that.

Another thing to keep in mind is that what started the problem might not be what's keeping it going today. Sometimes, the way we respond to sexual difficulty can make things even more complicated. For example, imagine a man who couldn't maintain an erection one time because he had been drinking. He might end up feeling ashamed or worried that he let his partner down. This fear of it happening again could become its own issue, even when alcohol isn't involved. In this case, the initial cause was a night of drinking, but the ongoing challenge could be tied to the stress and worry around it happening again.

Biological factors: Sexual difficulties can sometimes stem from biological factors, either directly or indirectly. When a medical condition, procedure, or medication directly affects sexual activity, it's considered a direct cause. For example, sexual function depends on a healthy supply of blood and nerve signals—both of which can be affected by conditions like diabetes. Physical factors that impact how a person feels can also have an indirect effect on sexual function. For instance, a widespread rash from an allergic reaction might leave someone feeling unattractive and miserable, which can reduce their desire for intimacy. While the rash doesn't physically prevent sexual activity, it can definitely impact someone's mood and confidence.

Psychological factors: Emotional and psychological factors can also play a major role in sexual health. Issues like depression, stress, body image concerns, anxiety, or past traumatic experiences can all negatively impact sexual function. Things like how someone feels about themselves, their body, their fears, and their past experiences all contribute to how they experience intimacy.

Situational factors: Sometimes, challenges with intimacy aren't about the individual at all—they're situational. Differences in sexual preferences, conflicts in the relationship, a partner's health issues, or environmental factors can all affect a couple's sex life. For example, work schedules might clash, or there might be a lack of privacy due to children or other adults in the home. These kinds of situations can make it hard to find time for intimacy, which can lead to a loss of interest in sexual connection over time.

Is there a sexual problem?
If your sex life is causing you or your partner stress, anxiety, or sadness, it might be worth exploring whether there's a sexual issue that needs addressing. If you're someone who struggles with an eating disorder, you might wonder if having a low sex drive is a problem. This is an important question, and the answer really depends on you. If your low sex drive isn't causing you any trouble or distress, then it's likely not a problem at all. It all comes down to how you feel about it. If it's not bothering you, then it's not a problem. But, it's also worth being honest with yourself. Sometimes low desire can be connected to things like trauma, anxiety, body image struggles, or even malnutrition.

Remember that everyone's sex drive is unique. Some people have a high interest in sex, while others don't, and that's perfectly okay. Being on the lower end of the spectrum isn't wrong or abnormal, no matter what messages we get from our hypersexual culture. When we talk about "sexual dysfunction," it's only an issue if it's an issue for you. It doesn't matter what society says is "normal" or what your friends claim they're doing. It certainly doesn't matter what we see in movies or porn. What truly matters is what feels comfortable and right for you.

If you and your partner(s) are happy with your sexual relationship, then there's no problem. On the other hand, if either of you feels worried or unhappy about any part of your sex life, that's when it might be worth seeking some help. It's not about how you compare to others; it's about whether you and your partner(s) are meeting each other's needs and expectations—realistic ones, of course.

If you're unsure about anything, that's okay. Keep reading, stay with me, and let's work through it together.

EXERCISE: Reflection

- Is sex ever painful for me? When, where, and with whom? Does this prevent me from having sex?
- Do I experience difficulties with my ability to orgasm?
- Do I have any concerns about any aspect of my body or my sex life?
- Do I have sexual fantasies? How do I feel about them? Am I comfortable sharing them with partners?
- How do I feel about the way I currently express myself sexually—frequency, practices, and so on? Am I feeling shame or confusion about my sexual expression?
- Is it possible that sexual dissatisfaction is the cause of my discontent with my partner?
- Am I unsure of myself or lack confidence in my sex abilities?
- Do I avoid sexual relations?

WHY EATING DISORDERS CAN AFFECT YOUR SEXUAL WELL-BEING

Eating disorders can take a toll on both the body and the mind. Hormonal imbalances, malnutrition, poor body image, low self-esteem, and mental health challenges are all factors that contribute to sexual difficulties. Low body weight, for example, can lead to reduced libido, lower testosterone, and decreased lubrication—all of which can affect sexual function.

For those with anorexia, this can be especially intense. People with anorexia may experience vaginismus (involuntary muscle tightening) or dyspareunia (pain or discomfort in the head or shaft of the penis, scrotum, vulva, vagina, pelvic floor muscles, or pelvis) making sex uncomfortable or even painful, and orgasms harder to achieve. Malnutrition affects brain function, which in turn impacts the whole body—including the reproductive system. When the brain isn't getting enough energy, it begins to prioritize essential processes, reducing hormone production (like estrogen and testosterone) that supports sexual desire and function.

Beyond the physical impacts, the mental and emotional aspects of eating disorders also play a big role. Distorted body image, dissatisfaction, and shame can create barriers to healthy sexual function. Many people with eating disorders feel uncomfortable in their own skin, making intimacy difficult. Worries about how a partner might perceive their body can cause anxiety, leading to avoidance of sex altogether.

Anorexia, bulimia, and binge eating disorder can affect people in slightly different ways when it comes to sexuality. According to a systematic review of research studies on sexual behavior in eating disorder patients, those with anorexia often report the highest levels of sexual anxiety and frequently avoid sexual activity due to negative body image and fear of judgment, while people with bulimia or binge eating disorder may tend to be more impulsive, which can sometimes lead to hypersexuality or casual sexual encounters (Castellini *et al.*, 2016). Their relationships may often feel unstable or conflict-driven.

Eating disorders can also impact self-pleasure. Many people with eating disorders report less frequent masturbation compared to those without these conditions. This may be tied to feelings of body dissatisfaction or, in the case of anorexia, a tendency to deny themselves any form of pleasure, including sexual. Overall, eating disorders can disrupt both partnered and solo sexual activities, making it harder for individuals to form healthy, fulfilling intimate connections. Partners may feel disconnected, and the person struggling with the eating disorder might feel unable to truly connect until they are on a path to recovery. In general, the physical and mental strain of eating disorders can make it difficult to feel connected, engage in sexual activity, or enjoy intimacy.

EXERCISE: Reflection

- Do any of these effects surprise me?
- What sexual effects have I experienced?

CASE EXAMPLE: John

Meet John, a 29-year-old man who faced bulimia nervosa for several years. His eating disorder started in his late teens, largely influenced by both societal pressures to have an athletic body and painful experiences of body shaming. John believed that being lean and muscular was the key to being valued, which led to cycles of binging and purging. These behaviors provided him with a temporary sense of control but ultimately affected his health and relationships.

John's eating disorder took a toll on his sexual health, leading to a loss of libido and difficulty with arousal. The shame he felt about his body and eating habits contributed to performance anxiety, making it hard to feel comfortable during intimacy. These challenges left John feeling inadequate, causing him to avoid sexual situations and disconnect from his body.

John's negative body image was closely tied to his ideas about masculinity. He felt pressured to achieve the "ideal" male body, believing that being muscular was the key to attractiveness and sexual competence. This need to conform to unrealistic standards made it difficult for him to feel confident or enjoy intimate experiences.

During his recovery, John worked with a therapist to challenge these unrealistic standards of masculinity and rebuild his relationship with his body and sexuality. He practiced mindfulness and self-compassion, learning to explore his desires without judgment. Open communication with his partner, Libby, was also a huge help. She provided a safe, non-judgmental space for intimacy, allowing John to feel more comfortable and connected.

John has made significant progress in his recovery. He no longer sees his body as something that needs to be perfected but rather as something that deserves care and respect. His confidence in intimacy has grown, and he now approaches it with a focus on connection and pleasure instead of performance. By embracing vulnerability and open communication, John has rebuilt intimacy with himself and Libby, leading to more fulfilling sexual experiences.

— CHAPTER 3 —

The Fallacy of Partial Recovery

GOALS

▶ Get to know the common experience of being in partial recovery from an eating disorder.
▶ Figure out if you might be in partial recovery yourself.
▶ Understand how partial recovery can affect your sex life and relationships.

IDENTIFY, DON'T COMPARE

While terms like "anorexia" and "bulimia" are widely recognized, the number of labels for food and body image issues has expanded significantly. A clinical diagnosis describes behaviors, feelings, and thought patterns, helping us understand shared traits and differentiate between "unhealthy" and "disordered" behavior, though this line is often blurry. Diagnostic labels can feel stigmatizing or oversimplified, reducing complex experiences to a single term. They describe but don't explain, shaping how we talk about eating disorders without always capturing their root causes or our personal relationships with food and self-image.

Comparing ourselves to stereotypes of eating disorders can lead us to dismiss our struggles (thinking, "It's not that bad") or cause us to stop short of full recovery (believing, "At least I don't meet the diagnostic criteria anymore"). But it's important to recognize that an eating disorder isn't about fitting a category; it's about acknowledging when thoughts and behaviors around food feel overwhelming or hopeless. While eating disorders may appear centered on appearance and eating habits, their deeper causes are unique to each person. Recovery isn't about the label—it's about shared understanding, connection, and healing beyond the diagnosis.

PARTIAL RECOVERY

Many people who have experienced sexual dysfunction because of an eating disorder recall having a healthy sex life before it all began. The good news is that *full* recovery can bring back normal sexual function. But here's the catch: recovery often stops before it's truly complete. Treatment can focus on stopping eating disorder behaviors without addressing everything else that needs healing. This leads to something called "partial recovery" or "quasi-recovery." It's that frustrating state of being "almost there" but not quite. Sometimes we recognize that we're not fully recovered, and sometimes we think we're done when we still have some healing to do.

Recovery isn't a one-size-fits-all term, and that ambiguity can be a challenge. For this discussion, let me explain what I mean by "recovery." While most of us agree that someone who still meets the diagnostic criteria for an eating disorder is not recovered, not meeting those criteria doesn't automatically mean you're fully recovered either. Recovery is more than just letting go of disordered eating behaviors—it means truly healing your relationship with food, your body, yourself, and others.

How is recovery defined?

Complete recovery can be hard to define, partly because only you can truly know once you've reached it. Even when you do recover fully, it's normal to still have occasional thoughts related to your eating disorder. The difference is that those thoughts lose their power. You can recognize them as disordered and choose not to act on them. Your relationship with food, exercise, and body image becomes similar to how it was before the eating disorder.

It's a common misconception that recovery ends once you reach a target weight and start eating more regularly. But there's so much more to it than that. Yes, reaching a healthy weight is part of the journey for some, but true recovery is about finding freedom in your mind and body. It's about no longer obsessing over your weight, feeling the need to control food, or constantly trying to change your body. Real recovery means experiencing a sense of ease with yourself that goes beyond just surviving.

If you've struggled with disordered thoughts for a long time, any reduction in symptoms can feel like a win—and it is. You might be able to focus more on other things, keep up with daily activities, and even feel somewhat stable. But this state, while better, is still just partial healing. And while you can continue to exist in that place, it's not truly living to the fullest.

There is no agreed-on definition of recovery. Experts and those with an eating disorder each have their own unique perspectives.

Recovery looks different for everyone, but I believe there are six key areas to consider:

1. Restoring a healthy-for-you weight.
2. Repairing any physical damage.
3. Developing new ways to cope with triggers.
4. Building a positive or neutral relationship with food.
5. Cultivating a positive relationship with yourself.
6. Fostering positive relationships with others.

Getting healthy again means achieving and maintaining a healthy weight, healing physically, and finding a new sense of normalcy in eating, coping, and relationships. Weight restoration is often the first step, but it doesn't end there. Recovery isn't just about hitting a specific body mass index (BMI) or being able to leave treatment. Gaining weight can be challenging, both mentally and physically, but it's crucial for rehabilitating your body and mind. Even if your BMI is technically "normal," you might still show signs of being undernourished or struggle with anxiety about gaining more weight. That's a signal that more healing is needed. Recovery is not about settling in the middle. The longer an eating disorder persists, the more damage it does—physically, mentally, and in relationships. Even after reaching partial recovery, many people continue to struggle with body image issues, anxiety, and certain disordered behaviors.

The bottom line? *True recovery means more than just "getting by."*

WHAT PARTIAL RECOVERY CAN LOOK LIKE
If you recognize yourself in any of these scenarios, you may not be fully recovered:

- Eating more than you did before but still not consistently honoring your hunger and/or eating an appropriate amount.
- Eating more foods than you did before but still labeling food as "good" and "bad" and avoiding "bad" foods much of the time.
- Having guilt or anxiety around food.

- Struggling to set healthy boundaries with others.
- Using exercise to "earn" or "make up" for what you eat.
- Having food rules about what, how much, or when you can eat.
- Frequent mood swings.
- Still largely defining self-worth by appearance or food habits, rather than feeling valued for other qualities.
- Continuing to hate your body.
- Struggling to rebuild trust with others.
- Fearing weight gain.
- Maintaining an artificially low body weight.
- Counting calories, weighing food, or using fitness apps.
- Struggling with self-acceptance.
- Wearing large, baggy clothes to hide your body.
- Weighing yourself often, just to know what you weigh.
- Having daily eating disordered thoughts or judgments.
- Seeing yourself primarily through the lens of the eating disorder, and struggling to separate from it.
- Not eating everything you're craving, or overeating what you're craving.
- Only eating foods like cake or cookies on special occasions like birthdays or holidays.
- Engaging in frequent or harsh self-criticism, especially related to food, weight, or appearance.
- Only eating fear foods if other people are eating them with you.
- Not allowing yourself to keep fear foods in the house.
- Eating food in secret.
- Not being fully aware of the situations, emotions, or people that trigger disordered thoughts or behaviors, or struggling to cope with them.
- Still relying on eating disorder behaviors or unhealthy coping mechanisms during stressful or emotional situations, without enough healthy alternatives in place.
- Not being able to have all of your fear foods.

When overcoming an eating disorder, many of us look for a middle ground, where we've managed to cease some of the most dangerous behaviors and move past the scariest moments, but maybe still keep a lower weight or avoid certain foods. It might feel as if we're doing fine—holding down a job, staying on top of school, and even having a social life. And in a culture that values thinness so much, it's easy to be tempted by this idea. But the truth is, partial recovery is an illusion. Many of the mental and physical symptoms of the eating disorder are still there, and the constant battle with those thoughts doesn't go away. So should we settle for this state of partial recovery?

Some people believe that fully recovering from an eating disorder is impossible—that the best we can do is "manage" it. And while it's true that there isn't a miracle cure, aiming only to manage the symptoms can mean missing out on true healing. Instead of just reducing symptoms, we *can* get to the root causes and aim for a full recovery.

ADDRESSING PARTIAL RECOVERY

If you're still experiencing negative consequences because of disordered eating, it means you're not fully recovered yet. I know this can be hard to hear, especially if you're just starting your recovery journey. Admitting where you are is a huge, brave step, and recognizing that a full recovery is possible is just as important. I understand how challenging it can feel, but please don't let yourself believe that partial recovery is the best you can do.

The idea that recovery isn't possible really bothers me. Yes, recovery is hard. It's uncomfortable and challenging, but that doesn't make it impossible. Recovery means continuing to take small steps forward. Partial recovery can feel like surrendering just short of victory. I want you to live the life you're capable of—the one you truly deserve. If you give in to the eating disorder, it will always be there.

EXERCISE: Reflection

- Is it possible that my weight is affecting my health?
- What thoughts or emotions are coming up for me in regard to weight or weight gain?

UNDERSTANDING STAGES OF CHANGE IN THE RECOVERY PROCESS

Making lasting changes to your behavior is challenging. It often takes a lot of time, energy, and emotional effort. When it comes to recovering from an eating disorder, the journey is rarely straightforward. Instead, it moves in cycles, with ups and downs along the way.

STAGES OF CHANGE MODEL
(PROCHASKA & DICLEMENTE, 1983)
Pre-contemplation
In this stage, we might not be ready to acknowledge that there's a problem. We may dismiss the idea altogether or downplay our need for help.

Contemplation
Here, we start to admit that we might need support, even if there's still a lot of fear around making changes. It's okay to feel scared—it means you're considering something important.

Preparation
Now, we're ready to make changes, but we might feel unsure about where to start. This is when we begin to develop specific coping strategies, like setting healthy boundaries, learning to manage negative thoughts and emotions, and figuring out how to take care of ourselves better.

Action
In this stage, we're ready to put our plans into motion. We start facing the behaviors head-on, even if it feels scary. We're willing to try new approaches and explore different ways of behaving.

Maintenance
Once we've been successfully and consistently working on our new behaviors, we enter the Maintenance stage. Here, we keep practicing our new habits, using our coping strategies, and focusing on self-care. We also take time to reflect on our lives, identify potential triggers, explore new interests, and live with a sense of purpose.

Relapse
Recovery isn't a straight path, and sometimes old behaviors resurface. This is why Relapse is often considered part of the Maintenance stage. It's a chance to learn, regroup, and continue moving forward—it's all part of the process.

The Stages of Change Model, also known as the Transtheoretical Model, describes the process people go through when trying to change a behavior. You might need to revisit a stage or two before moving forward again.

Sometimes, you'll even find yourself at different stages of recovery for different symptoms. For example, you could be in the Action stage for restrictive eating—working with a nutritionist and starting to eat in social settings—while still being in the Contemplation stage for body image, where you're just beginning to explore the impact of body checking or weighing yourself too often. Recovery is a unique journey for everyone, and that's what makes it both complicated and deeply personal. It's important to be patient with yourself as you navigate each part of this process.

ASSESSMENT: AT WHAT STAGES OF CHANGE AM I IN THE MAJOR AREAS OF MY EATING DISORDER?

Restrictive eating:

☐ Pre-contemplation   ☐ Contemplation
☐ Preparation   ☐ Action
☐ Maintenance   ☐ Relapse

Binging:

☐ Pre-contemplation   ☐ Contemplation
☐ Preparation   ☐ Action
☐ Maintenance   ☐ Relapse

Purging:

☐ Pre-contemplation   ☐ Contemplation
☐ Preparation   ☐ Action
☐ Maintenance   ☐ Relapse

Excessive exercise:

☐ Pre-contemplation   ☐ Contemplation
☐ Preparation   ☐ Action
☐ Maintenance   ☐ Relapse

Body image:

☐ Pre-contemplation   ☐ Contemplation
☐ Preparation   ☐ Action
☐ Maintenance   ☐ Relapse

- Do I have the resources and knowledge to make a lasting change successfully?
- Is there anything preventing me from changing?
- What might trigger a return to former behaviors?

Partial recovery is a common stage for many people with eating disorders. It's fine if that's where you are right now. Don't beat yourself up or give up hope. Full recovery from an eating disorder is not a linear process, and it is not a simple one. This is particularly important to note in light of how dysfunctional society's views on food and bodies are! Full recovery is attainable. This may sound trite, but it holds true. While it is important to stop the eating disorder behaviors, it is also important to address the thoughts and processes that underlie the behavior. This is where a lot of eating disorder treatments fall flat. From here, we will focus on the internal work that is often missed in eating disorder treatment.

CASE STUDY: Meena
Meena, a 39-year-old marketing executive, struggled with her relationship with food for years. Growing up in a household where dieting was the norm, she learned that being thin was tied to success. By college, her eating habits became restrictive, leading to a diagnosis of anorexia nervosa. After hospitalization, Meena entered an outpatient program, regained weight, and resumed work. On the surface, she seemed fine, but her thoughts were still dominated by fear of gaining weight and eating "bad" foods.

In this state of partial recovery, Meena's behaviors appeared healthy, but her mindset remained disordered. She ate only "safe" foods and compensated for any indulgence with exercise. Though no longer in immediate physical danger, she was not truly living. Her anxiety around food and body image began affecting her relationship with her partner, Marissa. She avoided physical closeness and struggled to connect emotionally, leading to tension between them. One night, after an argument about her refusal to eat out, Marissa told her, "It feels like there's a wall between us."

Realizing she needed deeper healing, Meena returned to therapy with a new goal: to heal her relationship with herself. She worked on letting go of control, finding self-worth beyond appearance, and enjoying food without guilt. Slowly, she made progress—eating previously feared foods, finding joy in movement, and opening up to Marissa. This journey was uncomfortable but ultimately brought them closer.

— CHAPTER 4 —

The Self-Control Spectrum

GOALS:

- ▶ Figure out if your coping habits tend to follow certain patterns.
- ▶ Explore what influences your unique coping style.
- ▶ Learn how your coping style impacts your relationships, and how it connects to eating behaviors and sexual patterns.

FINDING BALANCE

We can't put everyone with an eating disorder into the same box. Even with the same diagnosis, everyone is unique, with their own ways of coping and different experiences that shape their behaviors. Understanding our struggles—whether they're about food, emotions, or relationships—requires us to consider both how we attach to others and how we cope with stress. Parents who help their children feel secure often do so by openly talking about emotions. Kids raised this way learn early that their feelings matter, which boosts their empathy and helps them understand others better. These kids also learn how to self-soothe after stressful moments ("up-regulate") and how to rein in their excitement when needed ("down-regulate"). This gives them flexible control over their emotions—a kind of balance that helps them manage impulses without feeling overwhelmed.

Self-control is all about resisting our immediate desires or impulses for the sake of bigger goals. Many of us were raised to believe that more self-control is always better. Western culture tends to celebrate people who seem disciplined and able to hold back, and we often see impulsiveness as a flaw. Think of self-control as a spectrum. At one end, there's overcontrol—being too restrained, avoiding risks, and staying emotionally closed off. At the other end, there's undercontrol—being emotionally reactive and taking risks without thinking them through. Most of us fall somewhere in between, leaning a bit one way or the other but still managing to adapt. Emotional health is about flexibility and being able to switch gears depending on the situation. Of course, self-control isn't all bad—it's important for achieving goals, being responsible, and showing empathy. Finding that balance is key. Neither extreme—overcontrol nor undercontrol—is better. The goal is to be able to adapt, express, and regulate emotions in a way that fits the moment. It isn't just about "control" or lack of it—it's about learning when to hold on and when to let go.

UNDERCONTROL

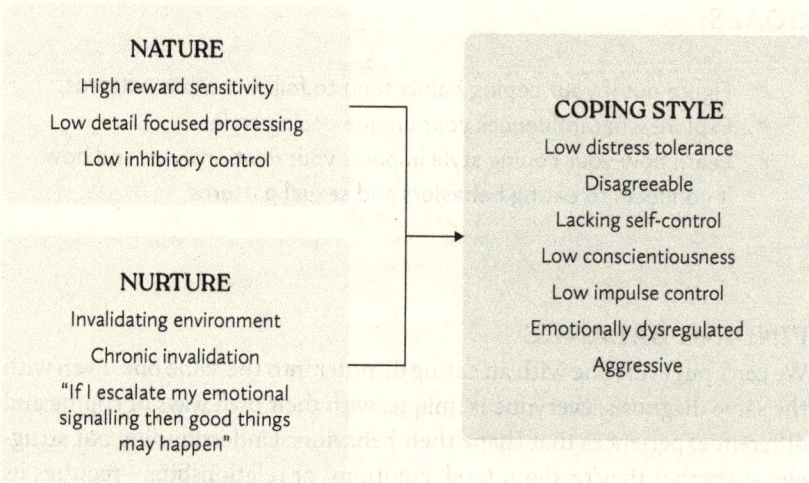

NATURE

High reward sensitivity

Low detail focused processing

Low inhibitory control

COPING STYLE

Low distress tolerance

Disagreeable

Lacking self-control

Low conscientiousness

Low impulse control

Emotionally dysregulated

Aggressive

NURTURE

Invalidating environment

Chronic invalidation

"If I escalate my emotional signalling then good things may happen"

Biologically determined personality traits reacting to environmental stimuli.
Biotemperament + INVALIDATING environment = maladaptive coping style

To regulate emotions, we first need to be aware of how we feel and then either change our response to those emotions or learn to accept and tolerate them. Those who are undercontrolled often describe feeling as if they're on an emotional roller coaster. They struggle to keep their emotions in check, sometimes acting out impulsively in ways that can be self-destructive. Their emotions can feel unpredictable, and they may find themselves in repeated cycles of emotional highs and lows. This kind of coping often makes it hard to maintain stable relationships, succeed at work, or focus on school. People who are undercontrolled tend to show their emotions outwardly. They might react strongly to situations and act on their impulses without much thought. Unfortunately, these impulsive actions often make things worse, adding to their stress or negative feelings. It's easy to see how this can become a cycle that is hard to break.

When emotions become too overwhelming, some people turn to binge eating as a way to cope. Binge eating can be a way to soothe distressing feelings, even if the person isn't fully aware of why they're doing it. It's a learned behavior that helps ease emotional pain, whether those feelings are "positive" (like excitement or happiness) or "negative" (like anger or worry), or even a mix of both.

OVERCONTROL

NATURE

Low reward sensitivity

High threat sensitivity

High inhibitory control

High anxious apprehension

High attention to detail

COPING STYLE

Masked inner feelings

Fake expressions

Preference for structure and order

Compulsive striving

Avoidance of unplanned risks

Distress overtolerance

Aloof and distant social signaling style

NURTURE

Self-control is imperative

Self-control is valuable

Focus on performance/achievement

Reinforced for appearing perfect

Reinforced for following rules

Mistakes are intolerable

"Always be prepared"

Winning is essential

"Never reveal weakness"

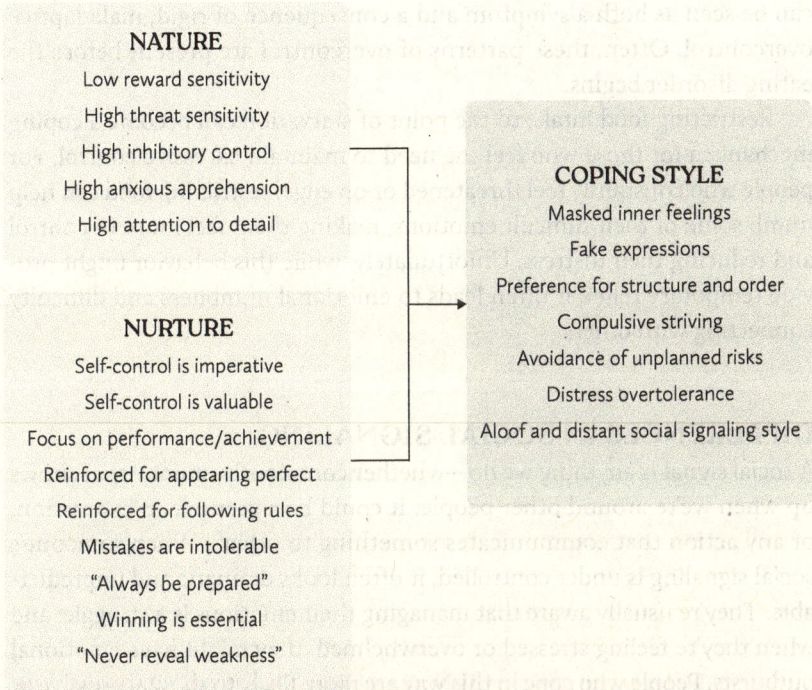

Biologically determined personality traits reacting to environmental stimuli.
Biotemperament + CRITICAL environment = maladaptive coping style

On the flip side, emotional overcontrol means having rigid and inflexible responses to emotions. People with this style work very hard, often subconsciously, to suppress, minimize, or rationalize their feelings. Their emotions might seem hidden or even nonexistent. They use excessive self-control as a coping mechanism, often presenting with a reduced emotional expression, avoiding risks, and becoming isolated and lonely. People with an overcontrolled coping style may feel disconnected from others, struggling to understand how to build close, meaningful relationships. They might say they have stable relationships—unlike those with an undercontrolled style—but if you take a closer look, you might notice that these connections often lack real depth or intimacy. They could be in committed relationships or even married, but these partnerships may feel empty of emotional, physical, or sexual closeness. Essentially, they may not be alone, but they still feel deeply lonely.

Many people with anorexia nervosa have an overcontrolled coping style. Research has shown links between anorexia and traits like social withdrawal, rigidity in thinking, a need for sameness, avoiding new experiences, a strong preference for structure, and perfectionism (Cassin & von Ranson, 2005; Fairburn *et al.*, 1999; Keel & Forney, 2013). Restrictive eating can be seen as both a symptom and a consequence of rigid, maladaptive overcontrol. Often, these patterns of overcontrol are present before the eating disorder begins.

Restricting food intake to the point of starvation can become a coping mechanism for those who feel the need to maintain excessive control. For people who constantly feel threatened or on edge, restricting food can help numb some of their difficult emotions, making them feel more in control and reducing their distress. Unfortunately, while this behavior might provide temporary relief, it often leads to emotional numbness and difficulty connecting with others.

DIFFERENCES IN SOCIAL SIGNALING

A social signal is anything we do—whether consciously or not—that shows up when we're around other people. It could be a gesture, an expression, or any action that communicates something to others. When someone's social signaling is under controlled, it often looks dramatic and unpredictable. They're usually aware that managing their emotions is a struggle, and when they're feeling stressed or overwhelmed, they might have emotional outbursts. People who cope in this way are more likely to show aggressive or antisocial behavior, as they tend to express their problems outwardly. This impulsivity can make their relationships unstable and volatile.

At the same time, they rarely try to tone down their positive emotions, which means they can be very expressive and full of energy. These individuals also tend to be less self-conscious in social situations and enjoy being the center of attention. Unlike some others, they aren't likely to spend much time planning or preparing for social events—they're more spontaneous and comfortable with just going with the flow.

On the other hand, people with overcontrolled social signaling usually come across as consistent and reserved. Their emotional expressions don't vary much—they tend to be calm and controlled, regardless of what they're feeling inside. They might avoid showing strong excitement or joy, and their expressions can sometimes seem muted or overly polite, even if they don't feel that way. Unlike those who are undercontrolled, overcontrolled individuals often take pride in their ability to keep their emotions in check, no matter the situation. For example, they might feel anxious on the inside but come across as composed or even indifferent on the outside, often downplaying their distress by saying, "I'm fine."

People with this overcontrolled style tend to dislike being the center of attention unless they've had time to prepare. This self-consciousness can sometimes make them hesitant to seek help for their mental health, and their inner struggles are often only known to their closest loved ones. When it comes to relationships and intimacy, these behaviors can create barriers, making it harder for them to connect with others emotionally. This can lead to feelings of isolation and loneliness, as their reserved social signals may unintentionally push people away.

BIOTEMPERAMENT MATTERS!

Let's talk about biotemperament and why it matters so much in understanding how we cope. RO-DBT and DBT both share a similar foundation: they focus on how our biological temperament and our environment shape the ways we cope with life. So, what exactly is "biotemperament"? Think of it as the genetic and biological tendencies we're born with—they influence how we see the world and how we handle our emotions. Just like some of us have blue eyes and others brown, our brains are all wired a bit differently. These differences shape how we experience the world around us.

For example, imagine someone who was born with a brain that tends to notice negative experiences more strongly than positive ones. This person might find it easier to see the thorns in a rose garden rather than the beautiful blooms. Now, picture that same person growing up in an environment that emphasizes self-discipline and avoiding mistakes. They might learn to hide their emotions and aim for perfection. This could mean they hold back from taking risks, always wanting to avoid making a mistake. To keep up the appearance of being in control, they might also mask their emotions, even when they're feeling really upset. Over time, they could become cautious about meeting new people, which might make them seem a bit distant or cold, even if deep down they're just trying to protect themselves. Understanding biotemperament helps us see why we act the way we do, and how our upbringing plays a huge role in shaping our responses. It's a blend of nature and nurture that creates our unique patterns of behavior.

WHY IS IT IMPORTANT FOR YOU TO KNOW YOUR COPING STYLE?

Before starting any kind of treatment, it's really helpful to ask yourself: does this fit my personality? Does this therapy help me make the changes I need for my mental health? You can get a better idea of where you stand by taking the assessments below to see if you lean more toward overcontrol or undercontrol. Don't worry—these are not measures of anything "wrong" with you. Having an overcontrol or undercontrol coping style isn't a problem in itself, and a high score in either doesn't mean you're in trouble. However, if you're dealing with challenges like an eating disorder, relationship issues, or concerns around intimacy, understanding whether you lean toward overcontrol or undercontrol can be really valuable.

ASSESSMENT: SELF-CONTROL

A. Behavioral Undercontrol Checklist

1. Impulsivity and risk-taking
   - ☐ I frequently act without considering the long-term consequences.
   - ☐ I sometimes engage in thrill-seeking activities, even if they are potentially harmful or reckless.
   - ☐ I struggle with resisting temptations, whether it's related to spending, food, or engaging in risky behaviors.

2. Difficulty regulating emotions
   - ☐ I experience frequent, intense emotional reactions that can be disruptive (anger, frustration, sadness).
   - ☐ I have trouble managing stress or anxiety, leading to outbursts.
   - ☐ I exhibit fluctuations in emotional states, sometimes shifting rapidly between high energy and low moods.

B. Behavioral Overcontrol Checklist

1. High self-discipline and restraint
   - ☐ I value punctuality and organization.
   - ☐ I prefer adhering to established plans or structures.
   - ☐ I follow strict dietary or lifestyle regimens.
   - ☐ I tend to avoid excess or indulgence in areas like food, entertainment, or spending.

2. Emotional control and suppression
   - ☐ I appear distant or unemotional in social interactions.
   - ☐ I tend to suppress negative emotions, such as sadness, frustration, or anger.
   - ☐ I strive to maintain control in both emotional and physical situations.
   - ☐ I feel anxious or upset when things are "out of control."

3. Disregard for social norms and rules
- ☐ I tend to challenge authority figures or societal expectations, often pushing boundaries.
- ☐ I sometimes engage in behaviors that are frowned on or outright against the rules.
- ☐ I have trouble following plans or obligations, often backing out at the last minute.

4. Difficulty with delayed gratification
- ☐ I seek instant gratification, often at the expense of long-term goals.
- ☐ I have a hard time sticking to goals that require patience or delayed gratification.

5. Lack of consistency in behavior
- ☐ I may be very productive at times but often neglect responsibilities when they feel uninteresting.
- ☐ I struggle to maintain effort over the long term, often abandoning tasks or projects.
- ☐ Decision-making can feel unpredictable, based on my current feelings or external pressures.
- ☐ I often swing between periods of activity and periods of inaction.

3. Perfectionism and high standards
- ☐ I set impossible standards for myself and others, leading to dissatisfaction.
- ☐ I constantly strive to improve and do not recognize or appreciate achievements.
- ☐ I become paralyzed by the possibility of making mistakes.
- ☐ I often avoid trying new things to prevent failure.

4. Rigid thinking and inflexibility
- ☐ I tend to view things as either right or wrong, good or bad, with little room for nuance.
- ☐ I am uncomfortable with uncertainty or ambiguity.
- ☐ I prefer familiar routines and may resist adapting to new situations.
- ☐ I struggle with spontaneity or deviation from the norm.

5. Hyper-self-monitoring and critical inner voice
- ☐ I regularly check in with myself, questioning my choices and actions.
- ☐ I experience excessive self-criticism for minor mistakes or perceived failures.
- ☐ I follow an internal code of behavior that might not align with social norms.
- ☐ I experience guilt, shame, or anxiety when not meeting my high standards.

6. Escaping stress through avoidance
   - ☐ I sometimes use substances (alcohol, drugs, etc.) to cope with stress or discomfort.
   - ☐ I engage in binge behaviors to numb feelings or distract from emotional pain.
   - ☐ I frequently engage in distractions (e.g., excessive social media use, gaming, overeating) to avoid facing difficult emotions or situations.

7. Difficulty coping with responsibility
   - ☐ I often avoid taking on adult responsibilities or facing challenges.
   - ☐ I have trouble taking care of mundane tasks like bills, work, or personal organization.
   - ☐ I focus more on having fun in the moment, with little concern for potential negative outcomes.

8. Disorganization and lack of structure
   - ☐ I am disorganized in terms of daily activities, personal space, or work habits.
   - ☐ I have difficulty planning or sticking to a schedule.

6. High need for control in social situations
   - ☐ I struggle to be emotionally vulnerable or open with others.
   - ☐ I avoid close relationships to maintain emotional distance and control.
   - ☐ I prefer to avoid confrontations, sometimes suppressing personal needs or desires to avoid disputes.

Total the checks in each column; the one with the most represents your dominant coping style. You are more prone to being under-controlled if you score higher in column A. You are more prone to being overcontrolled if you score higher in column B. A high score on either coping style does not necessarily mean that you are engaging in maladaptive overcontrolled or undercontrolled coping.

What is my coping style?

CASE STUDY: Jamie

Jamie, a 42-year-old, sought therapy after noticing that their coping hab-its negatively impacted their romantic relationship and ability to main-tain a balanced lifestyle. Jamie struggled with emotional undercontrol, leading to unpredictable interactions and disconnection from their part-ner. Jamie often used food as a coping mechanism, binge eating when feeling overwhelmed. This pattern extended into their romantic relation-ship, where they experienced cycles of emotional highs and lows, reacting impulsively to disagreements and sometimes withdrawing emotionally.

Understanding this helped Jamie realize that emotional flexibility was what they lacked. Jamie realized their goal wasn't perfect self-control but adapting their coping style. Through therapy, Jamie began identi-fying their patterns by reflecting on their eating behaviors and emo-tional responses. They learned techniques to regulate emotions without impulsive actions, practicing "down-regulating" when emotions got out of control. These strategies helped Jamie find a more balanced way of coping. By embracing flexibility, Jamie built a stronger connection with their partner, communicated their needs openly, and found healthier ways to cope with stress without using food. They learned to express emotions in a balanced way, helping their partner to better understand and support them.

CHAPTER 5

Sex-ED

GOALS

▶ Discover how attachments, coping mechanisms, eating behaviors, and sexual patterns evolve throughout your life.

▶ Understand how your past experiences have shaped the way you see yourself, connect with others, and engage in sexual relationships.

▶ Gain insight into why you hold certain beliefs, patterns, and behaviors that might be causing you pain or discomfort.

▶ Deepen your self-awareness around your own sexual development.

REFLECTING ON YOUR STORY

Our personal histories shape how we interact with the world, including our sexual relationships. Sometimes we aren't fully aware of how our past experiences influence us today. If you're struggling with intimacy, a therapist might ask you to explore your sexual history as a way to better understand yourself. This process can be like doing a bit of detective work to uncover things from your past that might still be affecting you.

In this chapter, I'll guide you through some of the questions I might ask in a sex therapy session. These questions are designed to help you gain insight into your sexual development and how your experiences have shaped your views of yourself, your relationships, and your sexuality. You decide what information you're comfortable sharing with others, whether that's your partner, therapist, or anyone else.

We'll take a journey through your sexual history from early life into adulthood, exploring how your attitudes and experiences around sex have changed over time—including before, during, and after any struggles with eating disorders. As you go through this chapter, remember there's no pressure to answer every question. Some questions might stir up difficult emotions, and that's okay. Take it at your own pace and engage with the parts that feel safe and helpful for you right now. If you find that some questions make you feel particularly vulnerable, that's often a sign they touch on something important for your current relationships. If you're working through this on your own and feel stuck, consider reaching out to a therapist. You don't have to do this alone, and there's no rush—go at a pace that feels right for you.

Pre-ED: Early experience sets the stage

Sexual development begins from birth, just like every other aspect of growing up. Children go through physical changes, but they also learn and absorb attitudes, beliefs, and behaviors about sexuality. Their knowledge and behavior are shaped by their age, what they observe from adults, and what they're taught, including cultural and religious influences.

Young children can be quite curious about other people's bodies, which can sometimes be surprising to adults. They may also discover that certain parts of their own bodies feel good when touched. As they spend time with peers, they start to pick up on gender roles. It's common for young kids to play games like "doctor" or imitate adult behaviors like kissing and holding hands. Children might try using "naughty" words or ask questions about topics such as where babies come from or the physical differences between boys and girls.

By the time they're in elementary school, kids become more aware of social norms and may start to feel more self-conscious or shy. They often want more privacy, especially around adults. Masturbation and sexual play are common, but children of this age usually keep it hidden from adults. As they approach puberty, many start looking for information about sexuality in media like TV, movies, or books to satisfy their growing curiosity about adult relationships. During adolescence, romantic and sexual interest in peers often starts to emerge.

Parents play a huge role in shaping their children's understanding of sexuality and body image. At every stage, kids need guidance, positive messages about boundaries, and open, supportive conversations about relationships and intimacy. Unfortunately, this doesn't always happen. There are lots of reasons why adults might hesitate to talk openly about these topics, including cultural or religious beliefs, personal discomfort, or simply not knowing how to start the conversation.

EXERCISE: Reflection

These questions are for your personal reflection. It's okay if not all questions apply to your experiences.

Experiences in early childhood

- How would I describe my childhood?
- To what extent did my family of origin share affection?
- Did the adult figures in my life show signs of emotional closeness, respect, and positive regard for one another? If so, how and how much?

Body messages from childhood

- How did I feel when I hit puberty?
- How did I feel about my physical changes during puberty?
- What body-related messages did my family generally communicate?
- What were the normative expectations placed on my body in my culture?
- In what ways did my sibling(s), friend(s), and/or the media influence my views on body image?
- When I was a kid, how did my parents approach conversations about bodies? Was there any discussion of different bodies?
- Could I ask questions about bodies if I wanted to? Did I get the information I needed?

Gender messages from childhood

- What gender-related messages did my family generally communicate?
- In my culture, what were the normative expectations placed on different genders?
- In what ways did my sibling(s), friend(s), and/or the media influence my views on gender?
- In what ways was I first aware of the differences between genders?

Sexuality messages from childhood

- How did my parents or other important adults in my life model marriage and sexuality for me? (Consider their views on commitment, intimacy, touch, and privacy.)
- Can I recall any times when I experimented with sexuality as a child? If my parents or caregivers found out, what was their reaction?

- Do I remember any early sexual experiences that were either positive or negative?
- How did I learn about sex—where, when, and from whom?
- What sexuality and sex education did I receive in school?
- What information about sex and sexuality did my parents teach me? Was anything useful? What was lacking?
- In what ways did my sibling(s), friend(s), and/or the media influence my views on sexuality, sensuality, and touch?
- To what extent did my religious upbringing shape my sexuality (thoughts and feelings about it) and my behavior?
- When I was a kid, how did my parents approach conversations about sexuality? Was there any sexual discussion? Possibly just implied or joked about? Was it forbidden?
- Could I ask questions about sex if I wanted to? Did I get the information I needed?
- What kinds of messages did they send about sexuality, nudity, touching others, contraception, premarital sex, having children, menstruation, and gender roles?

Pre-ED: A catalyst

For many people dealing with eating disorders, there's a belief that past abuse played a role in the development of their condition. In fact, about half of those struggling with anorexia report having experienced some form of physical, emotional, or sexual abuse. As a result, sexual experiences and self-image can be deeply impacted by these past traumas. While we don't completely understand how sexual trauma leads to an eating disorder, disrupted eating is often just one of the ways that broader post-traumatic stress symptoms show up. Sexual trauma can also stem from experiences that shouldn't be traumatic if our world were more compassionate—things like exploring gender identity, being part of the LGBTQ+ (lesbian, gay bisexual, transgender, queer, and others) community, having sex outside marriage, or simply existing in a way that some societies view with judgment or even punishment.

When trauma hits, the body and mind react in ways that make sense for survival. Eating disorders can often develop as part of this initial trauma response. Controlling food intake, for example, can feel like a way to regain some power or protection. Restricting food can help a person avoid feeling sexually attractive, create distance from overwhelming emotions like shame or pain, or even serve as a way to punish the body for not being able to "prevent" the trauma. These coping mechanisms can seem helpful, even logical, in the short term—a way to navigate through what feels impossible. For some, an eating disorder feels like the best, or maybe the least damaging, choice at the time. At least in the beginning.

ASSESSMENT: SEXUAL ABUSE HISTORY

What was your level of exposure to sexual abuse growing up, as an adult, or throughout your life?

This encompasses a wide range of experiences with sexual abuse, violence, and trauma, both overt and subtle, such as:

☐ being subjected to sexually explicit media without consent at any age

☐ being compelled, coerced, manipulated, seduced, or shamed into engaging in or receiving sexual touch, conversation, media, and/or intercourse

☐ hearing that your sexuality does not belong to you

☐ denigration, name-calling, or shaming of your gender, sexual orientation, body parts (especially chest, breasts, butt, genitals), or any type of sexuality

☐ being touched, hugged, tickled, cuddled, grabbed, pinched, smacked especially on your chest, breasts, butt, or genitals without consent or regard for boundaries, and/or being, coerced or shamed if you don't engage this way

☐ being made to share a bed with the parent because they need your attention or affection

☐ invasive or non-consensual sexual interest in your body, butt, genitals, and/or chest/breasts

☐ invasive questions or over-sharing around your sex life or their sex life

☐ putting constraints on your sexual identities by assuming that there is only one acceptable way to fantasize about, plan for, or otherwise organize sexual activity

☐ other:

Pre-ED: Body image contributes

For many people, the barriers to enjoying sex aren't always physical—sometimes, they're more about what's happening in our minds. Feeling uncomfortable or self-conscious about your body can make it really challenging to relax and enjoy intimacy. And this isn't just about people who have eating disorders; it's a common experience for many. These struggles often begin during adolescence or early adulthood, which is also a time when we start exploring our sexuality.

During these years, individuals typically become more self-aware of their appearance, and sometimes this heightened awareness turns into self-consciousness. Feminist theorists suggest that a lot of this pressure comes from how society often bases a person's worth on their attractiveness and sexual appeal. The portrayal of people in Western media—which often idealizes very specific body types—can make us feel as if we need to fit a certain mold to be desirable. This narrow beauty standard can lead many people to feel dissatisfied with their bodies, and in some cases, turn to harmful behaviors like disordered eating to try to fit in.

When body dissatisfaction takes hold, it can affect our sexual experiences in lots of ways. People who feel unhappy with their bodies often report having sex less frequently, experiencing fewer orgasms, and feeling less comfortable initiating sex. They might also avoid undressing in front of a partner, keep the lights off, or shy away from trying new things in bed because they're too preoccupied with how they look. On the other hand, people who feel good about their bodies tend to enjoy sex more—they often have higher sex drives, feel more confident, and are more comfortable expressing what they want.

ASSESSMENT: BODY IMAGE BEFORE THE EATING DISORDER
What was my body image like prior to my eating disorder?

Characteristics of a negative body image

- ☐ I had a distorted, inaccurate perception of my size and shape.
- ☐ I thought that only other people were attractive.
- ☐ I thought that my body size or shape was a sign of personal failure.
- ☐ I equated my weight or shape with my worth.
- ☐ I felt ashamed, anxious, and self-conscious about my body.
- ☐ I sometimes felt uncomfortable or awkward in my body.
- ☐ I spent an unreasonable amount of time worrying about my appearance, my weight, food, or calories.
- ☐ I sometimes avoided activities or places because of how I felt about my appearance.
- ☐ I avoided certain people because of the way I or they looked.

Characteristics of a positive body image

☐ I had an accurate perception of my size and shape.
☐ I celebrated and appreciated my natural body shape.
☐ I understood that a person's physical appearance says very little about their character and value as a person.
☐ I accepted my body and understood that all bodies are different.
☐ I refused to spend an unreasonable amount of time worrying about my appearance, weight, food, or calories.
☐ I felt comfortable and confident in my body.
☐ My appearance didn't determine my actions or behaviors.
☐ I felt comfortable around people of all shapes and sizes.

Pre-ED: Personality traits impact

Personality can be a tricky topic, right? Is it all about nature, or does nurture play a big part too? What makes us who we are, and does it really matter? When it comes to eating disorders and sexuality, these questions are especially important. It turns out that the same personality traits that are often linked to eating disorders may also be connected to certain sexual challenges. Many people with eating disorders attribute their sexual struggles to the disorder itself, but sometimes it has more to do with their personality. Personality traits linked to eating disorders can often influence how someone experiences sexuality. In a way, how a person interacts with their eating disorder often mirrors how they behave sexually. People with restrictive eating disorders often have a similarly restrictive relationship with sex, while those with binge-purge behaviors might use sex for other reasons—like to regulate their mood or to gain approval by meeting their partner's needs.

EXERCISE: Reflection

• Do my eating behaviors follow a pattern? Do they feel more constricted or impulsive?
• Is my sexual style more constricted or impulsive?
• Do I lean toward over- or undercontrol? Somewhere in the middle? Or both?

Pre-ED/Emerging ED: Depression demotivates/anxiety avoids

It's not always just the eating disorder itself that leads to a decrease in sex drive—other factors that come along with the eating disorder can play a big role too. Take depression, for instance. It can impact sexual function all on its own, and studies estimate that 33–50% of people with eating disorders also experience mood disorders like depression (Hambleton *et al.*, 2022). So, it makes sense that this could be another reason for a lower sex drive. Plus, the treatment for depression can be important to consider. Medications like selective serotonin reuptake inhibitors (SSRIs), which are often prescribed for both depression and eating disorders, are known to affect sexual function. Common side effects can include a reduced desire for sex and difficulty reaching orgasm.

EXERCISE: Reflection

- Did I have a diagnosis of anxiety or depressive disorder as a child or teenager?
- Did I take any psychiatric medication for anxiety or depression? Were there any side effects?
- If never formally diagnosed, did I experience symptoms of anxiety or depression?

Pre-Ed/Emerging ED: A new sexual interest

For many, an eating disorder can prevent the natural development of sexual experiences. It can create a barrier that stops them from participating in the activities that others their age might be experiencing. In fact, before the onset of an eating disorder, people with anorexia tend to have lower levels of sexual desire and activity, and their first sexual experiences often happen later compared to those with bulimia. This can lead to spiraling anxiety, especially when they compare themselves to others. Feeling inexperienced or anxious about their sexuality might make them hesitate to explore it at all, which only reinforces those fears.

EXERCISE: Reflection

- In what ways did I explore my own sexuality with or without the involvement of a partner?

- Socially and sexually, what was high school like? What were my dating experiences like for me?
- What were the context/age/thoughts/feelings of my first sexual experience? Were my thoughts and feelings about this experience positive, negative, or neutral at the time?
- When did I begin dating?
- How did my dating experiences help shape my view of my masculinity or femininity?
- How did they impact my view of sex?

Sexual identity is all about how you see your own sexuality. There are several components that shape this sense of identity, each playing an important role in how you understand yourself.

First, there's *gender identity*. This is your internal sense of who you are in terms of gender. It might match the sex you were assigned at birth, or it might be different. It's your own, innate understanding of your gender.

Next is *gender expression*. This is how you choose to show your gender to the world—through your clothing, hairstyle, voice, mannerisms, and activities. It's all those outward cues that communicate who you are.

Then there's *orientation*, which has a few layers:

- *Sexual orientation:* Who you're attracted to sexually.
- *Romantic orientation:* Who you feel romantic love for, which can be different from who you're sexually attracted to.
- *Erotic orientation:* What turns you on or brings you to orgasm—this could be different from your real-life encounters.
- *Relationship orientation:* This refers to the kind of romantic or sexual relationships you prefer, whether that's casual dating, monogamy, open relationships, swinging, polyamory, or something else.

Your sexuality isn't defined by who you have sex with or how often. Instead, it's about your feelings, thoughts, attractions, and behaviors. It's all about what draws you to others—physically, sexually, or emotionally. Sexuality is a deeply personal part of who you are, and exploring it can be exciting, liberating, and deeply rewarding. Figuring out your sexuality doesn't always happen overnight. It's something that can evolve over time, and it's okay if you're still figuring things out. Sexuality can be complex. There's no pressure to fit into any specific label—it's entirely up to you to decide what feels right.

While there are many terms to describe different aspects of sexual identity, you don't need a label unless it helps you feel understood.

> **AUTHOR'S NOTE: ON ORIENTATIONS**
> Sometimes, our sexual and erotic desires don't quite match up. It's totally normal to fantasize about things you might not actually want to do in real life. Despite what society might suggest, it's perfectly okay to have fantasies that stay just that—fantasies!

EXERCISE: Reflection

- What does this mean to me?
- What feelings are coming up right now?
- How would I describe my gender?
- How do I express my gender?
- Has my understanding of my gender changed over time?
- How would I describe my sexual orientation?
- Has my understanding of my sexual orientation changed over time?
- Did I ever experience discrimination, abuse, bullying, or other negative experiences due to other people's view of my sexuality or gender?
- How has my sexual identity (gender, expressions, orientations, etc.) been related to my eating disorder?
- How has my eating disorder impacted my sexual identity?
- Does my sexual identity affect my eating disorder?

Emerging ED/Active ED: Food and sex speak for us

For many of us who have struggled with eating disorders, it can be difficult to recognize and express our need for emotional support. As we move through recovery, we're encouraged to find new ways to express ourselves—and while this process is challenging, it's also incredibly rewarding. In therapy, we often begin to understand that the eating disorder may have been a way to communicate our painful emotions and unmet needs. Feelings like anger, guilt, inadequacy, loneliness, and fear often play a big role. And we might also realize that we longed for care and connection from loved ones but didn't know how to ask for it. The eating disorder may have become a way of expressing our unmet emotional needs when we couldn't find the words.

EXERCISE: Reflection

- What was my eating disorder trying to say then?
- What is my eating disorder trying to say now?
- What was my sexuality trying to say then?
- What is my sexuality trying to say now?

Emerging ED/Active ED: Malnutrition desexualizes

Malnutrition is a common consequence of eating disorders, especially those involving restriction. When the body doesn't get enough nutrients, it prioritizes survival, and non-essential systems, like reproductive function, slow down. Low levels of hormones like testosterone, estrogen, and progesterone—key players in sexual health—mean that people with restrictive eating disorders often experience a reduced sex drive.

Early weight loss, which often signals the onset of a restrictive eating disorder, might initially boost some people's sexual confidence because of the societal value placed on thinness. As malnutrition worsens, it causes significant shifts in hormone levels and neurotransmitter balance—changes that often lead to a noticeable drop in sexual interest and activity. Neurotransmitters, the brain's chemical messengers, are essential for regulating mood, behavior, cognition, and a range of bodily functions, including sexual desire. There are some specific physical factors at play too. People with vaginas who continue to have sex may struggle with vaginal dryness, lack of lubrication, or difficulty reaching orgasm—often due to a mix of physical and psychological reasons. This shift in hormones is similar to the changes that happen during menopause, and it can significantly affect sexual desire and experiences.

For those with penises, malnutrition can really take a toll on sexual health in a few ways. It can lower testosterone levels, leading to a reduced sex drive, and even make issues like erectile dysfunction more likely by affecting blood flow. Poor nutrition also impacts sperm quality, making it harder to maintain fertility. Plus, fatigue and low energy—common symptoms of malnutrition—can make intimacy feel exhausting rather than enjoyable.

EXERCISE: Reflection

- What were my sexual experiences during the beginning of my eating disorder?
- What was my relationship with my body at this stage?

Active ED: ED takes priority

If you're struggling with an eating disorder, you might notice that your focus has shifted almost entirely to thoughts about food, weight, size, and shape. It can feel as if there's no room left for anything else, and your connection to your own body starts to fade. The idea of being in touch with your body—whether it's for your own well-being or for intimacy with someone else—might seem distant, even repulsive. In these moments, it feels as if your whole life is wrapped up in managing hunger, ignoring bodily sensations, or dealing with the effects of starving yourself, like feeling cold, weak, or fatigued. Your appetite for anything beyond food—including intimacy—starts to disappear.

In this state, it's hard to connect to your body in a loving way, let alone share it with someone else. Eating disorders can create a barrier between us and the natural experience of sexual desire. Instead of enjoying intimacy and the vulnerability that comes with it, we may feel compelled to control every aspect of it. We might insist on keeping the lights off, avoiding nudity, or covering parts of ourselves we don't like. It can become impossible to feel fully present or experience pleasure without a sense of control.

In some cases, this desire for control can manifest in sexual activity as a coping mechanism. Rather than engaging in intimacy to experience connection and joy, some individuals might turn to sex as a way to distract themselves from overwhelming feelings. It can become a way to exert control over a part of themselves that feels otherwise out of control, or a way to gain validation that temporarily soothes emotional distress. However, this often leads to more disconnection from the true experience of sexuality and intimacy—making it harder to find healing, both in the body and in relationships.

EXERCISE: Reflection

- What were my body experiences during the worst of my eating disorder?

- What was my relationship with my body during the worst stage?
- What was my relationship with sex during the worst stage?

Recovery: Sex is a source of fear, comfort, healing, and pleasure, all at the same time

Research shows that, as you might expect, when other aspects of life start to improve during recovery, so does sexuality (Meguerditchian *et al.*, 2009; Morgan *et al.*, 1999). Studies tracking people through weight restoration and recovery found that sex drive increased as weight and mood stabilized. Gaining weight can be an uncomfortable and even frightening process, but it is often accompanied by an increase in sexual interest and a reduction in depression. Unfortunately, these studies tend to stop before participants reach an average weight, so we don't always get the full picture. But given that healthy relationships—romantic ones included—are often major sources of support during recovery, it's important to explore how sexual enjoyment can change and improve over time.

It's also fascinating to think about how emotional and sexual recovery are intertwined. For some, the experience of falling in love comes earlier than the return of lust or sexual interest. Reawakening one's emotional and sexual self can feel both thrilling and terrifying. Suddenly feeling all these intense, unpredictable emotions—like love—can be scary, but also wonderful. In many ways, it's like nourishing your emotional self just as you're nourishing your physical body in recovery. It is a sign of growing strength.

Giving yourself space to explore sexual desire can feel just as frightening as allowing yourself to eat something you've been craving. Or you might decide not to act on those desires if they feel unsafe or overwhelming—that's okay too. Experiencing new physical sensations, whether it's hunger, fullness, or a rush of desire, can feel strange and unsettling at first. But there's nothing inherently dangerous about reconnecting with your sexual self. You may worry about becoming self-indulgent or losing control—similar to fears about food and weight. This anxiety is natural, especially if you haven't had much experience with how our systems of desire and fulfillment tend to balance themselves out over time.

In eating disorder recovery, the approach is often to move slowly from a structured meal plan to more intuitive eating, based on hunger and fullness. It's a gradual process—both to avoid physical risks and to ease the emotional adjustment. The same idea can apply to sex. That doesn't mean you need to schedule intimacy in your planner—that might feel too rigid. Instead, think of it as a step-by-step process, one that you can move through at your own pace, gradually building comfort and spontaneity.

EXERCISE: Reflection

- What were my body experiences during early recovery?
- What was my relationship with my body during early recovery?
- What was my relationship with sex during early recovery?

EVERYTHING CHANGES AND EVENTUALLY FINDS ITS PLACE

Taking things slowly means being gentle with yourself, allowing for patience, and avoiding comparisons. Your journey is your own, and it will look different from anyone else's. Remember, how things are now isn't how they'll always be. Everything changes, and eventually, things do find their place. If your eating disorder is linked to traumatic experiences with sex, remember to be especially gentle and kind with yourself—and if you can, seek professional support to help you through. Treat yourself the way you would a dear friend: with compassion, care, and understanding.

As you move through recovery, you might notice that relationships of all kinds begin to shift. Ending a long-term illness can be disorienting, not only for you but also for those around you. You may find yourself stepping out of the role of "the sick one" and into someone entirely new—a person even you might not fully recognize yet. These shifts can put some unexpected strain on family and friendships. Some relationships will endure, others may drift away, and many will transform, just like you are. Letting go can be tough, but it's also a powerful part of this journey. The more you grow, the more you'll create space for new relationships that align with who you're becoming. Friendships, like romantic relationships, will take time, patience, and care—from both you and others. It might feel overwhelming to dive into dating, especially after a long time out of that world, and while hook-up apps might not feel quite right, low-pressure environments like coffee shops or even work connections might be better suited for where you're at.

Feeling confident in your sexuality can be especially challenging after an eating disorder. If you're connecting with someone who hasn't been through the same struggles, it's easy to assume they're more confident than they really are. The truth is, most people feel a little insecure, especially at first.

If it's your first time being intimate—or your first time in a long while—it might not be amazing right away. Like anything else, sex takes practice, and it's not always easy. Eating disorders often come with the need to be perfect, but recovery is about embracing the messy parts of life, too—including awkward or "bad" sex. Lean into the learning process. Explore, experiment, and take note of how far you've come. And if something doesn't feel right, don't hesitate to speak up or seek out what you need. Sex, at its best, is about connection—with others, yes, but also with yourself. Give yourself the grace to learn, grow, and enjoy the journey at your own pace.

EXERCISE: Reflection

- Where am I now? What is my relationship with my body, sex, and intimacy?
- As I look back over my personal sexual history, what would I change if I could?
- As I look back over my personal sexual history, what insights have I gained into my current sexual functioning and/or intimate relationships?
- What would I like to change the most about my current sex life and intimate relationships? Why are these issues the most important to me? Are they equally or more important to any current partner(s)?

HOW TO ASSESS YOUR SEXUAL SCRIPTS

We all have our own thoughts, feelings, and beliefs about sex. For some, talking about sexuality may feel awkward or shameful, while for others, it might be easier and more open—but many people fall somewhere in between. Sexual scripts are the internalized beliefs, narratives, and expectations we hold about sex, and they are influenced by our culture, upbringing, and personal experiences. From the moment we're born, we absorb society's expectations and norms—many of which are based on our gender. Girls are often taught to be nurturing and emotional, while boys are expected to be tough and not show feelings. As we grow, we develop our own sexual "scripts"—the set of ideas that guide how we think about and express our sexuality. To understand your own sexual scripts, it helps to understand the concept of sexual norms and the idea of social constructionism—the belief that we give meaning to the world around us through our experiences. As you explore your own sexual script, it's important to separate external messages from your personal feelings.

Sexual norms are the beliefs, behaviors, and attitudes about sexuality that society views as acceptable. These norms can change over time—for example, birth control is now widely available, whereas it used to be restricted. Sexual norms also vary across cultures; in some places, having multiple partners is common, while in others, monogamy is the expectation. Even if we don't agree with these norms, they still influence how we form our own beliefs about sex.

In the past 30 years, dating norms have shifted significantly toward increased acceptance of premarital sex, more casual hookups facilitated by dating apps, a greater emphasis on personal agency and communication in relationships, and a wider acceptance of diverse sexualities and gender identities, with the most notable change being the widespread adoption of online dating platforms as the primary way to meet potential partners.

Social constructionism suggests that our understanding of the world is shaped by shared experiences and assumptions. In the context of sexuality, the theory of sexual scripts explains that our attitudes and behaviors around sex are formed through cultural, social, and personal experiences. Understanding your own sexual scripts can help you feel more confident and self-aware, which benefits your relationships with others. Recognizing these scripts is the first step to changing them if they no longer serve you well. Remember, this is a personal and ongoing process—take your time and revisit these questions whenever you are ready.

EXERCISE: Exploring sexual attitudes and beliefs

The goal of this exercise is to get you to recognize and start working through any unhelpful or limiting ideas, values, or norms you may hold regarding sexuality. This aids in the formation of a positive sexual identity, which is crucial to the growth of a satisfying sexual partnership. You'll also be able to recognize the sex-positive and affirming beliefs, attitudes, and ideas you've developed.

Here are some questions to ask yourself in order to better understand your sexual scripts.

- What do I think about sex? How do I feel about it?
- What does sex mean to me? What is its purpose?
- What do I think about my body...all parts of it? Are there any parts I am uncomfortable with?
- What do I think about the bodies of other genders...all parts of them? Are there any parts I am uncomfortable with?

- What are my insecurities, vulnerabilities, fears, memories, and inhibitions regarding sex and sexuality?
- How do I feel about my body in different contexts (e.g., at the beach, in the bedroom)?
- What inhibitions or psychological barriers do I think I may have regarding sex?
- How important is sexuality to me?
- How do I honestly feel about having sex?
- Are there things in my sexuality that scare me?
- When do I feel the most shame?
- How comfortable am I communicating my sexual wants or dislikes?
- Do I feel confident exploring my sexuality?
- Do I expect each sexual encounter to be equally satisfying?
- What is the most enjoyable part of sex for me? The least enjoyable?
- What aspects of my sexual life do I value and would like to keep? To hold on to?
- What aspects of a sexual life would I still like to experience?
- What are my beliefs about the place of sexuality in a person's life?

ASSESSMENT: SEXUAL ATTITUDES

Mark one of the following for each item: positive, negative, or neutral, depending on how you feel about it.

Do I currently feel positive, negative, or neutral about:

- my genitals
  ☐ positive   ☐ negative   ☐ neutral

- my body
  ☐ positive   ☐ negative   ☐ neutral

- masturbation
  ☐ positive   ☐ negative   ☐ neutral

- mutual masturbation
  ☐ positive   ☐ negative   ☐ neutral

- oral sex
  ☐ positive   ☐ negative   ☐ neutral

- foreplay
  □ positive   □ negative   □ neutral

- vaginal intercourse
  □ positive   □ negative   □ neutral

- anal intercourse
  □ positive   □ negative   □ neutral

- erotic media (movies, books, web content)
  □ positive   □ negative   □ neutral

- pornography (movies, books, web content)
  □ positive   □ negative   □ neutral

- my sexual fantasies
  □ positive   □ negative   □ neutral

- my sexual orientation
  □ positive   □ negative   □ neutral

- my gender identity
  □ positive   □ negative   □ neutral

- my sexual appetite
  □ positive   □ negative   □ neutral

- my sexual interests and desires
  □ positive   □ negative   □ neutral

- others' perceptions of my sexual self
  □ positive   □ negative   □ neutral

HOW TO SHIFT YOUR SEXUAL SCRIPTS

Remember, exploring your sexual script is not about achieving perfection, but about understanding and embracing your unique path toward a fulfilling and positive sexual identity.

1. Explore your body

Take time to connect with your body and discover what feels good. This can start with solo exploration—touching yourself and noticing how different sensations feel in different parts of your body. If you have internalized negative messages about masturbation, this might feel uncomfortable at first, but over time, it can help you build a positive relationship with your body and your pleasure. Society often focuses on how we look, rather than how we feel inside. Reconnecting with your body can help you feel more comfortable in your skin and with your desires. Solo exploration is a powerful way to get to know your body and what brings you pleasure. You can also explore with a partner, sharing what feels good for both of you. If you feel uncomfortable or triggered by this exploration, it's okay to start slowly and seek support if needed.

2. Accept your thoughts

It's natural to want to push away uncomfortable thoughts, but trying to force them out of your mind usually makes them stronger. Instead, notice when these thoughts come up and name them. For example, if you feel shame about a sexual thought, acknowledge it: "I'm feeling shame right now." Recognize that it's okay to have these thoughts, and try to treat yourself with compassion. Accepting your thoughts, rather than fighting them, is a key step in changing your reactions to them. Remember that accepting uncomfortable thoughts does not mean agreement with those thoughts—it's about recognizing their presence and moving forward despite them.

3. Question your scripts

To shift your sexual scripts, you often need to challenge them head on. If you've always believed something like "pornography is wrong" but want to explore it now, try watching ethical porn and see how it feels ("ethical porn" refers to adult content that is produced with a focus on fairness, consent, and respect for everyone involved, both in front of and behind the camera). No script is inherently right or wrong—it's about what works for you. Evaluating your beliefs and experimenting with new ideas can help you determine which scripts are helpful and which ones are limiting.

4. Create new meanings

Your reactions reveal a lot about your sexual scripts. For instance, if your partner declines sex, you might interpret it as "They don't love me" or "I must look unattractive." Instead, consider other possibilities: "Maybe they're just tired" or "Maybe they have a headache." Shifting your interpretation can help you rewrite your script and foster healthier, more realistic perspectives.

EXERCISE: Goal setting worksheet

When clients first come to me for therapy, they frequently have very specific issues they want to address or symptoms that are upsetting them. However, they might also be bothered by other problems or even be unaware of some of them. This exercise is intended to assist you in identifying potential goals and help you consider areas you might want to work on. Jot your answers down in your notebook.

- Begin by listing any psychological symptoms or problems that are currently bothering you.
- Now, list any physical symptoms that are bothering you. Sometimes, physical symptoms may be connected to psychological issues.
- Write down any issues with body image that you would like to change.
- Write down any issues with disordered eating behaviors that you would like to change.
- Write down any issues with sex that you would like to change.
- How will you know when things are getting better?
- Write down the most important goal for your healing.
- List any other goals you have.

AUTHOR'S NOTE: ON MASTERY

Hey there, especially to my fellow overcontrolled copers, just a quick reminder: you don't need to master every single exercise in this book. Seriously, the goal here isn't to be the "best" at these skills. If you try an exercise a few times and it doesn't seem to click, that's totally okay! Not everything works for everyone.

Please don't feel that you have to succeed at every single thing just because it's suggested. The important thing is finding what works *for you* and what helps you move toward your goals.

CASE EXAMPLE: Emile

Emile, a 32-year-old trans man, sought therapy for intimacy issues and body image struggles. Raised in a conservative family, Emile described his childhood as loving but emotionally restrictive. Affection between his parents was rare, and discussions about bodies, sexuality, or emotions were taboo. His goal in therapy was to understand how his past experiences influenced his current relationships, sexual health, and self-worth. Emile explored his early family dynamics and identified that his parents rarely showed physical affection or emotional vulnerability. This lack of modeled intimacy shaped Emile's understanding of relationships. As an adult, he struggled to open up emotionally and feared abandonment. During puberty, Emile internalized negative body messages. He began feeling dysphoric in his developing body and guilty about his curiosity regarding sexuality. His eating disorder, which began at 16, was partly a response to these feelings. It allowed him to exert control over his body and desexualize it. As his weight dropped, his sexual desire diminished, and intimacy became a source of anxiety. He actively avoided intimacy, preferring to hide his body and feeling uncomfortable being touched.

As Emile moved toward recovery and gender congruence, his sexual interest increased, which both excited and terrified him. He began to recognize how his body image was intertwined with his sexual relationships. By reflecting on his sexual history and the connections between his eating disorder, gender identity, and body image, Emile gained a deeper understanding of himself. He learned that his intimacy struggles were not just about sex but also about his need for safety, autonomy, and acceptance. Emile's experience highlights how sexual scripts, shaped by cultural expectations and family dynamics, can impact sexual identity and relationships.

PART 2

Tame It

— CHAPTER 6 —

Wise Mind, Flexible Mind

GOALS

▶ Learn about the mind states associated with overcontrol and undercontrol.

▶ Identify which mind state you tend to operate from and how these mind states affect your thoughts, emotions, and behaviors.

▶ Learn the benefits of mindfulness, how to practice mindfulness depending on your coping style, and when to apply mindfulness skills.

Overcontrolled focus: Overcontrolled states of mind (Fixed Mind, Fatalistic Mind, and Flexible Mind)

Undercontrolled focus: Undercontrolled states of mind (Emotional Mind, Rational Mind, and Wise Mind)

WHAT IS MINDFULNESS?

Mindfulness can feel elusive—something you know is good for you, but what exactly is it? Is it a goal, a journey, or something else? A common misconception is that mindfulness means clearing your mind completely, but that's far from the truth. Instead, mindfulness is about accepting whatever thoughts or emotions come up, without judgment. Another confusion people have is between mindfulness and meditation. Meditation is a practice that helps calm the mind, while mindfulness is more of a way of being—staying present in the moment, whether you're meditating or just brushing your teeth. It's the simple act of "dropping in" to the present, wherever your thoughts may have wandered before. When we practice mindfulness while having a conversation, we give the person we're speaking with our full attention, fostering deeper connection.

Mindfulness and eating disorders

If you're struggling with eating disorders, it can often feel as if your mind is constantly at war with itself. Eating disorders can be overwhelming, often distorting reality and triggering harmful thought cycles. Mindfulness helps in calming the mind and creating a pause before acting on disordered eating behaviors. It provides a peaceful way to reconnect with your body and emotions, fostering healing and clarity.

Mindfulness-based therapy for eating disorders encourages us not to run away from difficult emotions, but to face them openly. It's not about trying to get rid of negative feelings but about being fully present with them. Over time, this helps reduce negative thinking patterns, improve emotional regulation, and increase awareness of hunger and fullness signals. It teaches us to respond rather than react.

Mindfulness and sex

Mindful sex helps us drop distractions, focusing on the moment, which enhances arousal and intimacy. When your mind and body are in sync, sexual performance and satisfaction improve. To reach peak arousal, we need to be fully engaged in the erotic experience—without distractions. But stress, anxiety, or even the pressures of daily life can interfere with our ability to be fully present during intimacy.

Practicing mindfulness during sex can help you let go of anxious thoughts and focus on what's happening right here, right now. This can lead to deeper arousal, more satisfaction, and a greater sense of connection with your partner(s). It's about continuously letting go of distractions and refocusing on your own sensations and your partner's touch, allowing pleasure to grow. This approach makes the experience richer, more enjoyable, and more connected, allowing you to overcome many common sexual concerns—like performance anxiety, body image issues, or communication barriers.

AUTHOR'S NOTE: ON MINDFULNESS AND HEALING FROM TRAUMA

Mindfulness is a powerful tool for healing from sexual trauma. After experiencing unwanted sexual acts, many people dissociate as a protective response—leaving them feeling disconnected from their bodies long after the trauma.

Mindfulness helps reverse this. By staying present and tuning in to current sensations and emotions, you begin to shift away from fear and disconnection. Because the brain naturally fixates on danger and negative memories, mindfulness helps rebalance your focus, grounding you in safety and the present moment.

Over time, it can restore a sense of control, connection, and peace within your body.

EXERCISE: Reflection

- What specific moments in my sexual experiences make me feel disconnected, and what might help me re-engage?
- Do I sometimes feel as if I am not present during sex or I am just going through the motions?
- Take note of any recurrent thoughts during sex (e.g., How does my body look? How long will this take? Does this feel good for my partner(s)? Are they judging me?).

The benefits of mindfulness for sex

Mindfulness can deepen your shared pleasure, improve your sexual performance, and help you become more in tune with your partner(s). Do you ever find your mind wandering during sex? You're definitely not alone. We've all had moments where we or our partner(s) seem distracted, and it's completely natural. Our minds have a habit of drifting, and sometimes we don't even realize how attractive we are to our partner(s). What could be more alluring than partners who're completely comfortable in their own skin? Practicing mindfulness, particularly focusing on acceptance, can help bring us back to the moment.

Imagine how it feels to know your partner is fully focused on you during sex. How does it change your experience when you're completely present— not thinking about the past or worrying about the future? Does it feel different? More intimate? More pleasurable? Mindfulness can also help set more realistic expectations for your sex life. Aiming for "perfect sex" all the time often results in disappointment. Our bodies aren't flawless, and what we see in pornography is far from reality. Acceptance is key to enhancing the quality of sex. This means embracing differences in libido, sexual preferences, and even moments when our bodies don't respond the way we'd like. Self-acceptance and acceptance of our partner(s) can be challenging, especially given the shame and secrecy often surrounding sex. Being gentle and realistic with ourselves is crucial. Mindfulness can help us bring empathy to our sexual experiences—for ourselves and for our partner(s).

Practicing mindfulness also fosters compassion for each other's sexual challenges. Many people in sexual or romantic relationships, regardless of gender, struggle to understand the experience of their partner(s). Slowing down, listening, and approaching these conversations with compassion helps create safety and trust. Compassionate conversations about sexual desires, concerns, and needs may feel vulnerable, but they are worth it for the intimacy they create.

Mindfulness can also indirectly improve your sex life by deepening your emotional bond. Taking a few minutes to hold each other mindfully, with compassion and acceptance, can help you relax and boost hormones like oxytocin and dopamine, which make us feel connected and safe. By being present with any of your five senses—touch, taste, smell, sound, or sight—you can become more attuned to your own body and your partner's, creating more satisfying sexual experiences.

Rather than rushing into intercourse, mindfulness helps us slow down and truly savor the experience, from foreplay to every touch. Many couples fall into routines, jumping straight to penetration, but there's so much more to explore. Savoring each moment, at your own pace, is what makes sex truly fulfilling.

COPING STYLE AND STATES OF MIND
Undercontrolled states of mind

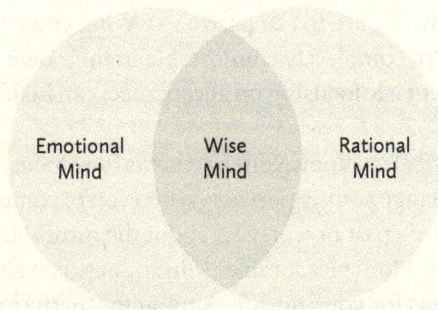

| Emotional Mind | Wise Mind | Rational Mind |

States of Mind: Undercontrol
Wise Mind helps you make decisions by balancing your Emotional and Rational Mind.

In Dialectical Behavior Therapy for undercontrol, we talk about three different mind states: Emotional Mind, Rational Mind, and Wise Mind (Linehan, 2014). Each of these mind states represents a different way of thinking and responding to the world, and a central goal in DBT is to help individuals shift from extreme states (Emotional or Rational Mind) into the balanced, integrated state of Wise Mind. The concept of mind states is central to understanding how individuals regulate their emotions and behaviors. At any moment, we can find ourselves in one of these states, which influence how we react and make decisions. Understanding these three can help you notice which one you tend to lean on, and what it feels like in your body when you do.

Emotional Mind

Think of a time when you've said something in anger or reacted out of frustration. That's your Emotional Mind at work—where feelings are in the driver's seat. When you're in your Emotional Mind, it's hard to think clearly or see things objectively. It's as if your emotions are running the show, sometimes making you act impulsively or say things you might regret later. The Emotional Mind can be overwhelming, but it's also an important part of who we are. It's what lets us feel deeply at special moments, like weddings or graduations. But when our emotions get too intense, they can cloud our judgment, making us reactive instead of thoughtful. People might describe you as "intense" or "hot-headed" when you're in this state, and it becomes tough to see things clearly or make rational decisions.

The Emotional Mind isn't always negative. It's what makes us passionate—whether we're standing up for something we believe in, writing from the heart, or loving deeply. However, when our emotions take over completely, it can be overwhelming and painful, leaving us anxious or scared. Everyday stressors like lack of sleep, being sick, overworking, or even just being hungry can make the Emotional Mind harder to manage. We all have moments when the Emotional Mind takes charge. It's part instinct, part learned response, shaped by all the experiences we've had in life. The key is learning to recognize it, so we can decide whether we want to let our emotions lead or find a better balance.

EMOTIONAL MIND
Thoughts

- Search for, interpret, favor, and recall information in a way that confirms your pre-existing beliefs
- Happen on autopilot
- Subjective opinion is all-encompassing and absolute in its personal significance

Emotions

- Anger
- Fear
- Anxiety
- Sadness
- Stress

Actions, urges, behaviors

- React aggressively or antagonistically
- Question or attack the other person's perspective
- Seek revenge
- Impulsive and reckless
- Very little deliberation or conscious effort
- Inner state and outer actions are difficult to control or override
- Fighting with someone you disagree with
- Taking an impulse trip without planning
- The urge to fight or flee
- Yelling or screaming at someone

Rational Mind

When you're in your Rational Mind, your focus is on thoughts rather than emotions. This means making decisions based on logic and facts, not feelings. In this mode, you rely on data, analysis, and careful planning to solve problems. You come across as calm, collected, and very goal-oriented—almost like an "inner professor" that's all about clarity and reason.

However, when you're fully in your Rational Mind, emotions often take a back seat, which can make you seem distant or even a little cold, especially in situations that call for empathy or emotional connection. It's as if your focus narrows entirely to the task at hand, and you might feel less in tune with your own feelings or those of others. The Rational Mind just thinks, assesses, and plans. It doesn't feel. It's the part of you that stays composed under pressure and can think clearly when emotions are running high. Everyone has this Rational Mind; it's just about learning when to call on it.

RATIONAL MIND
Thoughts

- Deliberate, done with careful consideration and foresight
- Not deciding until all information has been gathered
- Adhering to any and all the facts that you come across and ignoring anything not considered factual
- Making decisions based only on observable, external information, and not on anything derived from internal states

Emotions

- Considered irrelevant

Actions, urges, behaviors

- Research
- Plan
- Measure
- Ask
- Study

Wise Mind

Have you ever made a decision that just felt right, even if it didn't make complete sense to everyone else? That's your Wise Mind in action. The Wise Mind is the balance between two other states: the Rational Mind, which focuses on logic and facts, and the Emotional Mind, which reacts based on feelings. Instead of letting these two battle it out, the Wise Mind invites us to blend them, creating a calm space where emotions and logic work together.

Think of it like a Venn diagram—the Rational Mind and Emotional Mind are the two circles, and the Wise Mind sits in the middle, drawing from both. In this state, you can make decisions that respect your emotions without losing sight of reason. It's a place where you can act according to your values, while still considering your gut instincts and intuition. Of course, this balance isn't always simple. When you're overwhelmed by emotions, it might feel impossible to access your Rational Mind. Similarly, if you're stuck in your Rational Mind, it might seem hard to allow emotions in. To live in the Wise Mind, it's important to be aware of where you are at any given moment and work to bring both parts into harmony. Sometimes this means taking a break when your emotions are intense, or making room for empathy when you feel disconnected.

When we live in the Wise Mind, there's a sense of peace and balance. We trust our decisions, feel confident, and understand our next steps. Our emotions are welcomed, and our thoughts are clear. The Wise Mind isn't about perfection; it's about showing up for ourselves with honesty and respect, making choices that align with our values and improve our relationships. It feels calm, not chaotic; grounded, not hurried. It's when you know, deep down, that you're making the right choice—even if it's not the easiest one.

Overcontrolled states of mind

Coping mechanisms for people with overcontrolled tendencies can vary a lot. When it comes to handling life's challenges and making everyday decisions, those of us who lean toward overcontrol often shift between three different mindsets: Fixed Mind, Fatalistic Mind, and Flexible Mind (Lynch, 2018a). These mindsets emerge as ways to try to ease anxiety.

It's pretty common to respond with either a Fixed Mind or a Fatalistic Mind when we're feeling challenged—whether it's tough feedback, not getting what we want, or just the general overwhelm of life. When faced with unexpected changes or when told we need to adapt, many overcontrolling folks try to minimize or ignore what's happening. This is often just an attempt to feel less anxious, but it also makes it harder to learn new skills and grow in our flexibility.

Taking criticism is especially hard for those with overcontrolling tendencies. We often want to keep things predictable and orderly, and when faced with something new or uncomfortable, our instinct might be to dismiss or deny it. This makes change tough and can really stand in the way of building the adaptability we need to thrive.

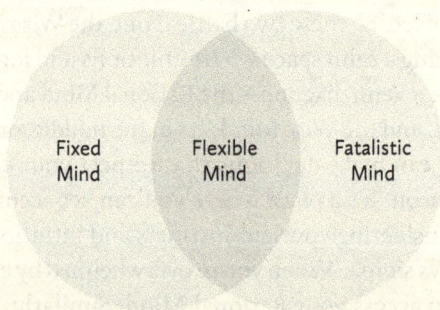

Fixed Mind | Flexible Mind | Fatalistic Mind

States of Mind: Overcontrol

Flexible Mind helps you adapt your behaviors and thinking for what is needed in the moment.

Fixed Mind

Meet the Fixed Mind—our inner "fighter." This part of us can be both a protector and, at times, the reason we feel stuck. For those of us who tend to be a bit more overcontrolled, getting into a fixed state of mind can often be tricky. It can make relationships harder because it prevents us from learning and growing from new experiences or feedback. The Fixed Mind is what shows up when we feel threatened, emotionally or otherwise. The Fixed Mind says, "I already know the answer, so there's no need for change." It's the voice that insists we do things perfectly every time and reminds us that there are "right" and "wrong" ways to do things—and we'd better do them right.

This is where the "fight" part of "fight or flight" kicks in. The Fixed Mind tries to shield us from anything it thinks might threaten our emotional well-being. Physically, you might notice tension or a sense of anger building up. Emotionally, it often feels like irritation, resentment, or anxiety. You may feel the urge to be stubborn, defend your actions, explain yourself, or try to control a situation. That's all the Fixed Mind trying to protect you, even if it's not always what's most helpful in the moment.

FIXED MIND
Thoughts

- Reject reality
- Reject what is uncomfortable
- React based on rules and past experience
- Experience denial or stubbornness
- Refuse to question beliefs, convictions, and intuitions
- Resist other points of view
- Resist any disconfirming feedback

Emotions

- Arrogance
- Resentfulness
- Pride
- Self-righteousness
- Over-confidence
- Frustration
- Anger
- Bitterness

Actions, urges, behaviors

- Explain, define, and justify behavior
- Quickly explain, justify oneself, or discount what is happening
- React aggressively or antagonistically
- Question or attack the other person's perspective
- Block or obstruct other person's goals or behaviors
- Become defiant, noncompliant, and uncooperative
- Seek revenge

Fatalistic Mind

We like to call the Fatalistic Mind our "escape artist." This part of us believes that there's no need for change because there's no solution. You know that voice in your head that says, "Screw it"? That's your Fatalistic Mind talking. It tells you that the situation is hopeless, that there's nothing you can do, so why even try? Just give up!

Imagine you've just started treatment, and recovery feels overwhelming and impossible. Your Fatalistic Mind steps in, urging you to abandon the effort and quit. Instead of openly resisting or pushing back, it tells you that giving up is the easiest path. By denying or lying to ourselves, we can feel justified in avoiding the hard work or the truth about what we're running from. In believing there's no solution, the Fatalistic Mind keeps us stuck. It often comes from feelings of failure or the desire to escape, to run away, or to ignore the issue at hand. Sometimes it even convinces us that nothing will go wrong if we just ignore the problem, despite all the signs telling us otherwise. It might make you think it's impossible to change, that others need to change first, or that problems will simply disappear if you wait long enough.

But here's the thing—having a Fatalistic Mind doesn't mean you're doing something wrong. It's not necessarily a bad thing. Observing this mindset without judgment can actually help us see when we're pushing ourselves too hard, when we might need to grieve, or when there are areas in our lives that need more attention. Sometimes, the Fatalistic Mind is trying to show us that something in our life needs to change, even if we're not ready to face it. Feelings like sadness, being unappreciated, misunderstood, or wanting to shut down are often signs that our Fatalistic Mind is active. Take a moment to tune in to your Fatalistic Mind. What is it trying to tell you? Sometimes giving it a little attention can help us understand what we really need.

FATALISTIC MIND
Thoughts

- "Even if I were open it wouldn't matter because there's nothing I can do"
- "Change is unnecessary because there is no answer"
- "What's the point?
- "Why bother?"

Emotions

- Unappreciated
- Invalidated
- Misunderstood
- Helpless
- Like a martyr or victim
- Resentful
- Bitter
- Cynical about change
- Numb/Shutdown

Actions, urges, behaviors

- Give up
- Disguised resistance to uncomfortable feedback:
  - Passive-aggressive responding
  - Pouting
  - Stonewalling/Silent treatment
  - Quietly delaying progress
  - Secretly planning revenge
- Silence
- Withdrawal
- Stop working toward goals

Flexible Mind

If you see yourself in the Fixed or Fatalistic Mindset, that's totally okay—honestly, it happens to the best of us. But now that you have this new awareness, you're in a great place to make some changes. Ask yourself how well that mindset has worked for you. What effect has it had on your relationships, health, body, and self-worth? Did it actually help you avoid discomfort?

These mental states can lead to distress and tension in our relationships because of the thoughts, feelings, and behaviors they bring out. But there is hope: the Flexible Mind. The Flexible Mind is like the antidote—a way to learn and grow without rejecting your past or falling apart. It means being adaptable, adjusting your thoughts and behaviors to fit the situation. It's about letting go of anything that holds you back—like fears, unhelpful habits, rigid beliefs, or unrealistic expectations of yourself, others, or the world.

With a Flexible Mind, we become willing to take risks, face the pain of the past, and fully embrace the present moment. It encourages us to honor our past and take responsibility while staying open to new experiences and learning from them. A Flexible Mind responds with openness and curiosity, allowing us to grow and thrive in the face of change.

EXERCISE: Identifying mind states worksheet

Think of a challenging situation you have been in. In your notebook, jot down your thoughts, emotions, and actions/urges that may have been linked to an unhelpful mind state.

- Thoughts
- Emotions
- Actions/Urges/Behaviors
- What mind state was I operating from?

MIND STATES AND MINDFULNESS

Being mindful of your different mind states is like giving yourself a gentle reminder to keep practicing those skills you're working on in everyday life. It's good to remember that while the roles of the Flexible Mind and Wise Mind in RO-DBT and traditional DBT overlap in some ways, they're also quite different. The Wise Mind emphasizes intuition and inner wisdom, while the Flexible Mind focuses on questioning our assumptions and viewing the world with compassion and curiosity.

Practicing mindfulness helps keep us from getting stuck in mindsets that don't serve us well. Mindfulness allows us to take the reins of our lives in a fresh, empowering way. When we're aware of our emotions, it becomes easier to manage them. The more we understand ourselves, the more we can grow and accept who we are. It's really about staying present, paying attention, and being intentional.

OKAY, SO *WHAT* DO I DO?

Mindfulness skills are divided into two types: the "what" skills and the "how" skills. The "what" skills are the actions you take to practice mindfulness, while the "how" skills are the way you carry out those actions.

The "what" skills

There are three "what" skills: observe, describe, and participate (Linehan, 2014). These are "what" you must do in order to practice mindfulness and be mindful. When you practice mindfulness, you connect with your Flexible or Wise Mind, which gives you more insight into who you are, what you need, and what you want. If you can't name what you're thinking or feeling, it's tough to know what you need. These skills will help you with that.

Observe

Observing is all about intentionally focusing your attention on the present moment. You can pay attention to both what's happening inside you and what's happening around you. While noticing your surroundings can be straightforward, the challenge is to do it without judging (that's the "how" skill). You can't truly observe things like another person's thoughts or feelings—though you might make a good guess based on their body language or tone of voice—because those are beyond the reach of your senses.

When observing internally, focus on these four areas: thoughts, emotions, physical sensations, and urges. Observation is about simply noticing what's happening inside and outside you, without holding on to it for longer than it takes to acknowledge it. There's no analysis or interpretation—just noticing what's there at that moment. Whether it's a thought, feeling, sensation, or desire, you're simply observing it.

Observing your thoughts and feelings without trying to change them can be the first step to building mindfulness. The idea is to allow yourself to fully experience what's happening—even if it feels uncomfortable—rather than pushing it away. This might seem counterintuitive since we naturally want to avoid emotional pain. But by observing our thoughts and feelings as they come and go, we give ourselves a chance to understand them better. You don't need to spend all day analyzing your feelings—just be open and curious for a little while. Let your thoughts and emotions flow, even if they're difficult, without trying to push them away.

Describe

To "describe" means putting what you observe into words. When you notice a thought or feeling, describing it means acknowledging it and naming what's happening. Practicing this skill with others can be as simple as silently describing what's happening around you—how someone looks, what they're doing, or how they're moving. Describing external experiences is about stating the "who," "what," "when," and "where."

Describing internal experiences can be trickier since they're more abstract. For instance, you could say, "A thought just came into my mind: I am practicing mindfulness." Or, if you're feeling sad, you might say, "I'm crying, and the corners of my mouth are turned down. The emotion I'm feeling right now is sadness." Describing urges works the same way—just acknowledge what's there without analyzing or interpreting it.

It's important to remember that you can't describe things you can't observe directly. For example, you can't describe what someone else is thinking. Even if they say something, you can only describe the fact that they said it, not necessarily what they were thinking. Separating what's observable from what's assumed can help lift the weight of unnecessary judgment. Sticking to the facts and describing without interpretation can give you clarity—for example, saying, "She is speaking in a sharp tone," instead of, "She is mad at me."

Learning to describe takes practice. At first, it might feel challenging, especially if you don't have the words to express what you're feeling. But over time, it gets easier, and you may find that just describing things without judgment helps you understand your experiences better.

Participate

To participate means to fully immerse yourself in whatever you're doing. When you participate, you're not overthinking or analyzing—you're just in the moment, completely engaged in the activity. Think about a time when you were so absorbed in something—maybe playing an instrument or a sport—that you forgot about everything else and just flowed with the experience. That's the kind of engagement we're talking about.

Mindfulness invites us to cultivate that sense of flow and presence in whatever we do. Participating is about throwing yourself into the here and now, letting go of thoughts about the past or worries about the future. This helps reduce the discomfort of negative emotions because we're meeting them head on rather than avoiding them. So, let yourself be in it—fully immerse, flow, and engage in what's happening right now.

EXERCISE: The Awareness Continuum (Lynch, 2018b)

Taking a look at the Awareness Continuum can help us compartmentalize our internal process and the external world so that we don't feel overwhelmed by either.

First, we use the pronoun "I" to emphasize that what we're describing is our own experience and not necessarily the experience of anyone else. It only applies to us; it is not universally true. The next line, "am aware of," conveys the idea that the things we are observing have entered our consciousness. A distance is created from the genuine sense of experiencing something when we are aware of it. We recognize that we are not the experience. Next, we give a sensation, emotion, thought, or image a name and add some context.

In this context, "sensation" means anything that a person can feel, hear, see, or smell. An "emotion" is a feeling, mood, urge, impulse, or desire. "Image" can mean anything from imagining the future to reminiscing about the past or even cognitive distortions like "mind-reading" (imagining what other people are thinking). Images in one's head are the focus here, not the physical world around us (which is the purview of "sensation"). "Thoughts" only address cognition in the present context.

We can begin to express what we are aware of aloud. As new ideas enter our consciousness, we gradually expand our repertoire of sentences to accommodate them. We simply tune in to the flow of consciousness and reflect aloud on our observations.

For example:

- I am aware of the sensation of seeing my partner looking at the woman across from us in the park.
- I am aware of thinking that she is more physically attractive than me.
- I am aware of imagining that my partner is comparing me to her.
- I am aware of thinking that I am not good enough.
- I am aware of the feelings of insecurity and rejection.
- I am aware of the sensation of seeing my partner's gaze on the ducks in the pond and not on the woman.
- I am aware of the emotion of relief that my partner did not notice the woman.
- I am aware of the thought that I am reacting based on emotions and cognitive distortions.

First, practice in non-threatening, neutral situations. You can use the Awareness Continuum later on when you need some distance from your experience, such as when you're having a terrifying mental image, when your emotions are too intense, or when your thoughts are stuck or repeating. When life seems to be getting too much for us, it's important to put some distance between ourselves and the situation. Truthfully, the most upsetting part of life isn't the world as we find it, but rather the extent to which we internalize the events that occur in it.

Try it by completing these sentences:

I am aware of . . . .

I am aware of . . . .

I am aware of . . . .

I am aware of . . . .

I am aware of . . . .

I am aware of . . . .

OKAY, SO *HOW* DO I DO IT?

Being mindful becomes much easier with the help of the "how" skills (Linehan, 2014). These skills guide you to keep your thoughts organized, focused, and aimed at reaching a specific goal. They help you let go of dwelling on the past or worrying about the future, so you can truly stay present in the moment.

The "how" skills
Non-judgmentally

Judgments are usually just unfounded conclusions that aren't backed by facts. Instead, try to simply observe and fully experience what you're doing without labeling it. Notice when you're adding your own opinions—it's something we all do, but it can often distort our view of things. Judgments tend to be short, vague, or sweeping statements, like "It's not fair" or "Things shouldn't be this way." Even if you're correct, those phrases are still expressions of personal opinion rather than facts. When you catch yourself making a judgment, gently redirect yourself to focus on the facts of the situation.

For example, instead of thinking, "My partner is being a jerk," notice that this is a judgment. Try to describe the situation more factually, such as, "My partner spoke to me in a harsh tone." Taking this non-judgmental approach allows us to open up to the present moment and all that it offers, including emotions like sadness or anger, and accept them as part of being human. Remember, it's not about labeling things as good or bad—they simply are. And if you catch yourself being judgmental, try not to judge that either!

One-mindfully
Being mindful means staying in the present and focusing on one thing at a time, rather than getting distracted by the past or worrying about the future. This is especially important when it comes to sexuality and intimacy. When you are fully present, you can actually *feel* more, connect more deeply, and tune in to your body and your partner(s). Mindfulness allows you to slow down, notice sensations, and respond to what feels good in real time, rather than performing or overthinking.

If your mind starts to wander, gently guide it back to the present task, whether that is your breath, your body, or your partner's touch. Even simple intimate moments can become more pleasurable and meaningful when you're fully there. Multitasking has no place in intimacy. Mindfulness invites us to truly inhabit the moment and experience sex as something we participate in, not something we rush through.

Effectively
Being effective is about doing what works to achieve your goals, not necessarily what you feel you "should" do or what you think is "right." It's about focusing on what's practical and helpful, even in intimate or vulnerable situations. In the realm of sexuality, this might mean communicating with a partner, even when it's uncomfortable, or choosing to rest and reconnect with your body instead of pushing through low desire or pain out of guilt or pressure.

Sometimes this means picking your battles—asking yourself if it's more important to be right or to feel safe, connected, or understood. Effectiveness may even require you to go against your own preferences or habits to support a deeper goal, like intimacy, trust, or self-compassion. It's not always easy, but letting go of the need to always be "right" can help you create the space for healing, growth, and meaningful sexual connection.

APPLYING MINDFULNESS TO SEXUALITY
Get busy with yourself (aka mindful masturbation)

If you want to improve your sexual experiences with a partner, spending more time on your own is a great place to start. When you're by yourself, there's no pressure to please anyone else, which makes it easier to focus fully on your own body and sensations. This is your time to explore and experiment, to find out what feels best for you and to enjoy the pleasure of your own touch. As you learn more about your body, you'll feel more confident and empowered, and you'll be better able to communicate what you enjoy when you're with a partner.

Solo play is also a beautiful way to deepen your connection with your body—emotionally and physically—and it can help you appreciate all the sensual pleasures it has to offer. When you practice mindful masturbation, you can shift your focus away from worries and toward the pure enjoyment of pleasure. And the best part is, these skills can translate to partnered sex too, if you want them to.

Remember, climax isn't the goal of amazing sex—whether you're on your own or with someone else. Orgasm is like the cherry on top, but the real sweetness is in the journey itself. So the next time you feel like rushing through to finish, try slowing down. Take your time, relax, and savor every moment. Your body is worth it.

EXERCISE: Mindful masturbation

Spend some time touching each area of your body, paying close attention to the sensations you experience. Is it pleasant and calming to touch your neck; is it stimulating and pleasurable to touch your chest/breasts and/or genitalia? Just how do you prefer to be touched? Which do you prefer, a gentle touch or a firm one? Do you prefer the sensation of using the oil or lotion, or would you rather go without it? What does the surface you are on feel like?

Remember to use all of your senses. What do you see? Do you find it sexually appealing to see or touch yourself? If you use any visual images while masturbating, take a moment to consider the image and what you find erotic about it. What sounds can you hear right now? Is the rhythm of your heartbeat and breath arousing? To get in the mood, perhaps you listened to some sensual music before you began.

The central concept is that of total immersion in the here and now. Your emotions and thoughts will likely fluctuate and stray. With those who have gone through sexual trauma, you might see some unwelcome negative emotions come to the surface. Always remember to take note of your thoughts and feelings without judgment, and then bring your attention gently back to the here and now.

Make time, set the mood, and ease into it

Take the time you need to unwind from the day's demands before diving into a sexual experience. Cancel any other plans, let yourself relax, and transition into the present moment. Whether you light scented candles, put on something that makes you feel good, or play your favorite music, create a setting that feels sexy to you. Think of it as a ritual if that helps. The key is to give yourself space to shift gears so you're fully ready. Even if it's spontaneous, sex can still be mindful—so don't stress if there's no time to plan.

Talk about it

How often do you talk about what you enjoy (or don't enjoy) in bed? Many people miss out on satisfying sex simply because they're hesitant to ask for what they want. Start by getting in touch with your own desires and then share openly with your partner in a judgment-free way. This could be before, during, or after sex. Being honest about what you need brings both freedom and pleasure. Discussing sex helps you stay present and connected with your partner. If you're comfortable, talk about what's happening in the moment. The more clearly you express your desires, the more likely you are to receive them.

Clear your mind

Many of us have myths and insecurities about our bodies or sexuality that make it hard to fully enjoy ourselves. It's tempting to overthink things, but that often backfires. Check in with yourself. Do you genuinely want to have sex right now? If you're feeling distracted or disconnected, it's okay. Communicate that to your partner and consider other forms of intimacy if that feels right. If you do want to be intimate, try asking yourself what you want to feel. Let your emotions flow through you and bring your full attention to the experience.

Handle distractions gently

Mindful sex means focusing on the pleasure your body is experiencing, but it doesn't mean distractions won't happen. Instead of trying to fight those thoughts, simply notice them, let them go, and refocus on an erotic cue. Some of my clients find it helpful to use a catchphrase to bring them back to the present. One client takes a deep breath and says "center" to herself, while another uses "bed, not head." There's no need to push your mind; instead, gently guide it back to the experience.

Practice mindfulness every day

Don't save mindfulness for the bedroom—everything is interconnected. Being present in your daily life helps you be more present during sex. For me, this means starting my day with a few minutes of meditation and reflection. I ask myself how I'm feeling in my body, where I might be holding tension, and where I need to focus my energy. In the evening, I do a similar check-in before winding down. Find what works for you, and let those moments of mindfulness make a difference both in and out of the bedroom.

WAYS TO PRACTICE MINDFULNESS ANYWHERE

Breathe with intention

Deep, intentional breathing is an incredibly simple yet powerful way to help your mind stay in the moment. It brings more oxygen to your brain and sends calming signals to your nervous system, making it easier for you to relax. Try taking a deep belly breath and notice how the air feels as it enters and leaves your nose. If your mind wanders, picture light and air flowing into your body with each inhale. This can help you be more present, not just in daily life but also during intimate moments with your partner. Try syncing your breathing with theirs to create a deeper sense of connection. Breathe in what you want—passion, love, connection—and exhale, letting go of any tension.

Disable your mental "autopilot"

Have you ever driven somewhere and barely remembered the journey? We go through so many routines on autopilot, and sometimes intimacy can become just another habit. Over time, even the things that once brought excitement can feel automatic if we aren't really present. To shake things up, focus on tuning back into your body throughout the day. It can be as simple as taking a few mindful breaths while waiting for a traffic light or feeling your body's sensations as you walk. Notice the rise and fall of your diaphragm, or the coolness of air passing through your nostrils. When your mind wanders (which it will), gently bring your attention back to your body. Over time, your brain creates new pathways that make staying present easier—including during intimate moments. This way, when your mind does drift during sex, you'll have the tools to return to your partner and the experience more quickly.

Engage all your senses

One easy way to practice mindfulness is to fully engage your senses in whatever you're doing—whether it's eating, showering, or taking a walk. Notice how things look, feel, taste, smell, and sound. For example, during a walk, you might focus on the sights, sounds, and scents around you, as well as how your body feels moving through space. It's okay if trying to tune in to all your senses at once feels overwhelming at first. Start with whichever sense feels most natural—maybe touch—then explore the others one by one. In the shower, listen to the water splashing, feel its warmth, notice the scents of your shampoo, and observe the bubbles forming and popping. Engaging all your senses can help ground you in the moment.

Mindfulness meditation

Meditation is a great way to develop mindfulness and learn to accept your thoughts as they come. If you're new to it, it's normal to feel restless or uncomfortable after just a few minutes. Our minds are used to constant stimulation! But over time, you might find that 15 or 20 minutes of meditation becomes your sweet spot.

Regular meditation can help you understand your own thoughts more deeply, which makes it easier to stay present when distractions come up. Meditation also reduces cortisol—the stress hormone that kicks in during "fight or flight" mode, diverting blood away from non-essential functions like sexual arousal. Less cortisol means less stress and a greater desire for connection. Mindfulness isn't about being perfect; it's a journey. Give yourself time to grow, and as you become more mindful, you may notice it's easier to navigate stress and discomfort, both in and out of the bedroom.

EXERCISE: Mindful meditation

Find a cozy spot where you won't be interrupted—somewhere that's quiet and free from distractions. You can either sit comfortably or stretch out on the floor. If you're sitting, try to keep your back straight but relaxed, so you can breathe easily without having to think too much about it.

Now, start by just noticing your breath. Feel the air as it moves in and out of your lungs, hear the gentle sound it makes, and notice how your heartbeat gradually slows, finding a calm and steady rhythm. It's completely normal for your mind to wander—that's just what our minds do! Don't be hard on yourself when it happens. Instead, just gently acknowledge the thought or feeling, let it be, and then bring your attention back to your breath.

To make it even more soothing, consider lighting a candle or some incense. You could also hold a grounding stone or a set of beads in your hand to help anchor you in the moment.

Mindful eating

Mindful eating is all about tuning in to your body and letting go of judgment around your eating habits—before, during, and after a meal. In the early stages of eating disorder recovery, this can be especially tough, as your body might not be sending clear signals about hunger or fullness. It might also feel overwhelming to focus on your body and your meals.

In times like this, mechanical eating—where you eat at regular intervals regardless of how you feel—can help you meet your nutritional needs consistently. If practicing mindful eating feels really distressing, you might find it helpful to work with a registered dietitian, mental health therapist, or recovery coach to support you through the process.

EXERCISE: Mindful eating

Bring yourself to the present moment as best you can. Take a second to notice if you're craving anything specific. Whatever you're craving, try not to judge it—just acknowledge it and respect it.

When you're ready to eat, settle in. Sit down with your meal or snack, and put away or turn off anything that might distract you— like your phone or the TV. Take a few deep breaths to feel calm and grounded.

As you eat, try to use all your senses to really enjoy the experience. Notice the texture of the food in your mouth, the different flavors, the aroma, and how it looks. If it's beautifully presented, take a moment to appreciate that. If it smells delicious, breathe it in. Let yourself savor it all.

Try to eat mindfully and without judging yourself. Every now and then, check in with your body to see how full you're feeling.

If you notice any uncomfortable feelings or thoughts popping up, recognize them, then let them pass. Our minds can feel hunger too, not just our bodies. When you feel both mentally and physically sat-isfied, allow yourself to stop eating.

CASE STUDY: Alex, Jordan, Casey, and Taylor

Alex, Jordan, Casey, and Taylor made up a close-knit polycule, each bringing their own strengths and challenges to the relationship. Alex, an artist, was deeply in touch with their emotions but sometimes found themselves overwhelmed by feelings like jealousy. Jordan, a teacher, tended to lean on logic and reasoning, often feeling emotionally distant. Casey, a therapist, practiced mindfulness daily and played a key role in helping the group balance emotions and logic. Taylor, an entrepreneur, had a hard time adapting when things didn't go as planned, often feeling stuck when things were out of their control.

Their relationship, though filled with love and connection, had its hurdles. Alex and Taylor, in particular, struggled with feelings of insecurity when one of them spent more time with someone else in the polycule. These feelings often triggered defensiveness or self-doubt, especially for Alex, who could get caught up in their Emotional Mind, and for Taylor, who sometimes shut down or reacted from a Fixed Mind state. When it came to sexual intimacy, Taylor got anxious about performance, while Alex tended to become distracted by self-judgment, making it hard to stay present with each other.

As a group, they realized that communication was key to navigating these challenges. Jordan, who had always relied on rational thinking, often found himself withdrawing when emotions ran high. It wasn't that he didn't care, but he was unsure how to navigate emotional conversations without feeling overwhelmed. This left Casey and Alex feeling disconnected, even though they deeply valued their emotional bond with Jordan.

Recognizing these patterns, Casey introduced mindfulness to the group as a way to help them stay present and manage their emotions. For Alex, mindfulness became a tool to pause and reflect before reacting. They began practicing the simple act of breathing deeply and asking themselves, *"What am I feeling right now?"* This small shift helped Alex notice jealousy or insecurity without immediately acting on it. This gave them the space to process those feelings, making it easier to talk openly about their needs and emotions with the others.

Jordan, who tended to default to logic, found mindfulness especially helpful in becoming more emotionally open. Instead of shutting down or distancing himself, Jordan began to practice vulnerability. He would say things like, "I feel disconnected right now—can we talk about it?" This small act of sharing his emotional state not only brought him closer to Casey and Alex but also allowed him to stay more present and connected in their conversations.

Taylor's experience with mindfulness was transformative. His tendency to get defensive or shut down in the face of feedback started to shift as he embraced self-compassion. Instead of resisting criticism, Taylor would remind himself, "I don't need to be perfect." This allowed him to stay more open to change and growth, both personally and within the polycule. He also started to practice mindfulness in sexual moments, letting go of the need to "perform" and simply being present with the sensations of intimacy.

Over time, mindfulness helped them build stronger emotional connections. Alex and Taylor learned to better manage their jealousy and emotional reactivity, while Jordan became more emotionally present and engaged. The group's communication improved, with everyone feeling heard and valued. In moments of sexual intimacy, mindfulness allowed each person to be more present, reducing distractions and deepening their connection. Without the pressure to "perform" or meet expectations, they found more joy in being with each other.

— CHAPTER 7 —

Let's Face the Facts

GOALS

▶ Learn how to ease your suffering and better cope during tough times.
▶ Discover all the options available to you in any situation.
▶ Understand the difference between radical openness and radical acceptance, and know when to use each approach.

Overcontrolled focus: Radical openness

Undercontrolled focus: Radical acceptance

RADICAL ACCEPTANCE

Radical acceptance, a powerful tool in Dialectical Behavioral Therapy, can be transformative when applied to healing from eating disorders and embracing one's sexuality. At its core, radical acceptance means fully acknowledging and accepting your reality without judgment (Linehan, 2014). This is especially important for individuals struggling with body image or sexual shame, as both often involve intense self-criticism and the need for control.

For those with eating disorders, radical acceptance encourages acceptance of the body as it is, even if it doesn't align with societal ideals. This doesn't mean neglecting self-care, but rather accepting the body in its current state as a starting point for healing. Similarly, individuals dealing with sexual shame can use radical acceptance to release the guilt or resistance they may feel toward their sexual identity, fostering self-compassion and understanding.

This practice also helps in acknowledging past trauma or painful experiences—whether related to body image or sexual experiences—without blaming or avoiding the truth. Acceptance of these realities, however diffi-cult, opens the door to growth and healing. It's a shift from self-loathing to self-compassion, empowering individuals to face their struggles with hon-esty, rather than denial.

Radical acceptance also offers a release from the constant need for con-trol. Both eating disorders and issues with sexuality often stem from an attempt to control one's body or desires. By accepting what you cannot change, you free yourself from the burden of perfectionism and control, creating space for healthier coping mechanisms.

Ultimately, radical acceptance is about embracing who you are in this moment, flaws and all, and recognizing that this self-acceptance is the first step toward real, lasting change. Whether in recovery from an eating disorder or in embracing one's sexual identity, accepting reality without judgment allows for deep healing and a shift toward self-compassion. These skills can guide us through intense feelings that might otherwise lead to actions we regret. While we can't always change a stressful situation, we can change how we respond to it, which is what distress tolerance is all about.

When faced with a challenging situation, you have four options:

1. Try to change the situation.
2. Change how you feel about it.
3. Accept it as it is.
4. Do nothing and continue suffering.

The first three options can help you feel better. The fourth, which is often the easiest but least helpful, keeps us stuck. How often have you complained without taking any action? We've all been there—it takes the least effort, but it doesn't make anything better. The third option, radical acceptance, is one of the most powerful yet challenging DBT tools. It's not radical acceptance if you're still blaming or resisting. You must let go of the "shoulds." Embrace reality as it is, even when it's difficult. That doesn't mean ignoring your feelings—you have every right to feel hurt or upset. Acceptance is about acknowledging what happened without letting it control or paralyze you.

The facts of your past and present are what they are, whether you like them or not. Avoiding the truth only prolongs your pain. To start healing, you need to acknowledge where you are right now. Pain is a signal that something needs attention, and denying reality doesn't make it go away. Radical acceptance can bring a sense of calm, even if it's difficult at first. It allows you to move forward, to change the parts of your life you find unfair or painful, starting from a place of truth.

THOUGHT PATTERNS THAT SIGNAL YOU MIGHT NEED TO PRACTICE RADICAL ACCEPTANCE

- I can't deal with this.
- This is not fair.
- Things shouldn't be like this.
- I can't believe this is happening.
- It's not right.
- Things should be different.
- Why is this happening to me?
- Why is this happening now?
- This is horrible.
- Why did this happen to me now?
- What did I do to deserve this?
- I can never catch a break.
- Bad things always happen to me.
- Nobody else has to deal with this.
- I wish things were different.
- I can't accept that this happened.
- I'm never going to feel okay about this.
- People shouldn't act the way they do.
- I can't get past what happened.
- This is terrible, and I'll never get over it.
- I shouldn't have to deal with this.
- Everything is working against me.

While it's normal to react to negative situations with emotions such as sadness or anger, blaming yourself or other people, or wishing that things could be different, will keep you stuck.

Why is acceptance so hard?

Acceptance can be difficult, and many of us struggle with it. We often confuse acceptance with approval or being "okay" with something, but that's not true. Acceptance simply means acknowledging reality rather than resisting it. It doesn't mean you're happy about what happened. It can be painful, and it's normal to feel that fear. By resisting reality, we remain stuck in a cycle of negative thinking or self-blame, which amplifies emotional distress and can lead to unhealthy coping mechanisms such as avoidance or substance use.

Accepting without judgment helps us move forward and experience peace. Radical acceptance isn't approval; it's acknowledging "this is what it is" without labeling it as good or bad. Letting go of the fight against reality can be the first step toward meaningful change. You can accept something while still working to make it better.

When radical acceptance is appropriate

- When refusing to accept what happened only makes your pain worse.
- If a difficult experience has left you feeling stuck or unable to move on.
- When there's no realistic way to improve or change the situation.
- If you've tried other ways of coping, but nothing seems to work.
- When something beyond your control has thrown your life off course.
- If you've experienced a significant loss – like losing a loved one, a job, or going through a breakup or divorce.
- When you find yourself suppressing emotions to the point that joy feels out of reach.
- If you often struggle to put your feelings into words.
- When you find yourself reacting with anger or frustration to things that seem small.
- If people around you have told you that it's time to let go of the past.
- After going through a traumatic experience that was beyond your control, or if you grew up in an environment of neglect or abuse.

> ### AUTHOR'S NOTE: ON RADICALLY ACCEPTING TRAUMA
>
> If you've experienced trauma, your safety always comes first. Before diving into radical acceptance, it might be helpful to work with a therapist to guide and support you. Radical acceptance can be especially challenging when it comes to trauma—it's completely okay if this journey takes time. The effects of trauma can be deep, and accepting what happened can be one of the most important steps you take. What happened to you is real, and acknowledging that truth is an act of courage and healing.

When radical acceptance is not appropriate

Radical acceptance isn't always the best approach. There are definitely times when it's better to take action and try to change your situation rather than simply accepting it as it is. Here are some examples of when radical acceptance might not be right for you:

- If you're in an abusive relationship.
- If you're being put in danger.
- If you're facing harassment, being taken advantage of, or not being treated fairly at work.
- If someone is treating you poorly or disrespecting you.
- If you're feeling burned out or unmotivated because of your current situation.
- If you're using acceptance as a way to avoid dealing with a problem.
- If you have some control over what's happening.
- If there's something you could do to make things better.
- If fear is holding you back from taking action.
- If you're always putting others before yourself just to avoid conflict.

In these situations, it's often more helpful to stand up for yourself, make changes, or seek help rather than trying to just accept things as they are. Radical acceptance can be powerful, but it's important to recognize when action is what's truly needed.

Ten steps for practicing radical acceptance (Linehan, 2014)

1. *Notice what's difficult:* Take a moment to observe when you're feeling stuck or struggling to accept something. This is the first step toward acknowledging your reality.
2. *Remind yourself:* Your reality is what it is, even if it's painful or not what you wish it to be. You can't change what's happened—the past is set—but you can decide how to respond.
3. *Reflect on how you got here:* Take a moment to understand what led you to this point. This isn't about blaming yourself—it's about recognizing the journey that brought you here.
4. *Engage your whole self in acceptance:* Use your body, mind, and spirit to practice acceptance. This might include mindfulness exercises, emotion regulation, or distress tolerance skills. (If you're looking for more, check out Chapters 6 and 9.)
5. *Write it out:* Consider writing down what steps you would take if you chose to fully accept the truth. What would your first step look like? What fears come up when you think about accepting this truth? Writing can help clarify your thoughts and intentions.
6. *Prepare for future challenges:* Acceptance isn't a one-time event—it's a practice. Mentally prepare yourself for situations that you know might be hard to accept in the future. This way, you'll feel more ready to navigate them.

7. *Notice your body:* Pay attention to any physical sensations, like tightness or tension, that come up when you are struggling to accept something. Use mindfulness techniques to stay present with these sensations (see Chapter 6 for some helpful practices).

8. *Validate your emotions:* You have a right to feel whatever emotions come up, whether it's sadness, disappointment, or grief. These feelings are natural, and it's okay to feel them.

9. *Look for meaning:* Even in the hardest moments, there is often some meaning to be found. This doesn't mean you need to be happy about it, but finding purpose or growth within your suffering can be powerful.

10. *Be kind to yourself:* Finally, remember to treat yourself with kindness. Acceptance can be difficult, and you deserve compassion as you work through it.

EXERCISE: Radical acceptance worksheet

What's making you upset? Jot down what happened in your notebook.

- Is there anything in what you have written that you have to accept as true? Is there any judgment or opinion? Such as, "This isn't the way things should be."
- Take a moment to reflect on this truth. "This is what happened," for example. What occurred, or what chain of events, brought about this reality?
- Consider this reality. Are you able to accept it in your mind? Is there anything you can tell yourself that will help you cope with this truth?
- Try to imagine how it would feel to accept it. If you were to accept this truth, how would your actions or behaviors change? Consider how everything would change if you were able to let go.
- Can your body accept it? Where are you resisting this reality? Where, specifically, in your body do you feel that burden? Can you feel any tension or pain in your body? Do you have the ability to let this go?
- Can you identify with feelings of dissatisfaction, melancholy, or loss at this time? Be still with that, admit it, let yourself feel it, and know that this is normal and acceptable. Record anything that stands out to you about these emotions or thoughts.

- What, in light of this harsh reality, gives life any meaning at all? This is a good place to refresh your memory on those points.
- Making a list of the benefits and drawbacks of accepting or rejecting this reality can help if you're having trouble doing so.

If you come across another problem, follow the outlined steps again.

EXERCISE: Radical acceptance coping mantras
Try repeating one of the following phrases to practice radical acceptance of a situation:

- It is what it is.
- So it goes.
- You have no power over me.
- This is how it has to be.
- I can't change the past.
- I can't predict the future.
- There is no point in dwelling on the past. It's already done and gone.
- I am strong; I will survive the present crisis.
- I can't go back in time.
- I can't control the past.
- Everything in the past has led up to this moment.
- Based on past events, everything is as it should be.
- I have no control over other people.
- I will not always agree with it or like it. That's okay.

Or create your own mantra! Some people prefer to use phrases from a favorite song or religious text.
Reflect on why those mantras resonate with you.

EXAMPLES OF RADICAL ACCEPTANCE IN PRACTICE
Dealing with a frustrating work situation:
"This is just a temporary setback. I can't change the situation, but I can choose how to respond."

Facing a disappointment in a sexual encounter:
"It's okay to feel sad, but I can accept that this happened and focus on moving forward."

When your partner says something hurtful:
"I can't control what they say, but I can choose how to react."

Managing a sexual difficulty or chronic illness:
"I can't change my condition, but I can manage it by taking care of myself."

Struggling with a personal loss or breakup in relationship:
"I can't change what happened, but I can choose how to move forward."

Facing anxiety or fear about sexual encounters or the future of a relationship:
"I don't know what will happen, but I trust that I will be okay."

Dealing with a difficult person or conflict in a relationship:
"This person is who they are, and I can only control how I respond."

Dealing with self-criticism or negative self-talk about your body or sexual performance:
"I am enough, just as I am."

Feeling overwhelmed by responsibilities or demands:
"I can only do my best in this moment."

RADICAL OPENNESS

Radical openness is NOT the same as radical acceptance. When we practice radical acceptance, we're learning to turn unbearable suffering into something more manageable—something we can live with. Radical openness, on the other hand, challenges how we perceive reality (Lynch, 2018a). It suggests that "we don't see things as they are—we see things as we are." Radical openness is about going beyond awareness. It's about actively seeking out the things that make us uncomfortable or that we usually want to avoid. Why? Because there's value in them; there's something to learn. It involves an intentional self-examination and a willingness to be "wrong," with the goal of growing and making changes if needed. It means not just assuming that our point of view is always correct.

This kind of openness requires us to take responsibility for our choices and actions. We can't just blame others, break down, hope that the world will change, or beat ourselves up as a way to avoid facing hard truths. Radical openness calls us to move beyond those old coping mechanisms. When we practice radical openness, we open ourselves to humility and a genuine curiosity to learn more. This can really benefit our relationships, but it's not always easy. It often involves letting go of beliefs or ideas about who we are. It's not something we can grasp purely by thinking about it; it takes deliberate practice, much like mindfulness. And as we keep practicing, our understanding of radical openness deepens and changes over time.

Radical openness invites us to question long-held beliefs about our bodies and self-worth. Many individuals struggling with eating disorders have deeply ingrained, often distorted, views about their bodies that might not reflect reality. By practicing radical openness, they can start challenging these perceptions, moving beyond the defensive, self-protective mechanisms they've used for years. This can be especially important in therapy, where individuals might need to confront deeply uncomfortable truths about their body image, identity, and sexuality.

Just as radical openness involves self-examination, it also invites us to explore our sexual identity with curiosity. It means being open to exploring what might make us uncomfortable, including our desires, boundaries, and past experiences. For individuals dealing with eating disorders, there might be a disconnection between their body and their sense of sexuality. Radical openness can help them challenge limiting beliefs about their sexual worth, attractiveness, and ability to experience pleasure. Both eating disorders and unhealthy sexual patterns can be coping mechanisms—ways to avoid deeper pain, emotional distress, or unmet needs. Radical openness can help individuals confront those avoidance strategies with a willingness to look beyond the surface. For someone struggling with an eating disorder, their control over food might be masking a deeper issue with self-worth or a need for control. By being open to the discomfort of exploring these deeper layers, they can start healing at a core level.

Radical openness requires humility—the acknowledgment that we might not know everything, and our perspectives may be flawed. Radical openness encourages vulnerability and self-compassion in the face of discomfort, which is crucial for breaking down those barriers of shame. The ultimate goal of radical openness is growth. In the context of eating disorders, growth could involve learning how to nourish the body in ways that feel loving and empowering. In terms of sexuality, it might mean exploring more authentic ways of expressing desire, intimacy, or pleasure. Radical openness challenges clients to move beyond old, stagnant patterns of thought and behavior, creating space for new, healthier habits.

Thought patterns that signal you might need to practice radical openness

- I need or desire to be right.
- I always try to go above and beyond.
- I need to perform well.
- Being vulnerable around other people is very uncomfortable for me.
- I feel like I have to rein in my emotions constantly.
- I struggle to be in the moment and take unplanned action.
- Expressing and experiencing anger are both challenging for me.
- I deny myself enjoyment in order to maintain my own high standards.
- When I make a mistake, I think it's only fair that I am punished for it.
- What I think of myself and what other people think of me are two entirely different things.
- I hold myself and others to strict moral guidelines.
- My tendency is to downplay my distress and maintain a stoic demeanor.
- I hardly ever feel satisfied with the work or performance I put forth.
- I put too much time into trying to get things right.
- I tend to be overly cautious and risk-averse.
- The strict rules I set for myself control every aspect of my life.
- Situations devoid of structure and order present a challenge to me.
- I'm constantly alert to what is out of place and feel compelled to make it right.
- Trusting others is difficult for me, and it takes a lot of time for someone to get to know the real me.

Radical openness is not something that can solely be understood intellectually—it requires direct and repeated practice.

AUTHOR'S NOTE: ON RADICAL OPENNESS

Radical openness means being willing to engage with discomfort or differing perspectives, without feeling pressured to agree or change immediately. Radical openness doesn't mean you have to agree, follow along without question, or say yes to everything. Sometimes, the best thing you can do is hold your boundaries, keep some distance, or choose not to change.

SELF-INQUIRY

We all have blind spots. Every one of us has implicit biases and limited self-awareness that we carry into every situation. That is why it's so important to stay open-minded and keep learning about ourselves. Growth requires the courage to question—and sometimes even change—our deeply held beliefs and assumptions. Self-inquiry is all about striving for truth, knowing that each new understanding is partial, fallible, and shaped by our biases.

Instead of blaming others or the world around us, self-inquiry encourages us to look inward and reflect on our assumptions, motivations, and actions. It asks us to stay open and introspective, even when we feel defensive or threatened. This means facing and learning from the experiences we'd rather avoid or ignore. By practicing self-inquiry regularly, we can start to see challenges not as obstacles but as opportunities to learn.

Short, consistent self-inquiry sessions are usually more effective than long, drawn-out ones, which can sometimes become about finding an answer or solving a problem. Focus on finding good questions rather than good answers. Self-inquiry isn't about ruminating or problem-solving—it's about genuine exploration. Writing down your reflections can be really helpful. Keeping a journal can serve as a reminder to return to the practice often and track how your questions evolve over time. Self-inquiry also means embracing healthy self-doubt. This isn't about blaming ourselves harshly or giving up, but about questioning ourselves with curiosity. It's a way to learn, not to criticize.

Three steps for practicing radical openness (Lynch, 2018a)

1. *Acknowledge discomfort:* Notice when something doesn't match your expectations—this can bring up feelings like frustration, anger, resistance, or numbness. Instead of trying to explain, defend, or distract yourself, simply acknowledge what's happening.
2. *Turn toward discomfort:* Use self-inquiry to lean into that discomfort and question your own assumptions and biases. Seek out what you don't know to learn from the constantly changing world around you.
3. *Show humility:* Stay humble and consider the needs of others. Aim to be flexible in your responses, adapting as you learn and grow.

EXERCISE: Examples of self-inquiry worksheet
Use your notebook to record your answers to these questions.

* What am I resisting?

- Is there something important for me to acknowledge or recognize about myself or the current moment?
- Am I finding it hard to question my point of view or even engage in self-inquiry?
- If yes, or maybe, then what might this mean?
- What am I preventing myself (or others) from acknowledging?
- What aspects of my life do I secretly take pride in?
- How have the suggestions of those who care about me been resisted in the past?
- How much resistance am I putting up while doing this exercise?
- What does this resistance suggest about my own openness to new ideas and perspectives, or my willingness to take an objective look at how I'm feeling?
- Do I think I already know everything there is to know about the circumstances I'm in?
- Do I feel as if I need to defend and explain my feelings or actions, even if they are self-critical or self-hating?
- Is it possible to view the circumstance or my own position in it in a different way? If so, am I ready to investigate what that might be? If not, what does this perhaps indicate about what I still need to learn?
- Is it challenging for me to evaluate my current viewpoints or my own actions?
- Is there a part of me that is adamant that it is correct or that its perspective is the correct one?
- Am I using this as another reason to criticize myself or show that I'm not useful or valuable?
- Does a part of me secretly hope that I will fail? In that case, what might I have to learn?
- Is there a different way I could react to myself right now? How might this improve my life or the lives of those around me?
- Am I ready to try something new without using failure as an excuse to be hard on myself?
- If I take the time to stop and listen to my thoughts and feelings, what is it that I am afraid of hearing?
- How much consideration have I given to what I need right now? What might I still need to learn?
- In this moment, what do I require most? Do I want to know what I need if I'm unsure of what I need? If not, what does this tell me about my potential requirements?

- What am I afraid might happen if I were to drop my perspective momentarily?
- What am I trying to communicate when I harshly blame myself, others, or the world?
- How does my harsh judgment of myself or others impact my relationships?

DON'T BELIEVE EVERYTHING YOU THINK AND FEEL

We all have moments when we mistake our thoughts or feelings for reality. When we hold on to certain thoughts long enough, they start feeling like "the truth." It can be hard to see things any other way, right? Our thoughts directly impact our emotions, and when those thoughts are negative or critical, they can drag us down. We often think we're seeing the truth, but really, we're just reinforcing negative beliefs that keep us stuck.

Have you ever thought that your partner was mad at you, just because they were quiet? Or maybe you've assumed that if you didn't get everything "right," you failed completely. These are examples of cognitive distortions— ways our minds trick us into seeing things in a negative, exaggerated light. They tend to become automatic, especially during difficult times, and can be hard to break. By learning to identify these unhelpful thoughts, we can work through the struggles they create and start feeling more in control.

Cognitive distortions can play a big role in how we see our bodies, weight, and even our relationships with food. In fact, these types of thoughts are often at the core of eating disorders. Negative thoughts about food and body image can lead to disordered behaviors, creating a cycle where negative thoughts trigger negative feelings, which then reinforce unhealthy behaviors. Treatment for eating disorders often starts by addressing behaviors like irregular eating patterns or extreme dieting. But even when these behaviors improve, distorted thoughts can linger. Recovery is about recognizing these patterns and choosing to change them for the better.

COMMON COGNITIVE DISTORTIONS (BURNS, 1980)

All-or-nothing thinking: Viewing situations in black-and-white terms, without recognizing any middle ground.

Overgeneralization: Making broad, sweeping conclusions based on a single incident or piece of evidence.

Mental filter: Focusing solely on negative aspects of a situation and ignoring any positive parts.

Disqualifying the positive: Dismissing positive experiences or achievements as unimportant or accidental.

Jumping to conclusions: Making assumptions without evidence, including mind-reading or fortune-telling.

Magnification (catastrophizing): Blowing things out of proportion and expecting the worst possible outcome.

Minimization: Downplaying or undervaluing positive qualities or achievements.

Emotional reasoning: Believing that negative emotions reflect objective reality (e.g., "I feel it, therefore it must be true").

"Should" statements: Holding yourself or others to rigid, unrealistic standards ("I should always be perfect").

Labeling: Attaching negative labels to yourself or others based on behaviors or mistakes.

Personalization: Taking responsibility for events outside your control or blaming yourself for things that aren't your fault.

Blaming: Focusing on the other person's mistakes or flaws while ignoring your own role in the situation.

These inner dialogues can sometimes mislead us about our relationships. Cognitive distortions can create misunderstandings, heighten conflict, and damage intimacy. They often make us see situations in the worst possible light, affecting how we interpret our partner's words or actions. Your feelings are shaped by how you think, not necessarily by what's actually happening. When we let distorted thinking dominate, we might end up hurting our relationships without even realizing it.

The key to healthy relationships is psychological flexibility—being open to different perspectives and seeing beyond our own immediate reactions. Many times, the filters through which we see our partners—like fear, jealousy, or past hurt—can distort reality, leading us to make poor choices or react in unhelpful ways. Learning to step back and look at our thoughts objectively can make all the difference. Let's look at some real-world situations where cognitive distortions show up in our relationships.

SOME EXAMPLES OF COGNITIVE DISTORTIONS IN ACTION
Overreacting to our partner's intentions

When she's around you, she's unusually quiet and distant. You might think she's mad at you, or worse, that you did something wrong. Your low self-esteem is triggered by her neglect. You either lash out at her, or you pout for a long time. But in reality, she's just had a tough day at work and needs some space.

Obscuring a person's true character

A co-worker or employer is too harsh in their criticism of you. You internalize their criticism, which makes you feel horrible about yourself and makes you dislike them more and more. In reality, it is they who have the problem, not you.

Erroneous interpretations of other people's behavior

You feel that a man spends a lot of money on you because he cares about you and wants to provide for you. Because he wants to control, dominate, and own you, he establishes intimacy and commitment with money.

Self-doubt!

You don't get a call back from a new girl. There are times when you think you did something wrong and beat yourself up for not being "enough." However, the truth is she has a girlfriend or a wife, and she is not being truthful with either of you.

Irrational judgments of others

When a man is self-serving, emotionally detached, and violent to you, you disregard his harmful actions and commit to a relationship with him.

Misinterpreting others

Someone is outgoing, nice, and makes you feel like their new best friend, and another is quiet and reserved and you categorize them as unfriendly and uninteresting. Once you get to know them, you see that the dull person is incredibly dependable and wise, while your new BFF is arrogant, fake, and untrustworthy.

EXERCISE: Identifying cognitive distortions worksheet
Jot down your answers to these questions in your notebook.

What *feelings* am I experiencing (emotions and physical sensations)?
Example: Anxiety, body is tense.

What *thoughts* are associated with my feelings?
Example: "My partner doesn't want to have sex with me because they think I'm too fat."

Is there a *cognitive distortion* there?
Example: Mind-reading, jumping to conclusions, personalizing.

CASE EXAMPLE: June
June, a 54-year-old marketing executive, had recently gone through a breakup. She had been in a 15-year relationship and envisioned spending her life with her partner. The end of the relationship left her feeling devastated, questioning her worth, and experiencing intense emotions like sadness, anger, and hopelessness. June had always believed that the end of a relationship meant personal failure. It was uncomfortable for her to question this belief because it made her vulnerable, bringing up feelings of shame and inadequacy. However, with her therapist's support, she began to challenge this long-held perception. She leaned into the discomfort, realizing that relationships could end for many reasons and that an ending wasn't necessarily a reflection of her value.

Practicing radical openness also involved June examining her own role in the breakup. This was particularly challenging, as it meant facing the ways in which her actions or behaviors may have contributed to the relationship's difficulties. Instead of blaming herself or her partner entirely, she worked on understanding her part without judgment. By acknowledging her role, she gained insights into patterns she wanted to change and behaviors she wanted to improve in future relationships. This level of self-examination allowed her to take responsibility for her growth and become more open to making meaningful changes.

CHAPTER 8

No, Fat Isn't a Feeling

GOALS

▶ Discover the thought and behavior patterns that keep you stuck in an unhealthy body image.

▶ Learn how to challenge and change those patterns to start feeling better about yourself.

▶ Understand how a negative body image can affect your sex life—and explore ways to build body confidence and satisfaction.

Overcontrolled focus: Check for rigid rules or high standards that affect body image

Undercontrolled focus: Check for emotion-based reasoning or emotion-based reactions to your body

WHAT IS BODY IMAGE?

Body image is all about how you see, think, and feel about your body. It's your personal relationship with your appearance, including how comfortable you feel in your own skin. "Body image satisfaction" refers to how happy you are with the way you look. This concept extends beyond size and shape to encompass other important aspects like skin color, facial features, and how your body aligns with societal expectations based on gender identity or cultural norms. For BIPOC (Black, Indigenous, and People of Color) individuals, body image issues may be compounded by the challenges of colorism, racism, and stereotypes that affect perceptions of beauty. Similarly, gender-expansive individuals may experience difficulties with body image as they navigate societal pressures related to gender presentation, which may not align with traditional or binary gender expectations.

Struggling with negative body image can lead to feelings of depression, loneliness, and low self-esteem. It can also trigger an obsession with weight loss, muscle gain, or an increased risk of developing eating disorders. These struggles are not one-size-fits-all but intersect in unique ways depending on an individual's race, gender identity, and other personal factors. Body image is fluid—it can improve with time and effort, and a positive body image isn't about perfection. It's about accepting and embracing your uniqueness, no matter your shape, size, skin color, or gender expression.

The four aspects of body image (Cash & Smolak, 2011)

- *Perceptual:* How you perceive your body. Sometimes, the way you see yourself isn't quite how you actually look.
- *Affective:* How you feel about your body. It's about how satisfied or dissatisfied you are with your weight, shape, or specific parts of your body.
- *Cognitive:* The thoughts and beliefs you have about your body. For instance, you might think you'll be happier once you reach a certain weight or get more toned. These kinds of beliefs can lead to an unhealthy focus on appearance.
- *Behavioral:* How your feelings about your body affect what you do. If you're unhappy with how you look, you might avoid social situations or turn to risky behaviors like excessive exercise or disordered eating to try to change your appearance.

EXERCISE: What is true about my body image right now? (Cash, 2008)

Characteristics of a negative body image:

- ☐ I have a distorted, inaccurate perception of my size and shape.
- ☐ I think that only other people are attractive.
- ☐ I think that my body size or shape is a sign of personal failure.
- ☐ I equate my weight or shape with a sign of my lack of worth.
- ☐ I feel ashamed, anxious, and self-conscious about my body.
- ☐ I sometimes feel uncomfortable or awkward in my body.
- ☐ I spend an unreasonable amount of time worrying about my appearance, my weight, food, or calories.
- ☐ I sometimes avoid activities or places because of how I feel about my appearance.

☐ I avoid certain people because of the way they or I look.

Characteristics of a positive body image:

☐ I have an accurate perception of my size and shape.
☐ I celebrate and appreciate my natural body shape.
☐ I understand that a person's physical appearance says very little about their character and value as a person.
☐ I accept my body and understand that all bodies are different.
☐ I refuse to spend an unreasonable amount of time worrying about my appearance, weight, food, or calories.
☐ I feel comfortable and confident in my body.
☐ My appearance doesn't determine my actions or behaviors.
☐ I am comfortable around people of all shapes and sizes.

EXERCISE: Reflection

Perceptual: How do I see myself and my body?

Affective: How do I feel about myself and my body?

Cognitive: How do I think about myself and my body?

Behavioral: How do I behave with regard to myself and my body?

WHY IS HAVING A POSITIVE BODY IMAGE SO HARD?

If you've ever struggled with your body image, you're definitely not alone. There are so many different reasons why this happens, and most of them go way back. From early childhood, we start to form our first impressions of ourselves, shaped by what we see, hear, and experience. Your body image today is influenced by everything from your past experiences to the cultural messages you receive every day. Let's explore why feeling good about our bodies can be so challenging.

Cultural factors

Many people struggle with body image, often due to deep-rooted influences starting from childhood. Our perceptions are shaped by experiences and cultural messages that idealize narrow standards of beauty. Cultural norms, media portrayals, and societal expectations, often driven by oppressive systems, promote unrealistic ideals that fuel shame and feelings of inadequacy. Industries like fashion, beauty, and diet benefit by making us feel we must change ourselves. These unrealistic standards are also perpetuated by edited and curated social media images, which lead to harmful comparisons. Studies show that social media use can contribute to negative body image, bullying, and mental health struggles, especially among adolescents.

Family environment plays a significant role too. Negative comments from caregivers during childhood can lead to lasting issues with body acceptance, impacting self-esteem and even intimacy. Other factors, such as puberty, aging, trauma, or societal stigmas related to weight and appearance, can further complicate how we feel about our bodies. Understanding that these pressures are external—not inherent—can be a powerful first step toward embracing ourselves as we are.

COMMON SOURCES OF BODY IMAGE ISSUES

- The rise of social media use and the resulting societal emphasis on image and beauty.
- Images that have been digitally edited, manipulated, and/or retouched being widely used.
- Stigma attached to being overweight; discrimination against fat people.
- Exposure to images in the media that represent unrealistic and limited ideals of appearance.
- Being taunted, criticized, or victimized by bullying because of one's weight or appearance, especially in adolescence.
- Colorism, which is prevalent among people of color and is characterized by the idealization of lighter-colored skin.
- Minority stress caused by long-term experiences of victimization, racism, and discrimination.
- Gender dysphoria and the wider social pressure to look a certain way because of binary gendered appearance ideals.

Interpersonal experiences

Body image messages can come at you in different ways—sometimes they're direct, like when someone tells you to lose weight, and other times they're more subtle. For example, you might pick up on the idea that it's normal for adults to be self-conscious about their appearance just by watching how others talk about themselves. Constant body-shaming comments or jokes can really hurt a person's self-esteem over time. Even positive comments can backfire if they make you feel that your worth is tied only to how you look or if they create pressure to always look a certain way.

Physical changes

Puberty is a time when our bodies go through big changes, and for many of us, this can lead to feeling overly focused on how we look. Whether you go through these changes earlier or later than your peers can also affect how you feel about yourself. Changes like gaining weight or dealing with acne can make you feel less attractive, which can be tough on your self-esteem. Interestingly, research shows that even after people clear up their acne or lose weight, they don't always feel better about their bodies.

Puberty can be especially challenging for gender-diverse individuals because the physical changes often don't align with their true sense of self. Growing facial hair, developing breasts, or a deepening voice can feel as if the body is betraying who they are, making it difficult to feel comfortable or connected to their own body. Society's rigid expectations about how boys and girls "should" look can add pressure, and these changes might push someone into a category they don't identify with, leading to body image struggles and lowered self-esteem.

EXERCISE: Reflection

- Have I ever found myself making comparisons to physically attractive people? Or even people who are not conventionally attractive?
- Who was the subject of the comparison? How were they selected? Were they representative of people of my age and gender or not?
- How was the person assessed? What body parts were the focus of the comparison, and how were they evaluated?
- Have there ever been times when I scrolled through social media sites, such as Facebook and Instagram, and suddenly felt bad about my body?
- Is there a part of my body that I wish I could change?
- Have I ever thought that my life would get better if I lost weight or had a particular body shape?
- Has my body ever affected my mood?

- Have I ever tried making changes to my looks in hopes of being more physically attractive?
- Have I ever engaged in activities I don't enjoy, such as going to the gym for hours or eating foods I don't like, to lose weight?
- Have there ever been social events that I avoided or missed because of how I felt about my body?

EXERCISE: What impact has my body image had on me?

If you struggle with body image issues, you likely know how deeply they can impact your overall well-being. The following emotions and behaviors are common ways people may be affected by or cope with body image concerns. However, it's important to note that not everyone with body image struggles will experience all of these. Which of these resonate with you?

- ☐ Low self-esteem
- ☐ Lack of confidence
- ☐ Stress
- ☐ Social avoidance
- ☐ Isolation
- ☐ Reduced intimacy with others
- ☐ Decreased motivation to seek help
- ☐ Perfectionistic tendencies
- ☐ Repetitive negative thoughts
- ☐ Increased spectatoring
- ☐ Mental health issues such as depression, anxiety, and body dysmorphic disorder
- ☐ Eating disorders/disordered eating
- ☐ Sexual avoidance
- ☐ Low sexual arousal
- ☐ Orgasm difficulties
- ☐ Lack of sexual desire
- ☐ Passivity/reduced assertiveness
- ☐ Reduced physical activity
- ☐ Suicidal ideation and self-harm

- ☐ Coping behaviors like smoking, drinking to excess, or substance use
- ☐ Going to extreme lengths to change your appearance (including anabolic steroids, unregulated diet pills, and laxatives)
- ☐ Reduced academic and career aspirations and performance

Other:

IS BODY IMAGE AFFECTING YOUR SEXUAL SELF?

We live in a world where mirrors are everywhere and apps let us manipulate how we look. The pressure to present ourselves a certain way can make it hard to appreciate our bodies for what they do rather than how they look. These unrealistic standards can affect our feelings about ourselves—even in the bedroom. Research shows that negative body image is one of the biggest barriers to sexual pleasure and responsiveness, second only to relationship problems. But here's the thing: you don't have to feel great about your body all the time to enjoy a fulfilling sex life. In fact, experiencing sexual pleasure can boost body image, improve self-esteem, and even aid in healing. And as you work on improving your relationship with your body, your sexual experiences will likely become more enjoyable too.

Many of us worry about our appearance during sex. Concerns about cellulite, muscles, chest size, belly size, penis size, body hair, or just not being "sexy enough" are normal, but they can distract us from enjoying the moment. These worries consume energy that could otherwise be used for connection and pleasure. It's helpful to remember that our partners often have their own insecurities too. The first step to feeling more comfortable is understanding what influences your body image and learning ways to build self-esteem.

How does body image influence sex?

The following are two of the most common ways that body image affects sex: mental distraction and sexual confidence.

Mental distraction: Negative body image often leads to mental distractions during sex. Instead of being fully present, we might get caught up in non-sexual thoughts about how we look. This mental distraction can reduce sexual satisfaction, make it harder to reach orgasm, and affect our ability to connect with our partner. Feeling self-conscious also impacts how we perceive our partner's thoughts about us, which can lead to avoiding sex altogether.

Sexual confidence: Body dissatisfaction can also reduce sexual confidence—the belief in our own sexual qualities and ability to talk about sexuality openly. Sexual confidence plays a big role in creating satisfying experiences and fostering intimacy with our partner(s). Without it, we're more likely to hold back, avoid initiating intimacy, and miss out on deeper connections.

EXERCISE: Reflection

- Am I ever insecure about my appearance during sexual activity?
- Am I ever embarrassed about the way I look naked?
- Do I ever get distracted by negative thoughts about my body during sex?

BODY POSITIVITY OR BODY NEUTRALITY?

Negative body image can be a lifelong struggle, affecting not just you but potentially future generations too. That's why movements like body positivity and body neutrality have emerged, offering alternative ways to break free from harmful societal standards. The body positivity movement is all about embracing self-love and challenging unrealistic beauty standards. It's a powerful rejection of the idea that there's only one "ideal" way to look. Thanks to social media, many people—especially women—are being encouraged to let go of self-consciousness, celebrate their authentic selves, and post photos without edits or filters. But body positivity isn't without its challenges. Some feel that it has missed the mark on inclusivity, leaving out certain bodies, genders, and ethnicities. Others find that striving to always feel positive about your body can be exhausting and unrealistic.

If body positivity feels overwhelming or unattainable, body neutrality might be a better fit. Body neutrality focuses less on how your body looks and more on what it does for you—keeping your heart beating, helping you breathe, and all the other incredible things your body accomplishes every day. This approach takes the pressure off needing to love every part of yourself and instead focuses on acceptance. It's a more accessible way to find peace with your body, no matter what shape or form it takes.

Ultimately, the choice is yours. For some, body neutrality feels freeing and achievable, while others may find joy and empowerment in body positivity. Both paths are valid—it's all about what feels right for you. In fact, both approaches can coexist and people may shift between them depending on their needs. For example, some days, body positivity might feel empowering, while on others, body neutrality might feel like a more achievable goal. Do what works best for you.

EXERCISE: Reflection

- What are my thoughts about body positivity?
- What are my thoughts about body neutrality?
- Which sounds more appealing to me: body positivity or neutrality? Why?

"FEELING FAT"

It's normal for us to have moments of discomfort with our bodies, but it's important to challenge the negative feelings that come from these moments. Ever said or thought, "I feel fat"? It's a phrase we often hear, yet it's not really a feeling at all. "Feeling fat" is actually about much more than physical weight; it's the way we experience discomfort in our bodies or emotions. The truth is, it's used to describe a complex state of being that's influenced by our internalized beliefs about weight, body image, and worth. We're usually talking about something else. It could be guilt after eating, feeling sluggish, or not fitting into unrealistic beauty ideals. Instead of expressing what's really going on—like feeling lonely, unloved, or anxious—we label it as "fat" because it's become shorthand for feeling not good enough.

Breaking this cycle means being honest about what we're really feeling. Are we tired, insecure, or ashamed? Finding the right words helps us get the support we need and avoid perpetuating harmful stereotypes about bodies and weight. Remember, everyone has days when they need extra care and support—it's okay to reach out and be honest about what's truly bothering you, rather than falling back on "feeling fat."

When someone is struggling with an eating disorder, it often feels as if their body and their life are completely separate—like two things that will never connect. What they might not realize is that the way they feel about their body is deeply linked to what's happening in their life, whether now or in the past. It's a huge insight that's easy to overlook. Many people think that "feeling fat" is just a feeling that comes out of nowhere or has to do only with their weight or how their clothes fit. If you take a closer look, you might realize that you're stressed about work, struggling in a relationship, feeling overwhelmed, or maybe experiencing sadness or anger. These feelings can get tangled up with how you see your body, making it a target for emotions that feel too hard to deal with directly.

Sometimes "feeling fat" is a way to avoid confronting these difficult emotions. Shifting your focus from your body to what's actually happening in your life is key to healing. It's natural to want a distraction from tough emotions now and then—but for many of us, this distraction can become all-consuming.

When all of your energy is focused on "fixing" your body, you end up ignoring the real challenges making you feel depressed, angry, or overwhelmed. You might believe that if you just lost weight or changed how you look, you'd feel better. And maybe you would—but not for long. Losing weight or changing your body won't magically solve problems at work or in your relationships. It won't erase deeply held beliefs such as "I'm not good enough" or "I'm unlovable." It won't make people stay when they want to leave.

To truly address what's going on, you have to understand what's really wrong. It's not your body that's the problem—it's the emotions and experiences behind those body image struggles. The things you dislike about your body are often reflections of suppressed emotions or old wounds you've tried to ignore.

If you've been using food or your body as a way to cope, it's understandable that your body might be affected. But changing your body won't fix the underlying issues. The real journey begins when you start to identify the emotions and experiences you've been avoiding. It's not easy to let go of the coping mechanisms that have helped you manage stress or feelings of inadequacy. But change is possible—and it starts by increasing your awareness of how you've been using food and body image to cope. This is where true healing begins.

What if every time you "feel fat" you were to ask yourself: "What am I really feeling?"

EXERCISE: Reflection

- Have I ever felt "fat"?
- What does feeling "fat" mean to me?
- Are there any common emotions, people, or situations that trigger this "feeling"?

EXERCISE: Feeling fat check-in

When you experience the thought of "feeling fat," take a moment to pause and reflect further on what else may be happening.

- Am I feeling physical discomfort?
- Am I feeling emotional discomfort?
- What am I trying to avoid dealing with?
- Do I know what I am really feeling? What is it?

BODY CHECKING AND BODY AVOIDANCE

Body checking is when you constantly examine your appearance or weight, while body avoidance is when you go out of your way to avoid doing so. People with eating disorders might swing between these behaviors, or even do both at the same time, avoiding certain areas of the body and hyperfocusing on others. They are both rooted in overthinking about shape and weight and can vary in how intense they are.

Body checking

Body checking can take many forms, including:

- *Weighing:* Stepping on the scales daily, or even several times a day, to track weight changes.
- *Measuring:* Using a tape measure to check body parts like the waist or hips.
- *Wrapping:* Using your hands to check the size of your wrists, stomach, arms, or thighs.
- *Tracing:* Running your fingers along areas like collarbones or hip bones to see if they feel different.
- *Pinching:* Grabbing parts of your body to feel for fat or changes in firmness.
- *Mirrors and photos:* Constantly checking yourself in mirrors or photos to examine your appearance.
- *Comparing:* Comparing your body to past photos, other people, or images online.
- *Seeking reassurance:* Asking others for validation about your appearance or obsessively checking how clothes fit.
- *Focusing:* Paying excessive attention to specific parts of your body.

Everyone's version of body checking looks a bit different, but it often stems from a desire to feel better about certain parts of our appearance. It might feel like a way to get some control or relieve anxiety. For example, checking the size of a body part after eating might give a temporary sense of comfort that things haven't changed. The problem is that body checking rarely gives us the reassurance we're hoping for. It's a bit like Googling your symptoms—instead of feeling better, you end up more anxious and fearful. Body checking might bring a fleeting sense of relief, but often it just makes the worries and self-criticism worse.

In sexually intimate moments, this preoccupation with appearance can make it nearly impossible to relax or feel present. The individual may become hyperaware of their body, distracted by thoughts of how they look, which can interfere with arousal, lubrication, and orgasm. Beyond the physical discomfort, body checking often creates an emotional disconnection—feeling emotionally removed from one's partner because of a perceived lack of attractiveness or fear of judgment. This disconnection erodes intimacy, trust, and vulnerability, essential components for a fulfilling sexual experience.

EXERCISE: Reflection

- Do I engage in any body-checking behaviors? Which ones are the most common for me?
- What do I hope to feel or avoid when I engage in body-checking behaviors?
- What am I looking for in these behaviors?
- How do I feel before body checking and after body checking? Do I actually get what I am looking for?

Body avoidance

Body avoidance is when someone tries to avoid seeing or thinking about their body, especially their shape or weight. It's kind of the opposite of constantly checking or scrutinizing your body, but the underlying worries about weight and appearance are still very much there. This avoidance doesn't help in the long run because it keeps those worries alive and sometimes even makes them worse. When we avoid our bodies, we miss the chance to challenge the fears and negative beliefs we have about our size or shape. Instead of learning to think in a more balanced way about our appearance, we get stuck in a cycle of fear.

Here are some common examples of body avoidance:

- Avoiding or covering mirrors.
- Looking away when passing reflective surfaces like windows.
- Not looking at yourself when getting dressed.
- Wearing loose or baggy clothes to hide your shape.
- Avoiding weather-appropriate clothing, like wearing long sleeves or pants in hot weather.
- Not going clothes shopping.
- Skipping activities like swimming or dancing that might draw attention to your body.
- Avoiding close physical contact with others.
- Refusing to look at photos of yourself.
- Avoiding touching your own body.

Individuals engaging in body-avoidance behaviors often distance themselves from intimacy, withdrawing from sexual encounters due to insecurity about how they look. This avoidance can lead to emotional and physical disengagement in relationships, as partners are left without the opportunity to connect intimately. In sexual situations, feelings of discomfort or anxiety about one's body can reduce arousal, desire, and sexual enjoyment. The lack of intimacy also makes it difficult to communicate openly about sexual needs, fostering frustration and unfulfilled desires.

While some body avoidance behaviors might feel helpful or necessary during certain stages of recovery, the goal is eventually to move toward body acceptance or body neutrality. For many people, avoiding their body entirely can actually make their preoccupation with it even stronger in the long term. The ultimate aim is to live a life where your size or weight isn't controlling your happiness or daily decisions.

EXERCISE: Reflection

- Do I engage in any body-avoidance behaviors? Which ones are the most common for me?
- What do I hope to feel or avoid?
- What am I looking for in these behaviors?
- Do I actually get what I am looking for when avoiding my body?

Why body checking and body avoidance make us feel worse
We end up hyperfocusing on our weight and shape: When we focus on something intensely, our brain becomes trained to notice even the tiniest details.

The problem is that weight and shape naturally fluctuate, which makes it easy for us to overthink those small changes and stay stuck in a cycle of worry.

We're not great at judging our own body: How we see our weight and shape can be influenced by so many things—our mood, what we've eaten, how full we feel, or even recent images we've seen in the media. It's also hard for us to accurately remember how our body looked or felt in the past, so we may assume we "look bigger" without any real evidence.

We tend to look for "problems": When we're preoccupied with our body, we often look for things that confirm our fears—like signs of weight gain. And because our brains are wired to find what we're looking for, we might notice only the things we don't like, completely missing our body's strengths and positive qualities.

We compare selectively (and unfairly): Think about who you're comparing yourself to. Is it everyone around you, or just those who seem to fit an "ideal"? When we compare ourselves to a small, often unrealistic group—like photoshopped or filtered images—we're setting ourselves up to feel worse. These comparisons aren't fair, and they don't reflect the full range of beauty that exists.

OVERCOMING BODY CHECKING AND AVOIDANCE
The first step is to become more aware of your body-checking or body-avoidance habits.

Identify the current state and function of these behaviors in your life

EXERCISE: Assessment
In your notebook, write down your answers to the following questions:

- In what ways am I checking or avoiding my body and weight?
- Which body parts? How often per day?
- How am I feeling after body checking, during body checking, and after body checking?
- How does it affect my mood?

- How does it affect my eating disorder behaviors?
- How does it affect my sexuality?

Make an effort to fight the urge to check your own body

Here's some great news: we all have the ability to learn and create new habits! It might not always be easy, and there will definitely be some discomfort along the way, but it's absolutely possible to shift your brain's default from body checking to something healthier. Imagine you're starting to make a new trail through the forest. At first, it's tough going—the path is barely there, and your brain doesn't naturally know to take it. But the more you walk that path, the clearer it becomes, until one day it feels like second nature. Meanwhile, the old path grows over and fades away as you use it less and less. This is the magic of rewiring your brain: with consistent, focused effort, you can see real changes. It's not instant, but it's worth it. Every single one of us has this capacity for change, and you can get there step by step, with patience and persistence.

EXERCISE: Urge surfing worksheet (Linehan, 2014)
Write your answers to these questions in your notebook.

- Why do I feel I need to body check right now?
- How uncomfortable would I be if I could not check or avoid my body?
- What can I do in this moment instead?

Determine which checking and avoiding habits you'd like to improve

Look at your answers to the question above: In what ways am I checking or avoiding my body and weight?

EXERCISE: Body checking and avoidance
In your notebook, write down any body checking or avoidance behaviors you'd like to work on. Be as specific or broad as you need to be—this list is for your eyes only.

Next, choose just one or two behaviors to focus on right now and then revisit the list as those behaviors improve.

Establish objectives for changing these behaviors

Think about ways to gradually limit these behaviors, then adjust your goals as you go.

Here are a few ideas to get started:

- *Reduce frequency:* For example, try checking only twice a day instead of five times.
- *Limit the behavior:* Maybe cut down to once a week instead of every day.
- *Eliminate it completely:* If you're ready, consider stopping altogether.
- *Postpone the behavior:* See if you can delay checking a little bit longer each time.
- *Increase engagement (if you tend to avoid your body):* Spend more time with your body gently, for example applying lotion or wearing clothes that make you feel comfortable.

EXERCISE: Objectives

- Can I think of some tiny steps I can take today to start resisting the urge to check or avoid?

Write these down in your notebook and try to focus on only one or two at a time. Revisit the list as those behaviors improve.

Change your environment

Once you understand what tends to trigger body checking, you can make small changes that might reduce it or even make it go away entirely. For example, you could:

- put away or remove your scales
- move mirrors to different locations, or limit the number you have
- get rid of any measuring tools.

Even these small adjustments can make a big difference, helping you gradually reduce body-checking behaviors and ease the focus on negative thoughts about your body.

Remember, the idea is to start with simple, achievable goals and then slowly build on your progress. You've got this!

EXERCISE: My body-checking and avoidance triggers worksheet

Jot down in your notebook your answers to the following questions:

- What are some objects that trigger an urge to check or avoid my body (mirrors, tape measure, photos, etc.)?
- What are some places that trigger an urge to check or avoid my body (beach, mall, etc.)?
- What are some people that trigger an urge to check or avoid my body (friends, partners, etc.)?
- What are some situations that trigger an urge to check or avoid my body (live streaming, dates, scrolling social media, etc.)?
- What are some thoughts that trigger an urge to check or avoid my body (e.g., "I overate" or "My partner thinks I'm huge")?
- What are some emotions that trigger an urge to check or avoid my body (sadness, guilt, etc.)?
- What are some other things that trigger an urge to check or avoid my body?

EXERCISE: Managing discomfort

When you feel the urge to engage in body checking, it's important to acknowledge the discomfort without letting it control you. Here are some helpful strategies to manage that discomfort and resist the urge to body check.

Mindful breathing: Try deep, slow breathing to calm your body and mind. Inhale for a count of four, hold for four, and exhale for four. This simple technique can help you stay grounded and interrupt the urge to check your body.

5-4-3-2-1 grounding exercise: When you're feeling overwhelmed, try this exercise to reconnect with the present moment:

- Name 5 things you can see.
- Name 4 things you can feel.
- Name 3 things you can hear.
- Name 2 things you can smell.

- Name 1 thing you can taste.

Affirmations: When negative thoughts arise, counter them with positive affirmations. Remind yourself: "I am more than my appearance," or "My worth is not defined by how I look."

Engage in a positive distraction: When you feel the urge to check, try engaging in an activity that takes your mind off your body. Take a walk, dive into a book, or immerse yourself in a hobby that isn't related to appearance. It's a great way to refocus your energy.

Challenge the thought: Pause and ask yourself, "What am I really feeling right now?" Often, the urge to body check stems from anxiety or insecurity. By identifying the underlying emotion, you can address it more directly, instead of focusing on your appearance.

Mindful self-compassion: Be kind to yourself when these feelings arise. Instead of judging yourself for feeling anxious or checking your body, try saying, "It's okay to feel this way. I'm doing my best right now." Self-compassion can help you navigate discomfort with care and understanding.

IMPROVING GENERAL BODY IMAGE

Having a healthy body image doesn't have to be some far-off dream. There are real, practical steps you can take to start shifting your mindset and feeling better about yourself.

Identify where your body image issues come from

Take a moment to think back to some of your answers in Chapter 5: when was the first time you felt unhappy about your body? It probably wasn't some random feeling that just popped up out of nowhere. Was there a specific moment or a certain person who planted that idea in your mind? Maybe it was a comment from a family member, something you saw in the media, a teacher, an ex-partner, or even your own thoughts. Understanding where those feelings started can help you start to let go of them.

EXERCISE: Reflection

- What external influences have impacted my body image (family, community, society, media, etc.)?
- What was the effect it had on me? (Think about both positive and negative influences.)
- How is my body image linked to my sexuality and sensual self?

Shift your focus

Shift your focus to what makes you amazing. Think about your strengths, talents, and unique traits—there's so much more to you than just your appearance. Are you kind? Creative? Funny? Do you love art, dancing, learning, or helping others? What do you like about yourself?

EXERCISE: Reflection

- What do I appreciate about myself?
- What makes me unique?

Talk to yourself as you would talk to someone you care about

When it comes to your body, try talking to yourself as you would to a friend. We're often so much harsher on ourselves than we'd ever be on someone we love. It can feel strange at first, especially if you're used to negative self-talk, but starting small can make a big difference. Studies show that changing how we speak to ourselves really works. Begin by noticing those critical thoughts, and slowly swap them for words of gratitude or even just neutrality. Over time, this shift can help you cultivate self-compassion and a more positive relationship with your body.

EXERCISE: Negative thoughts worksheet

Take a day to record every self-critical thought you have about your body.

Then challenge each thought with four questions:

1. Does the thought contribute to my stress?

2. Where does it come from?
3. Is my thought a logical one? Is it distorted?
4. What is a more positive or fact-based thought?

Write your findings down in your notebook.

Stand your ground with others

It's okay to set boundaries with others when it comes to your body. Prepare a few responses to have on hand for unwanted comments. Try something like, "Why do you feel the need to say that?" or, "How would you feel if someone said that to you?" You could also keep it simple with, "Yes, I'm aware" or, "Your comments aren't helpful." The goal is to stand firm and remind others that their opinions about your body are unnecessary.

EXERCISE: Responses to unhelpful comments

- What can I tell someone who makes unwanted comments about my body?
- Are there certain people in my life who tend to make these comments? Who?

Start moving

Moving your body can be a great confidence booster. Whether it's dancing, yoga, or just going for a walk, find something that feels good and enjoyable. It's not about changing how you look—it's about embracing what your body can do for you and experiencing the joy of movement. And remember, it's not about "shoulds." If movement feels like a chore or a punishment, it's not going to help you feel better. Instead, focus on activities that make you happy, help relieve stress, and let you feel at one with your body.

Shift your focus to fun and wellness instead of appearance

BMI has often been used as a measure of health, but it doesn't tell the whole story, especially for athletes, pregnant people, or older adults. Rather than fixating on numbers, focus on how you feel and aim to nurture every part of your well-being: mental, emotional, cardiovascular, and sexual health. Working out or moving your body should be fun, not a chore. The more you enjoy it, the more likely you'll stick with it.

Be grateful for your body

Being grateful for what your body can do can go a long way toward improving body confidence. It takes practice, but focusing on what you appreciate about your body can reduce negative feelings and help you feel more present—both in everyday life and during intimate moments. The benefits to your overall well-being, including sexual confidence and satisfaction, make it well worth the effort.

EXERCISE: Reflection

- What do I appreciate about my body?
- What does my body do for me?

Carefully consider the things you expose yourself to

Social media can have a big impact on how you feel about your body. One of the best things you can do for yourself is to filter what you're exposed to. You don't need to put up with content that makes you feel bad. Take a moment to unfollow or mute accounts that contribute to negative body image, even if they belong to friends or family. You deserve a feed that lifts you up, not one that drags you down.

CASE STUDY: Maria

Maria, a 32-year-old trans woman, has been in recovery from anorexia nervosa for two years. Her journey toward gender affirmation began at 28, coinciding with a deepening struggle with her eating disorder. Transitioning provided a sense of identity alignment, but also intensified her desire to control her body, leading to restrictive eating habits. Maria's struggle for control was influenced by societal expectations of feminine beauty and her need for validation, contributing to severe body image issues that affected her health and relationships.

Maria's eating disorder significantly affected her sexuality. During the height of her disorder, she felt disconnected from her body and experienced little sexual desire. She often dissociated during sexual encounters, focusing on how her body appeared to her partner, leading to shame and dissatisfaction. Physically, malnutrition reduced her libido. She also experienced vaginismus, causing pain during penetration, which reinforced avoidance and anxiety around intimacy.

Before transitioning, she felt disconnected from her physical self. Hormone replacement therapy and gender-affirming surgeries helped align her appearance with her gender identity, but lingering body image issues continued to impact her sexual health. Despite physical changes, Maria struggled to accept her body as a source of pleasure and connection.

Maria's recovery involved reconnecting with her body and sexuality through self-compassion exercises, learning to nurture rather than control her body. She explored her sexual desires through self-pleasure, discovering what felt good without external pressure. Therapy helped her unpack layers of shame around her gender and sexuality and shift her focus from pleasing her partner to understanding her own needs. Maria's partner, Jayden, played a crucial role in her healing by providing a supportive, non-judgmental space for intimacy. They rebuilt trust through non sexual connection, such as cuddling, gentle touch, and open communication. This gradual approach helped Maria feel more comfortable and allowed her to reconnect with her sexuality at her own pace.

Maria has made significant progress in feeling more connected to her body. She no longer views her body solely as something to control or validate her gender but as a source of pleasure, connection, and vulnerability. She has learned to explore her sexuality without shame, recognizing it as an evolving part of who she is. By embracing her desires and vulnerabilities, Maria is building a sexual identity that feels authentic, free from societal standards or the limitations of her eating disorder.

— CHAPTER 9 —

Accept the Feelings, Address the Behavior

GOALS

▶ Learn about the function of emotions.
▶ Understand and identify your own emotions.
▶ Learn to effectively express emotions.
▶ Reduce emotional vulnerability.

Overcontrolled focus: Emotional expression

Undercontrolled focus: Emotional regulation

FEELINGS!

At some point, we've all found ourselves frustrated with our emotions, wondering why we feel so deeply or why we react the way we do. It can be tempting to see all emotions as "bad" or as something we need to push away. But the truth is, our emotions aren't enemies to be avoided—they actually play a crucial role in our lives. Our emotions help us find meaning in our experiences. When something stirs up an emotional response, whether it's a positive or negative feeling, it's a sign that it matters to us. Without our emotions, our ability to care for others and connect—both with them and with ourselves—would be deeply limited. Emotions enrich our relationships and deepen our understanding of the world around us. In essence, they make our lives more vibrant and meaningful.

It's important to remember that emotions, in themselves, aren't good or bad—they simply are. They serve essential functions in our lives, helping us understand ourselves, make decisions, and connect with others. While it might seem like our emotions are the main source of our pain and struggle, it's not as simple as labeling them as "bad." Often, we have a tendency to remember the negative emotions more vividly. This can make it easy to forget all the moments when emotions bring joy, love, or connection into our lives. Even if it doesn't always feel that way, emotions are much more than just a source of distress—they're key to living a full and connected life.

EMOTIONAL OVERWHELM

Emotions can be complicated, confusing, and overwhelming. They can even feel a little scary at times. Are you having trouble navigating your feelings? You might be carrying some mistaken beliefs about emotions that are making things harder for you—affecting your behavior, relationships, and overall emotional well-being. When we try too hard to push our feelings away, we often end up making things worse for ourselves. Instead, it's important to learn how to work with our emotions, not against them, if we want to lead a fulfilling, balanced, and productive life.

Every eating disorder involves some level of difficulty with managing emotions, though how this looks can vary from person to person. Emotional dysregulation is a term that describes these challenges, and it can apply across a range of situations and diagnoses. It might include any of these:

- Struggling to recognize your own emotions.
- Not understanding what you're feeling.
- Difficulty noticing emotions when they come up.
- Challenges understanding others' emotions.
- Trouble expressing emotions to others.
- Struggling to regulate your emotions effectively.
- Being highly sensitive to emotions.
- Having intense emotional reactions.
- Difficulty showing emotions non-verbally.

If your relationship with your emotions isn't as cooperative as it could be, you might notice some of these signs:

- Suppressing your emotions by burying them or trying to push them away.
- Constantly distracting yourself from your feelings (e.g., through social media, work, or other activities).
- Using substances, binge eating, or other behaviors to numb your emotions.

- Avoiding people, places, or situations out of fear of being overwhelmed.
- Criticizing yourself for feeling the way you do.
- Letting emotions completely take over your decisions and actions.

Getting a better handle on emotions helps us respond to them in healthier ways, makes it easier to tolerate discomfort, and puts us in a better position to adjust our emotional states when needed—whether we want to "turn them up," "turn them down," or simply stay balanced while we're feeling them. For some of us, intense emotional experiences are a regular part of life. People who have experienced trauma, those with an undercontrolled coping style, or those who are naturally more sensitive often deal with overwhelming emotions. When these feelings become unbearable, it's easy to resort to what we call "regrettable actions" to try to get rid of them. Engaging in behaviors like binge eating, purging, or seeking unhealthy sexual encounters can be attempts to manage overwhelming emotions, but they rarely provide lasting relief, instead leading to feelings of guilt, shame, and further emotional dysregulation.

The problem with these regrettable actions is that they often make things worse in the long run. While these actions might provide a short-term release, they often leave us feeling worse about ourselves—thinking, "I can't handle this," "Something's wrong with me," or "I'm broken." These harsh self-judgments can bring on more negative emotions like guilt and shame, and they can also make us more sensitive to others' opinions, leaving us even more vulnerable to overwhelming feelings.

Learning to work with our emotions is a key part of emotional well-being. In general, we have three options for dealing with difficult emotional states: we can express them, suppress them, or let them run their course. Developing the skills to make thoughtful choices about which approach to take can make all the difference.

Why is emotional regulation so hard?
Impediments to the effective use of emotional regulation skills fall into two broad categories: *biological factors* and *present or immediate factors*. A combination of both types of factors is often the cause of difficulties in controlling emotions or using emotional regulation skills.

Biological factors
Some of us are simply wired to feel emotions more intensely than others. Let's explore three main biological challenges:

- *Hypersensitivity:* Some people are naturally more sensitive than others—they feel things deeply and express emotions strongly. This means they often have *too many emotions* to process at once, or those emotions feel as if they're coming in at full speed. This can lead to more discomfort, distress, or emotional overwhelm.

- *Hyper-reactivity:* When you're hyper-reactive, emotions tend to trigger impulsive reactions before you have time to fully process them. It's as if your emotions get the jump on you, making it tough to pause and decide how you actually want to respond.

- *Slow return to baseline:* After feeling intense emotions, some people can quickly come back down to their "normal" state, but others stay at that high intensity for longer. When emotions linger, it makes staying calm and regulated much harder.

Present or immediate factors

Building the skills for long-term emotional stability takes time and practice, but there are immediate, day-to-day factors that can make it even more challenging to regulate emotions. Here are a few that might resonate:

- *Lack of skill:* Sometimes, we simply don't have the tools we need. If we weren't taught as kids how to deal with emotions in a healthy way, it can be hard to figure out on our own. If people dismissed our emotions when we were young, it might leave us feeling confused about how to manage them now.

- *Reinforcement of behavior:* Our environment plays a big role in how we behave. Sometimes, intense emotions get reinforced by the people around us, especially if our strong reactions get us what we need or want. On the other hand, attempts to manage emotions might get ignored or punished, making it tempting to give up on trying.

- *Moodiness or rapid mood swings:* When your current mood is driving your actions, rather than your wiser, more balanced self, emotions can feel as if they're in charge. Rapid mood changes can make it difficult to stick with healthy emotional responses.

- *Emotional overload:* Ever feel so overwhelmed that you just can't think straight? That's emotional overload—when emotions are so high that

it's hard to function, let alone use the skills you've learned. When this happens, it's best to start with distress tolerance techniques to bring the intensity down a notch.

- *Emotional "myths" or false beliefs:* False beliefs about emotions can keep you from managing them effectively. If you feel ashamed of your emotions or believe that intense emotions are just "who you are," you might not be motivated to learn new skills.

- *Lack of understanding of your own feelings:* If you don't know exactly what you're feeling, it's hard to regulate it. Sometimes emotions are all jumbled together, making it tough to know what to focus on.

THE ROLE OF INVALIDATION AND VALIDATION

People with eating disorders often struggle with how they handle their emotions. Some may express their feelings in an intense, unfiltered way, which often happens when their emotional needs have been neglected. This can make others label them as irrational or unpredictable. To avoid this, many overcontrolled individuals learn to do the opposite—suppressing their emotions to appear calm and in control. But both of these approaches can lead to feeling misunderstood and not getting the help they need. Experiences of emotional invalidation—such as being told "You're overreacting"—can exacerbate feelings of shame and isolation, making it harder to process emotions.

Validation is about accepting, understanding, and valuing someone's feelings. It's letting them know they're safe to be themselves, and that their emotions are okay. When we validate someone, we're not just listening—we're showing that we genuinely see them, understand them, and accept them for who they are. This can be as simple as actively listening, giving a nod of understanding, or even offering a comforting hug. When someone feels validated, their painful emotions often ease. But when feelings are ignored or dismissed, they tend to grow stronger and more overwhelming.

What is an invalidating environment?

It's common to feel disconnected when your emotions seem more intense than those of the people around you. You might hear things like "You're too emotional" or "You're too sensitive" from friends, family, or co-workers, making you feel misunderstood or even judged for expressing your feelings. Repeatedly hearing that you're "overreacting" or that your emotions are "inappropriate" can lead to self-doubt. Over time, you might start punishing yourself or rejecting your own emotions, losing trust in your feelings altogether.

Invalidation like this can take a serious toll, both emotionally and physically. Research shows that being invalidated can lead to increased heart rate, higher blood pressure, and more difficulty managing emotions (Schreiber & Veilleux, 2022; Shenk & Fruzzetti, 2011).

This kind of response, when widespread or prolonged, can be deeply harmful. One way to start healing from invalidation is to understand how your experiences have shaped your emotional regulation and your sense of self.

The impact of invalidation can range from minor misunderstandings to more severe, deliberate actions. On the milder side, most family conflicts happen because of unintentional miscommunication. Even in loving families, a child who's particularly emotionally sensitive might not always feel understood. The same goes for adult relationships—sometimes we just miss each other's needs, and over time, feeling misunderstood can make you question whether there's something wrong with you.

As we move further along the spectrum of invalidation, things can get more serious. Experiences like bullying, rejection, neglect, or emotional abuse are much more harmful, as they are often intentional. Environments where sharing your feelings is met with extreme, inappropriate reactions—where you're told your emotions are wrong or don't make sense—create deeply invalidating conditions. Invalidation prevents problems from being noticed or resolved. Often, a child in this kind of environment is simply told to control their emotions without being given the tools or support to do so.

It's important to note that an invalidating environment doesn't always involve abuse or neglect. Even well-meaning families can unintentionally invalidate a child by dismissing, judging, or mocking their feelings. Without empathy, a child can come to feel that their emotions and thoughts are entirely unjustified. This can leave them struggling to identify their feelings, distrusting themselves, or even turning to unhealthy coping mechanisms.

When a child's emotional needs aren't met, they often express themselves even more intensely—but what they really need is validation. Unfortunately, this can lead to a cycle where heightened emotions are the only way to get a response. A child may learn, unconsciously, that only strong reactions will get their needs met. On the other hand, some environments push for emotional suppression and stress achievement as the measure of success—this can be equally invalidating, just in a different way.

EXERCISE: Experiences of invalidation
Check the box next to examples that match your experiences.

Examples of invalidation
Feel or look differently:

- ☐ Lighten up
- ☐ Get over it
- ☐ Don't cry
- ☐ Don't make that face
- ☐ Don't worry
- ☐ Stop looking so sad
- ☐ Don't get angry

"Should":

- ☐ You should be excited
- ☐ You should feel thankful
- ☐ You should be happy
- ☐ You should just drop it
- ☐ You shouldn't worry so much
- ☐ You should feel ashamed of yourself
- ☐ You shouldn't say that

Your perception is wrong:

- ☐ I'm sorry you feel that way
- ☐ You've got it all wrong
- ☐ I do listen to you
- ☐ That is ridiculous
- ☐ I was only kidding
- ☐ It's not personal

Minimizing:

- ☐ You're okay!
- ☐ It's not that bad
- ☐ You just had a lousy day, that's all
- ☐ There is no reason to feel unhappy about this

- [ ] There is no need for alarm
- [ ] That's life
- [ ] Shit happens

Isolating:

- [ ] The only person who feels that way is you
- [ ] Why should it concern you if it doesn't bother anyone else?
- [ ] You are making everyone else miserable
- [ ] Don't you ever think of anyone but yourself?

Reasoning:

- [ ] There is no point getting upset!
- [ ] You are not being rational
- [ ] It doesn't make any sense to feel...
- [ ] But if you really think about it....

Limiting or intolerance:

- [ ] Are you still upset over that?
- [ ] You should be over that by now
- [ ] Quit your crying!
- [ ] Get over it!
- [ ] Forget about it
- [ ] This is getting really old
- [ ] I am sick of hearing about it
- [ ] Go to your room if you plan to cry
- [ ] I'm not having this discussion

Invalidating actions:

- [ ] Punishing/grounding
- [ ] Keep checking a watch or phone
- [ ] Quickly attempting to end the discussion
- [ ] Eye-rolling
- [ ] Abruptly leaving a conversation
- [ ] Totally ignoring someone who is trying to communicate
- [ ] Disrupting a speaker's train of thought

Defending or explaining

☐ I am sure he didn't mean it that way!
☐ You just took it the wrong way
☐ I am sure she was trying to help
☐ Maybe she was just having a bad day
☐ Maybe it is because...
☐ That is because...
☐ Of course, because you...
☐ Well yeah, because they...

Name-calling or labeling:

☐ "Dramatic"
☐ "Cry baby"
☐ "Whiner"
☐ "Emotional"
☐ "Sensitive"
☐ "Drama queen"

Philosophizing:

☐ That's life
☐ Shit happens
☐ Time heals all wounds
☐ This too shall pass
☐ Every cloud has a silver lining
☐ You will understand when you are older
☐ There is a reason for everything

Oversimplification:

☐ You need to exert more effort
☐ It's possible that you could make some positive changes if you tried
☐ Perhaps if you had more social interactions outside the house, your mood would improve
☐ It's a matter of personal choice whether or not you allow yourself to experience joy

EMOTIONAL LEAKAGE

People who are overcontrolled often experience what we call "emotional leakage," where their emotions spill out in unexpected ways (Lynch, 2018a). The downside of having great self-control is that it can lead to habits that aren't always sustainable. Overcontrolled individuals tend to bottle up their feelings for so long that eventually, the pressure becomes too much and everything bursts out. When this happens, their inner feelings are revealed with more intensity than they'd like. These emotional leaks often feel out of character, can happen in public, and may leave the person feeling embarrassed or guilty afterward. You might see shouting, name-calling, or other dramatic displays of emotion—similar to those who are typically more undercontrolled.

However, unless it's followed by self-criticism or harm to oneself or others, emotional leakage isn't necessarily a problem. It's completely okay to show others how you truly feel, even if those emotions are negative. In fact, people who express their emotions openly are often seen as more trustworthy and emotionally connected to others. For overcontrolled people, though, emotional leakage is usually followed by self-criticism because they have strong rules about when and how to express their emotions. When these rules are broken, it can lead to frustration and self-blame.

Clients have shared examples of what we call "high-intensity leakages," like cutting someone off aggressively in traffic, berating a server for getting an order wrong, or storming out of a meeting. They've also talked about "low-intensity leakages," such as smiling at someone's misfortune, "forgetting" to invite someone to an event, or pretending not to notice when someone needs help. High-intensity signals can often be mistaken for emotional dysregulation, so it's important to consider the timing, place, and frequency of these moments.

If you relate to this, remember that it's human to feel overwhelmed at times, and emotional leakage is part of that. The goal isn't to be perfect, but to understand yourself with compassion and recognize when you need support.

EMOTIONS HELP US

Emotions are more than just feelings; they serve a valuable purpose in our lives. While pure logic can sometimes fall short, emotions play a critical role in decision-making, motivating our actions, communicating our inner world, and helping us form deep connections with others. Let's explore how.

The function of emotions
They help us make decisions
Our emotions are often faster than our thoughts. They can guide us to act quickly, especially in critical situations. Imagine trying to logically assess the danger of a speeding car—you'd probably already be in trouble! Emotions allow us to react instinctively. They also act as important signals, letting us know when something is worth paying attention to—like curiosity urging us to explore, or anxiety telling us to tread carefully.

They motivate our actions
Emotions are powerful motivators. They prepare us for action, whether it's the "fight, flight, or freeze" response, or the inspiration to pursue joy or defend something important. Anger can drive us to make changes, joy keeps us energized, and even anxiety can push us to do our best. Without emotions, we'd lack the motivation to overcome challenges or achieve our goals.

They communicate our inner experience and signal our intentions to others
Emotions communicate what we're experiencing to others, often without words. Facial expressions, body language, and tone of voice can say a lot more in an instant than a long explanation. These non-verbal signals strengthen our connections, helping us feel seen and understood. However, it's important to remember that not everyone expresses emotions the same way—different people, including those on the autism spectrum, might use unique ways to share their feelings, like writing or art.

AUTHOR'S NOTE: ON NON-VERBAL EMOTIONAL EXPRESSION
Not everyone expresses emotions in the same way, and that's okay. For some people, non-verbal emotional expression can be really helpful, but it can be a challenge for many autistic individuals. Their way of communicating non-verbally might be different from what most people expect. The truth is, there are so many ways to share how we feel without using words or facial expressions. Some people find comfort in writing, typing, or channeling their emotions through music, poetry, art, or even dance. All of these are beautiful and valid ways to express yourself.

They facilitate the formation of strong social bonds

Our ability to mirror others' emotions, even without realizing it, is part of what helps us connect. When we see someone smile or grimace, our own brains mimic that feeling. This shared emotional experience is what allows us to comfort each other, laugh together, or rally for a cause. Emotions are the glue that binds us in both joyful and challenging times, creating empathy and solidarity.

AUTHOR'S NOTE: ON EMOTIONAL REASONING

It's helpful to see emotions as tools—they can guide us, connect us, and teach us about ourselves. However, it's also crucial to remember that "feelings aren't facts." Just because we feel something deeply, it doesn't always mean it reflects reality. When in doubt, pause and check the facts.

SOME EMOTIONS AND THEIR PURPOSE

Love: Love often signals that things are going well and that we feel a joyful, strong connection in a relationship. It's a reflection of positive growth and bonding.

Guilt: Guilt can be a sign that we've hurt someone or let them down, and it's a reminder to make amends. If you feel guilty, it may mean that a relationship needs attention or repair.

Anger: Anger is often a cue that we've been wronged. It can guide us to take action, like addressing an issue or venting to a trusted friend or family member. It's an emotion that helps us stand up for ourselves.

Shame: Shame, though uncomfortable, serves to reveal our faulty core beliefs. For example, someone might feel shame after being excluded from a group, which might point to a belief like "I'm not wanted." Becoming aware of these beliefs helps us work through them.

Anxiety: Anxiety comes in two types: productive and non-productive. Non-productive anxiety can feel overwhelming and makes it hard to function because it's out of proportion to the situation. On the other hand, productive anxiety is a natural motivator that helps us plan, meet deadlines, or prepare for challenges.

Sadness/Grief: Sadness or grief naturally makes us want to reach out to others for support, and having someone to lean on can be incredibly comforting. When we lack that support, processing these feelings becomes harder. Remember, when we share our grief, it invites support from others, while pretending to be fine can often leave us feeling worse.

Happiness: True happiness shows that something is going well. It's also possible to feel moments of happiness even during challenging times, showing our resilience and capacity for joy.

EXERCISE: Reflection

- Can I recall situations in my life when I typically experience these emotions?
- What actions or urges do I find myself having when I experience these emotions? Are there any patterns?
- How do I want to respond to these emotions differently moving forward?

GOOD? BAD? NEITHER!

There's really no such thing as "good" or "bad" emotions. Emotions are just... emotions. Sure, some feel a lot better than others, but each one plays an important role and carries its own message. That said, emotions aren't always accurate. Learning to listen to them can help you figure out whether they're giving you the right information.

Sometimes we feel emotions that seem to come out of nowhere. We might feel shame even when we've done nothing wrong, or guilt without a clear reason. Fear can pop up even when we aren't in real danger. We can even feel happiness in situations that aren't good for us, like a toxic relationship. Even when your emotions don't seem to match the situation, they're still trying to tell you something important.

Feeling unnecessary guilt? It could be a sign that you need to work on setting boundaries. Experiencing fear that doesn't make sense? It might mean there's an opportunity for growth if you push yourself a little further. Understanding your emotions gives you the power to decide whether they line up with what's actually happening around you.

MISTAKEN BELIEFS ABOUT EMOTIONS

Sometimes, our relationship with our emotions can become strained because of the mistaken beliefs we hold about them. While emotions play a meaningful role in our lives, many people have misconceptions about what emotions are and how they should be handled. Some might think that emotions are the most important part of who they are, while others see them as something to suppress or ignore. It's important to remember that these beliefs are not facts, and they can negatively impact our emotional well-being.

You might recognize a few of these beliefs in yourself or those around you. Often, our misconceptions about emotions are so deeply ingrained that we may not even realize we have them. Some of us were taught that emotions are always negative and should be suppressed, while others were raised to believe that emotions are the only things that define us. These "all-or-nothing" ideas about emotions can be misleading, and it's helpful to remind ourselves that emotions are neither entirely good nor entirely bad. Emotions are a fundamental part of life, and they can bring both positive and negative experiences.

If you notice that some of these beliefs feel true to you, take a moment to reflect on whether they are genuinely serving you. Are these beliefs helping you regulate your emotions, or are they holding you back? Sometimes these misconceptions come from a more rigid way of thinking—where emotions either "are" or "aren't" something absolute. Instead, try approaching your emotions from a place of balance, where both feelings and facts coexist, without invalidating your experience.

Even if these beliefs aren't entirely wrong, treating them as absolute truths can lead to unhelpful thinking patterns. Emotional regulation isn't about denying the positive side of our emotions or amplifying the negative; it's about embracing the full spectrum of what emotions bring to our lives, in a way that serves us best.

EXERCISE: Mistaken beliefs about emotions

Consider whether any of these statements strike a chord with you as you read them. You may have been acting in accordance with them unconsciously. Check the box next to each myth you believe is true or somewhat true.

☐ We make our best decisions when emotions are kept out of it.
☐ In every situation, there is a right way to feel.
☐ Being emotional means being out of control.
☐ Emotions should be controlled.

☐ Letting others know what I am feeling inside is a sign of weakness.
☐ Most people dislike emotional people.
☐ Negative feelings are bad and destructive.
☐ Feeling happy or excited is naive or childish.
☐ Love is only a chemical reaction.
☐ It is important to never let another person know what you are really feeling inside.
☐ Some emotions are really stupid.
☐ Some emotions are useless.
☐ All painful emotions are a result of a bad attitude.
☐ Painful emotions are not really important and should be ignored.
☐ People who feel happy are liars.
☐ I shouldn't feel this way if others don't agree with me.
☐ The finest gauges of my emotions are those around me.
☐ Instead of trying to control or calm my emotions, giving in to their extremes might lead me far.
☐ Being creative takes a lot of energy and a lot of feelings that you can't always control.
☐ I will not have my feelings manipulated; doing so would be dishonest.
☐ Emotional truth, not factual truth, is what really counts.
☐ All that matters is that people act on their own desires.
☐ The mark of a completely liberated person is one who acts only on the basis of their feelings.
☐ These feelings make me who I am.
☐ It's because of my emotions that I've gained so much respect.
☐ Nothing triggers my emotional responses.
☐ Follow your gut feeling no matter what.
☐ Some feelings are considered inappropriate for one gender more than the other ("boys don't cry" or "anger isn't ladylike").

EXERCISE: Self-inquiry on myths

Self-reflection can begin with the examination of any one of the myths listed above. Keep in mind that self-inquiry does not presume that something is wrong, bad, or dysfunctional just because it is examined.

• What might I need to learn from this myth?

- What might this myth be telling me about myself and my life?
- How open am I to thinking differently about this myth or changing the myth? If I am not open or only partly open, then what might this mean?
- How does holding on to this myth help me live more fully?
- How might changing this myth help me live more fully?
- What might my resistance to changing this myth be telling me?
- What do I fear might happen if I momentarily let go of this myth?

EMOTIONAL EXPRESSION

We've all heard about feeling overwhelmed by our emotions. Maybe you've had one of those moments—crying in the restroom at work, feeling completely drained, or yelling out in frustration. It's something many of us can relate to. For a lot of undercontrolled copers, emotions often sit just below the surface or spill out in all directions. On the other hand, overcontrolled copers seem to keep it all together, showing a picture of perfect emotional control. Overcontrolled individuals often suppress emotions, leading to emotional leakage or acting out in unhealthy ways. In the context of eating disorders or compulsive sexual behaviors, this can manifest as excessive restraint in emotional expression, only to have emotions surface explosively later.

ASSESSMENT: EMOTIONAL EXPRESSION

- Do you mask your feelings whenever possible?
- Have you been told you have a serious or flat expression?
- Does your partner or friends want you to show more emotion, but you don't know how?
- Do others have trouble telling when you are joking or being sarcastic?
- Do your true feelings and your outward expressions contradict themselves?

If you answered "yes" to any of the above questions, you might have become too good at controlling your emotions. Overcontrolled people often struggle to express their feelings and rarely let others in. Some suppress their emotions by maintaining a blank expression, while others hide behind a false smile. For example, someone might look composed while internally grieving, or appear calm while feeling anger or resentment. Usually, emotions are pushed down after they've already surfaced internally. This kind of suppression targets the part of emotion that conveys our feelings to those around us, which means its effects are felt not just within us, but also in our relationships.

Since overcontrol is often unrecognized, people around us may miss the signs that we're in distress. Limiting emotional expression can lead to disconnection from others and, ultimately, isolation. Even positive emotions, like excitement or enthusiasm, are stifled. We can't selectively suppress our feelings; when we shut one emotion down, others get blocked too. These coping habits often cause social difficulties, including decreased support, intimacy, and satisfaction.

Have you ever felt uneasy around someone who constantly wears a fake smile or keeps a serious, neutral expression? It's natural—our minds are wired to recognize and distance ourselves from unwelcoming individuals. Our capacity for emotion and vulnerability is what connects us. People who are emotionally reserved or closed off find it difficult to build close relationships.

To build deep, lasting relationships, we need to show vulnerability. When we don't trust someone, we put up a facade to protect our true thoughts and emotions. But when we open up and share our inner world, we're signaling two powerful messages: "I trust you" and "I'm like you." This doesn't mean expressing feelings carelessly—context is key. Sometimes, it's wise to keep our emotions to ourselves. We will explore emotional expression as it relates to interpersonal connectedness more in the next chapter.

EMOTION REGULATION SKILLS
PLEASE skill (Linehan, 2014)
PLEASE is an emotional regulation tool that helps reduce the chances of acting out when feeling unpleasant emotions. It focuses on self-care practices that are always important but become essential during times of emotional stress, trauma, anxiety, or depression.

P & L: Physical health and iLlness
Take care of your physical well-being. Listen to what your body is telling you—if you feel unwell, make it a priority to rest and take care of yourself. Consider vitamins, relax your muscles, and make doctor's appointments promptly. Follow the doctor's advice and take prescribed medications as directed. Even if you feel fine, regular checkups are important to stay on top of your health.

E: Eat a balanced diet
Eating regularly and healthily can help maintain your energy levels and stabilize your mood. Make sure your meals are balanced, with fruits, vegetables, and plenty of water.

A: Avoid mood-altering substances
Use substances like alcohol sparingly, or limit them to weekends. Avoid illicit drugs, as they increase emotional vulnerability during and after use. Even caffeine and marijuana should be used in moderation to keep emotions steady.

S: Sleep and rest
Get enough sleep—ideally between eight and ten hours each night. Keep a regular sleep schedule, even on weekends, and practice good sleep hygiene: reduce screen time before bed and keep the lights low to signal to your body that it's time to rest. If sleep doesn't come easily, rest as best you can.

E: Exercise or movement
Move your body in a way that feels good and is comfortable for you. Exercise naturally releases mood-boosting chemicals and helps release pent-up energy or stress. Aim for 20–30 minutes a day, but start small if you're new to it—even a few minutes makes a difference.

Opposite action

Sometimes, it's better to control your emotions than to act on them right away. The DBT skill called "opposite action" helps you do just that—go against what your emotions are pushing you to do (Linehan, 2014). This can be helpful when your feelings don't match the facts or when acting on them won't get you the outcome you want. Opposite action lets you choose behaviors that align more with how you'd like to feel, rather than how you actually feel in the moment. But make sure you're using this skill for emotions you genuinely want to change—not just because someone else wants you to.

When you're just starting out, it's best to practice with less intense emotions. Begin by noticing your feelings and identifying the action urge that comes with them. Then, ask yourself if your emotion fits the situation and whether acting on it would really be helpful. Do you want to feel something different? If yes, choose the opposite action and commit to it fully. Use words, facial expressions, body language, thoughts, and actions that express the opposite emotion. Stick with it until your original feeling starts to lose its intensity. Once you get the hang of this, you can apply it to more intense emotions to get even better at managing your reactions.

Remember, opposite action is most useful when your emotions aren't in line with what's really happening, or when they're not helping you reach your goals. If your feelings are causing more harm than good, try a different way of responding—you might be surprised at the difference it makes.

OPPOSITE ACTION

Find the action that goes against what our common emotions make us want to do.

Emotion: Anger
Urge: Attack
Function: To defend or attack
Opposite action: Show kindness/concern or walk away/gently avoid.

Emotion: Shame
Urge: Hide, avoid
Function: To isolate
Opposite action: *Justified:* Make your behavior public. Apologize. Make amends for the wrongs done, or take steps to stop and right similar wrongs done to others. Aim to never make that mistake again. Learn to live with the repercussions. *Not justified:* No apologizing. Repeat the actions that make you feel ashamed. Make your personal characteristics or behavior known.

Emotion: Fear
Urge: Run or hide
Function: To escape danger
Opposite action: Approach. Look around slowly. Explore. Stay involved with it. Build courage.

Emotion: Sadness
Urge: Be inactive
Function: To avoid contact
Opposite action: Approach. Avoid avoiding! Get active (run, jog, walk, or do other active exercise).

Emotion: Disgust
Urge: Reject or distance ourselves
Function: To avoid discomfort
Opposite action: Push through and get through the situation.

Emotion: Guilt
Urge: Repair violations
Function: To seek forgiveness
Opposite action: *Justified:* Apologize and mean what you say. *Not justified:* No apologizing. Repeat the actions that make you feel guilty. Make your personal characteristics or behavior known.

Emotion: Envy
Urge: Try hard to gain or obtain
Function: To fight injustice and inequality
Opposite action: List the things for which you are grateful. Inhibit destroying what the other person has.

Emotion: Jealousy
Urge: Regain affection of a partner or friend
Function: To protect
Opposite action: Let go of controlling others' actions. Share. Stop spying or snooping.

Emotion: Love
Urge: Increase contact and physical proximity
Function: To keep attached, connected, and surviving
Opposite action: *Not justified:* Stay away from the person, animal, or thing. Avoid dwelling on the person, animal, or thing in your mind. Remind yourself of the reasons why love isn't justified.

CASE STUDY: David

David, a 32-year-old man, sought therapy after struggling with binge eating and compulsive sexual behavior. He had been battling anxiety and guilt for years, but his unhealthy coping mechanisms had become more frequent in recent months. David grew up in a household where emotions were rarely discussed. His parents often dismissed his feelings, telling him to "man up" whenever he expressed sadness or frustration. This left David feeling confused about his emotions and unsure of how to cope with them. He internalized the belief that emotions were a weakness and that expressing them would make him vulnerable or unworthy.

In his early adulthood, David's unresolved emotional issues began to manifest in unhealthy behaviors. He turned to food to numb overwhelming feelings of anxiety, guilt, and loneliness. Binge eating became his way to cope after particularly intense emotional moments, such as when he felt rejected by a partner or failed to meet his own high expectations at work. But afterward, he often experienced shame and disgust, which only intensified his emotional turmoil.

David also struggled with compulsive sexual behavior, using casual encounters to fill the emotional void left by his inability to express his emotions. These encounters provided temporary relief but left him feeling more disconnected and empty afterward. He couldn't help but criticize himself for "not being able to control himself" and for seeking validation from others in this way.

Therapy helped David recognize the patterns of emotional dysregulation that fueled his behaviors. He learned that his deep emotional sensitivity, combined with the lack of emotional validation he experienced as a child, made it difficult for him to manage his feelings in a healthy way. David realized that when he suppressed his emotions—especially feelings of sadness, frustration, or anger—they often erupted later in the form of binge eating or compulsive sex.

As he explored these behaviors in therapy, David was introduced to emotion regulation skills. He began to practice identifying his feelings early on, labeling emotions instead of ignoring them. He also worked on challenging mistaken beliefs he had about emotions—like the idea that expressing vulnerability was a weakness. With time, David learned to express his feelings in healthy ways, like talking openly with his partner or journaling when he felt overwhelmed.

David's journey wasn't easy, but with ongoing therapy, he was able to reduce the frequency of his binge eating and sexual behavior. By learning to better understand and regulate his emotions, David began to form healthier connections with others and himself. His newfound emotional awareness not only helped him cope with difficult feelings but also gave him the tools to make decisions that aligned more closely with his long-term goals.

CHAPTER 10

Getting Intimate
(without Undressing)

GOALS

▶ Learn the value of creating intimate relationships.
▶ Identify any personal social signaling deficits that are impacting interpersonal connections.
▶ Learn effective social signaling and communication skills.
▶ Learn how to improve existing relationships, create fulfilling new relationships, and recognize toxic or unhealthy relationships.

Overcontrolled focus: Interpersonal connectedness and radical openness

Undercontrolled focus: Interpersonal effectiveness and radical acceptance

VULNERABILITY. IS. NECESSARY. FOR. HEALTHY. RELATIONSHIPS

Healthy relationships require us to give up some control and allow ourselves to be vulnerable, which can feel scary—especially if being vulnerable brings back memories of past risk, discomfort, or hurt. It's understandable if feeling this way seems unbearable. But here's the truth: you deserve to experience loving and honest relationships.

A lot of my work involves helping clients recognize how harmful isolation can be and supporting them in taking steps to reconnect with others in healthy ways. Allowing relationships into your life and giving yourself permission to truly enjoy them can be a powerful part of full recovery.

This means being open to different types of relationships and exploring what kinds of connections feel right to you. Pay attention to how you feel in different social settings: which people make you feel comfortable? What activities do you love sharing with others? How much time do you actually want to spend with certain people? There's no one-size-fits-all model for friendships and relationships. As long as they're genuine and healthy, they can take many forms. This process might feel easy, or it could take some time. Be gentle with yourself as you navigate this. You're on your own path, and it's okay to take the time you need to figure things out.

On intimacy

Intimacy is about the ability and willingness to be close to someone else while also being open to their closeness in return. When we think of intimacy, we often link it to something sexual, but it's so much more than that. Intimacy can show up in many different ways in a relationship, from emotional to physical, to intellectual connection. Eating disorders can deeply affect all these forms of intimacy, not just the sexual kind.

TWELVE TYPES OF INTIMACY (CLINEBELL & CLINEBELL, 1970)

- *Sexual intimacy:* Sharing your fantasies, desires, and physical pleasure with each other.
- *Emotional intimacy:* Opening up and sharing your deepest feelings.
- *Intellectual intimacy:* Having the space to discuss even tough subjects without feeling ridiculed or dismissed.
- *Aesthetic intimacy:* Bonding over the beauty in life—whether it's art, music, nature, or theater.
- *Creative intimacy:* Planning and creating things together—such as making future plans, taking a course, or starting a project.
- *Recreational intimacy:* Sharing hobbies and activities you both enjoy, helping to keep your relationship fun. Finding ways to spend quality time together helps you stay connected beyond the routines of daily life.
- *Work intimacy:* Working together on shared responsibilities, like taking care of the household or supporting each other's goals.
- *Crisis intimacy:* Supporting each other through tough times,

---

deepening your connection. Facing challenges together can make you feel closer and build a stronger bond.

- *Conflict intimacy:* Resolving differences and disagreements in a healthy way that brings you closer rather than pulling you apart.
- *Commitment intimacy:* Working toward something meaningful together, whether it's starting a family, volunteering, buying a home, and so on.
- *Spiritual intimacy:* Sharing your thoughts and feelings about life's deeper meaning.
- *Communication intimacy:* Expressing your needs and expectations openly, and feeling heard, which fosters understanding and closeness without judgment.

While it's possible for partner(s) to be intimate in all 12 ways mentioned above, not everyone is or even wants to be. Relationships don't require us to fulfill every type of intimacy. Many of us meet some of our intimacy needs outside our sexual relationships. We all have interests and hobbies that aren't always shared with our partner, and connecting with others for those activities can lead to meaningful, long-term friendships—which is wonderful, as long as everyone is informed and on board. Partners can support each other in this, too.

You don't need to engage in all 12 types of intimacy, but understanding how they interconnect can help build a solid, healthy relationship. For example, sexual intimacy can be hard to achieve if there isn't a connection on other levels first. Emotional and sexual intimacy are important, but other forms of intimacy also play a big role in creating a strong bond. When you cultivate different types of intimacy, you open yourself to more respect, love, and understanding in your relationship.

EXERCISE: Reflection

- Are any of the 12 types of intimacy surprising to me?
- What are some examples of ways I've experienced each type of intimacy in my relationships?
- Which types of intimacy do I value most?
- Which types of intimacy do I value the least?

- Are there any types that I have not nurtured as much as I would like?
- How many different types of intimacy do I believe my partner(s) and I share?
- Which type of intimacy is causing me the biggest conflict right now?
- What about in the past?

Blocks to intimacy

- When you expect intimacy to "just happen."
- When you place blame on each other for failures or conflicts.
- When expectations and boundaries are not communicated.
- When no vulnerable thoughts and feelings are being shared, and communication is only superficial.
- When there are negative communication patterns (poor listening, ineffective conflict resolution or problem-solving strategies, criticism, and defensiveness).
- When a partner devotes the bulk of their efforts to things like work, family, household tasks, and other concerns, and they neglect the relationship.
- When your closeness suffocates one another.
- When a partner stops providing support, affirmation, and acts of kindness.
- When one partner does not treat the other with the same consideration that one would want to be shown to them.
- When a partner is too scared to be themselves around a certain person.
- When you are fearful of someone hurting you in any way.
- When one partner frequently invalidates another.
- When disagreements typically involve one partner making demands of the other and the other partner responding by pulling away.
- When trust is violated in any way.

EXERCISE: Reflection

- What are the common barriers to intimacy in my relationships?

Interpersonal effectiveness

Interpersonal effectiveness is all about how we connect and interact with others. It's the set of skills that helps us maintain relationships, ask for what we need, set boundaries, and foster deeper connections. Whether it's expressing our needs clearly, maintaining a relationship that matters to us, or sticking to our values, being effective in our interactions helps us achieve our goals while honoring ourselves and others.

Our communication skills play a big role in the quality of our relationships and our interactions. The way we communicate affects our well-being, self-esteem, and confidence. And just like any other skill, there's always room to grow—even the best communicators can get better.

Interpersonal connectedness

Humans are social by nature, and we all have an instinctive need to build meaningful connections with others. These connections—or interpersonal connectedness—give us a sense of belonging, purpose, and shared identity. It's about feeling emotionally close to others, and it's the opposite of feeling lonely.

What's interesting is that the feeling of being connected isn't just about how many people are in our social circle or how much support we get. It's about how connected we *feel*. You can feel lonely in a room full of people or feel deeply connected even when you're alone. Of course, having fewer friends or struggling with relationships can make it harder to feel connected, but it's really about whether our unique social needs are being met. Everyone's needs are different; some people are energized by lots of social interaction, while others, like introverts, might need less to feel fulfilled. Ultimately, it's about finding what works for you.

THE NEUROSCIENCE OF SAFETY AND CONNECTION

We evolved as social beings to feel protected and bonded to each other. Understanding how our nervous system works can help us make better choices during conflict and strengthen our relationships with those we care about. Our nervous system includes the central nervous system (the brain and spinal cord) and the peripheral nervous system. The peripheral system has two main parts: the somatic nervous system and the autonomic nervous system. The somatic nervous system is voluntary, controlling movements like muscle contractions. The autonomic nervous system, however, handles involuntary processes like heart rate and digestion. It has two branches—the sympathetic nervous system (SYNS) and the parasympathetic nervous system (PSNS).

The SYNS is all about action—it primes the body for physical activity like fighting or fleeing. This "fight or flight" response focuses our energy on survival by speeding up our heart rate and diverting resources away from things like digestion. On the other hand, the PSNS is about rest and relaxation—it takes over when we're at ease, like after a meal, reducing the heart rate and promoting recovery. Our autonomic nervous system is always at work, whether it's in a state of action or rest.

When we sense danger, our bodies prepare us to deal with it in some pretty recognizable ways:

- Our heart rate and breathing speed up to get more oxygen and blood to our muscles.
- Our muscles tense, ready for action.
- Non-essential functions like digestion and sexual functioning are temporarily paused.
- We sweat to help us stay cool.
- Adrenaline is released to boost our energy.
- Cortisol, the stress hormone, helps reduce pain but can also make it harder to think clearly.

Our two main survival mechanisms—the sympathetic nervous system (fight or flight) and the parasympathetic nervous system (freeze, flop, dissociate)—evolved to keep us alive in threatening situations. Here's a quick look at these automatic responses:

- *Fight:* This could be verbal (like saying "no") or physical (pushing or struggling).
- *Flight:* Running away, hiding, or backing off to put distance between you and the threat.
- *Freeze:* Staying still and silent. Many people freeze during traumatic events like sexual assault—it's an instinctive response, not a sign of consent. Animals often freeze to avoid being seen by predators.
- *Flop:* Similar to freezing, but instead of muscles tensing, the body goes limp. This response can minimize physical pain, and the mind may dissociate to help cope.
- *Fawn/Friend:* Appeasing a potential threat, negotiating, or calling for help. This instinctive response is about survival and does not imply consent.

All these responses are natural, automatic ways our bodies protect us from harm.

Many people are familiar with the concept of "fight or flight." So, it can feel confusing, frustrating, or even shameful if, in a moment of danger, you didn't fight back or immediately flee. But just like fight or flight, other responses to danger—freeze, flop, and fawn/friend—are instinctive, and we don't choose which one we experience. Understanding these responses can help make sense of your own feelings and reactions.

AUTHOR'S NOTE: ON SEXUAL ASSAULT

It's important to remember that many people who experience sexual assault or rape don't put up a fight. And there are many understandable reasons why you might not be able to physically or verbally resist. *None of these responses mean that you're at fault—and you never need to explain why you didn't fight back. Consent is never implied by not resisting, and you did what you needed to do to survive.*

Our "social brain"

Imagine trying to connect with the world around you while feeling constantly on edge. It wouldn't make for very successful friendships. People with a tendency for overcontrol often bring defensive behaviors into social interactions without even realizing it, which can further isolate them. When you're feeling uneasy and want to share a problem with your partner, your voice or facial expressions might tense up without you even realizing it. Your partner, in turn, picks up on your discomfort and might respond with defensiveness or anxiety. This is because our nervous system is always scanning for threats—even when there isn't an immediate danger. Historically, humans have needed to pick up safety cues from others before deciding if a new person was safe to approach. This need for social connection while staying safe led to the development of a third subsystem: our ventral vagal complex, often called our "social brain" (Porges, 2011).

This part of our nervous system helps us read and respond to social cues like a calm voice or a friendly smile. These "social safety cues" are essential for feeling secure and relaxed around others. When our social brain is in tune, we feel open, flexible, and ready to connect—we're in our friendly state, eager to explore and interact. It quiets our defensive instincts, making it impossible to feel both peaceful and threatened at the same time.

Social safety cues fall into five categories, and we are always in one emotional state or another (Lynch, 2018a):

- *Safety cues* make us feel secure, loved, and connected. Our body feels relaxed and calm.
- *Novel cues* are unexpected stimuli that prompt us to assess their importance. The body feels alert and focused.
- *Rewarding cues* bring positive or pleasurable emotions. The body feels energized and powerful.
- *Threatening cues* signal danger, making the body feel tense, agitated, and hot.
- *Overwhelming cues* activate our emergency shutdown system, leaving us feeling numb and detached.

When one emotional system is active, the others tend to be inhibited. Understanding how these cues impact us can help us navigate our emotional landscape more effectively.

The great news is that when we're feeling anxious or stressed, we can actually activate this part of our brain through simple actions. Instead of over-analyzing, we can take action to calm ourselves. We can take a few deep breaths, use mindfulness, or try repeating a calming affirmation to ourselves. Engaging in any self-soothing behavior can help activate our social safety cues.

By engaging our social safety system, we naturally calm our physiology and enhance our ability to connect with others. This system helps us communicate with warmth and friendliness—the muscles in our throat, ears, face, and even our diaphragm all play a role. When our social brain is active, our heart rate slows, and we breathe more deeply. We feel more comfortable initiating eye contact and physical touch, and we can be more genuine with our emotions. This isn't just useful for resolving conflicts; it helps us feel more connected. When we're calm and true to ourselves, we can open up, listen better, and form deeper bonds with others.

EXERCISE: Activate the social brain in minutes by releasing tension (Big 3 + 1) (Lynch, 2018b)

- Step 1: Take a deep breath.
- Step 2: Raise your eyebrows.
- Step 3: Engage a warm closed-mouth smile.
- (+1): Lean back in your chair (if you are sitting).

CUE EVALUATED AS				
Safe	**Novel**	**Rewarding**	**Threatening**	**Overwhelming**

	Safe	Novel	Rewarding	Threatening	Overwhelming
ANS system triggered	Social-safety system on	Social-safety system withdrawn	Social-safety system disengaged	Social-safety system disengaged	Social-safety system disengaged and withdrawal of SNS responses
Primary action urge	Urge to socialize	Urge to stand still	Urge to approach or pursue	Urge to flee or attack	Urge to give up
Autonomic responses	Body relaxed Breathing slow and deep Heart rate slow	Body freezes Breath held	Body animated Heart and breath rate faster	Body tense Breath fast and shallow Fast heart rate Sweating	Body immobile Heart rate drops Pain threshold increased
Emotion words	Approachable Relaxed Sociable Open	Attentive Focused Curious	Excited Elated Motivated Goal driven	Anxious Irritated Defensive	Numb Disinterested Detached Non-reactive
Action or expression	Effortless eye contact and facial expressions Listening to and touching others	"What is it?" Stopping Looking Listening	Expansive gestures Insensitivity to others' expressions and social cues	Constrained facial expressions Tight gestures Monotonic voice Averted gaze or stare Fight or flight response	Flat unexpressive face Monotonic and slow speech Dissociate Swoon Faint
Social impact	Social signaling enhanced	Social signaling capacities momentarily suspended	Empathic perception impaired Still expressive	Both empathy and pro-social signaling impaired	Withdrawn Social signaling irrelevant

Neuroception

EXERCISE: Labeling emotions worksheet (Lynch, 2018b)

Be on the lookout for experiences and events linked to changes in body sensations and mood states, and use the following skills to identify which of the five emotional response systems may have been involved. Check the relevant boxes or write your answers down in your notebook. The emphasis is on pinpointing the name of the emotion you may have been experiencing.

1. Think about the event that triggered your emotional response.

2. Tune in to your body to identify the emotional system that was triggered.
My body felt:

☐ relaxed and calm (social safety cue)
☐ alert and focused (novelty cue)
☐ energized and powerful (rewarding cue)
☐ tense, agitated, and hot (threatening cue)
☐ numb and detached from reality (overwhelming cue).

Describe any other body sensations.

3. Tune in to how you socially signaled:

☐ easily made eye contact (parasympathetic social safety system)
☐ easily expressed my emotions (parasympathetic social safety system)
☐ had an easygoing tone of voice (parasympathetic social safety system)
☐ touched or reached out to someone (parasympathetic social safety system)
☐ stood still and gazed intently (novelty-evaluative system)
☐ listened carefully (novelty-evaluative system)
☐ was expressive, talkative, or used expansive gestures (SNS excitatory arousal system)
☐ had to make an effort to listen to others (SNS excitatory arousal system)
☐ may have missed something important that another person said or did (SNS excitatory arousal system)
☐ found it difficult to smile without feeling fake (SNS defensive arousal system)
☐ had a flat facial expression (SNS defensive arousal system)
☐ averted my eyes, or stared intensely (SNS defensive arousal system)
☐ had a flat tone of voice (SNS defensive arousal system)

- [ ] used constrained hand gestures (SNS defensive arousal system)
- [ ] had constrained, emotionless body language (parasympathetic shutdown system)
- [ ] had slow body movements (parasympathetic shutdown system)
- [ ] had a low rate of speech and flat tone of voice (parasympathetic shutdown system)
- [ ] stared vacantly (parasympathetic shutdown system).

Note any other social signals.

4. Observe your action urges and desires in order to label your possible emotions.

I wanted/desired to:

- [ ] run away/flee (fear)
- [ ] hide my face or disappear (shame)
- [ ] repair or make amends (guilt)
- [ ] isolate and deactivate (sadness)
- [ ] push away or expel (disgust)
- [ ] exert my superiority (dominance)
- [ ] harshly gossip about someone (unhelpful envy)
- [ ] reject help from another (bitterness)
- [ ] pursue (pleasurable dominance)
- [ ] give up but blame it on others (bitterness)
- [ ] revenge (envy)
- [ ] block a person from getting to know someone I feel very close to (jealousy)
- [ ] stand still or freeze (novelty)
- [ ] socialize (contented love)
- [ ] explore (curiosity)
- [ ] attack (anger).

Record other emotional response tendencies or reactions.

5. Identify the function of the emotion, remembering that it may have more than one.

My emotion:

☐ helped me make a decision
☐ motivated my actions
☐ communicated my inner experience and signaled my intention
☐ helped me get closer to someone and/or experience empathy with someone.

Record any other functions of the emotion.

Getting "stuck"

So, even when we know logically that we're safe, our nervous systems might disagree—especially if we have a history of trauma that makes us wary of close relationships. You might have found a wonderful new partner and feel excited about the possibility of intimacy. But at the same time, alarm bells may be ringing in your brain. Even if you really want closeness, these alarms can lead you to pull away, need lots of personal space, or feel restricted sexually. Sadly, when we withdraw like this, it often causes others to pull away from us too.

For someone with a well-regulated nervous system, feeling threatened means seeking social support. If a child's nervous system develops normally, they learn to turn to safe, secure people when they feel unsafe—whether that's being held, talking it out, or getting help to calm down. But what if those safe people weren't there? What if your parents or caregivers were absent, intoxicated, overwhelmed, or traumatized themselves? In those situations, we might develop a nervous system that stays activated for far too long, even without real danger, leading to attachment wounds, intimacy avoidance, and a variety of mental and physical health issues. To manage our anxious systems, we might learn to isolate ourselves instead of seeking comfort from others, because people start to feel frightened. When a loved one is upset or we feel uncomfortable, intimacy can feel like a threat—something to avoid. It can be incredibly hard to reach out for help in moments like these, which is why many of us isolate instead. Without a healthy nervous system that knows how to reach out for connection during moments of threat, intimacy becomes something we fear, even though we crave it. People stuck in this state are less likely to reconnect and repair relationship rifts compared to those with secure attachments. This might look like someone needing days or even weeks of isolation after feeling triggered before they're ready to engage again. Unfortunately, for those who need more immediate repair, this delay can lead them to give up on the relationship altogether.

AUTHOR'S NOTE: ON TRIGGERS AND MEMORIES

After a traumatic experience, our minds often hold on to the details in terms of how we felt and what we sensed at the time. So, even if we're completely safe in the moment, our brain might still kick into "fight, flight, freeze, flop, or fawn" mode if something in our environment reminds us of that original traumatic event. It could be a certain color, a familiar smell, or even a particular sound that sets things off.

This is what people mean when they say they feel "triggered." It's actually quite common for survivors of sexual violence. When this happens, the anxiety, panic attacks, nightmares, and flashbacks are all very real—and they can be overwhelming. One thing that can help during these moments is to remind yourself that the danger has passed, and at this moment, you are safe. Your mind is just making a connection between something now and something from the past, and your body is reacting. Grounding and mindfulness can help you stay present and remind your brain that you are safe here and now. See Chapter 8 to review grounding exercises and Chapter 6 for mindfulness techniques.

UNDERSTANDING BOUNDARIES

Boundaries define who we are and shape our interactions with others. They help us understand what we feel, what we own, and what we're responsible for, while also clarifying what we expect from others. Clear boundaries communicate how we want to be treated, what we will and won't tolerate, and how close we're willing to let others get—both physically and emotionally. They exist to protect us from harm and prevent others from taking advantage.

Rigid boundaries: "I will never tolerate any form of criticism, even constructive."

Flexible boundaries: "I may sometimes be open to feedback but will voice when I feel uncomfortable."

Without boundaries, we can lose touch with our sense of self, our needs, values, and priorities. When there's nothing to separate us from another person, our sense of identity fades. What we think, feel, and believe, as well as our goals and passions, are uniquely our own. But sometimes others find our uniqueness threatening or confusing, and they may pressure us to conform. When we let others define us, we lose our authenticity. In emotionally entangled relationships, we often make choices based on what our partner wants or what others think is right, rather than deciding for ourselves. Boundaries help us avoid this by defining who we are and allowing us to live authentically. They protect our well-being and prevent us from overworking, overcommitting, overgiving, or being taken advantage of—all behaviors that conflict with our values and priorities.

Healthy boundaries also have a direct impact on how we feel emotionally. Setting and sticking to them can be challenging, especially if you grew up in a chaotic or dysfunctional household where boundaries were unclear. Secure boundaries feel safe and comforting. They allow us to choose what to let in and what to keep out—keeping out negativity and hostility while opening ourselves up to love, acceptance, and intimacy.

If you were raised with clear boundaries, you likely learned how important they are and how to set them. But if boundaries were never modeled for you as a child, learning to establish and communicate them as an adult can be more challenging. Remember, it's never too late to start setting boundaries that protect your well-being and honor your authentic self. This process may feel uncomfortable and unfamiliar at first, but with time and effort, you can develop a strong sense of individual identity.

Remember boundaries are *not:*

- demands
- ultimatums
- mean
- selfish
- fixed.

EXERCISE: Reflection

- Who modeled unhealthy boundaries for me?
- Who modeled healthy boundaries for me?
- What were these boundaries like?
- How have the boundary problems in my childhood family made it difficult for me to set boundaries now?
- Did they impact my communication style, self-esteem, sense of safety, or ability to trust? How?

Identifying your boundaries

The first step to setting healthy boundaries is knowing what matters to you—what you value, and what you're comfortable accepting or rejecting in any situation. Boundaries can be easier to navigate when broken down into these seven categories (Harper, 2019a):

Physical boundaries: These relate to your preferences for physical contact—who, when, where, and how. Physical boundaries cover things like your personal space, bodily autonomy, and privacy. They're communicated through your actions: what you wear, how you move, and what physical contact feels okay to you.

Sexual boundaries: These boundaries are about both the physical and emotional aspects of sex, including your likes, dislikes, and what feels safe and comfortable for you. They also cover your preferences for the language around sex, including humor or specific terms. Sexual boundaries extend beyond physical acts and shape how you express your sexuality overall.

Emotional-relational boundaries: These involve not only protecting your own feelings but also respecting others' emotions. Emotional boundaries help define your sense of self. When someone is judgmental, abusive, or dismissive of your emotions, they're violating your emotional boundaries.

Intellectual boundaries: These boundaries are about respecting each other's thoughts, ideas, and beliefs. They also include the freedom to explore knowledge and learn. A healthy intellectual boundary involves respecting different perspectives, even if they aren't your own. Dismissal or invalidation of your ideas by others is a breach of this boundary.

Spiritual boundaries: These relate to your beliefs, whether religious or otherwise, and how you choose to express them. Spiritual boundaries protect your right to practice your faith (or not) in your own way. If someone coerces you into or prevents you from spiritual practices, they're crossing your spiritual boundaries.

Property boundaries: These are about what belongs to you, both physically and materially. If you feel pressured to lend, give away, or spend money in ways that don't feel right to you, it's likely a property boundary is being crossed.

Time boundaries: Your time is precious. Time boundaries help you decide how you want to spend it and protect your right to say no when demands are unreasonable. Violations happen when you take on too many commitments or others place unfair demands on your time.

Boundary violations

Boundaries can be tricky, and the lines between different kinds of boundary violations aren't always clear. Sometimes, it's pretty straightforward—like when someone takes your pen without asking, which is just a property boundary violation. But other times, multiple boundaries get crossed all at once. For instance, if someone asks for your help organizing a surprise party, they might be pushing your intellectual and time boundaries, and maybe even a few emotional ones too.

Cheating in a monogamous relationship can involve multiple types of boundary violations, depending on the nature of the infidelity. These violations may be explicit (clearly breaking an agreed-on rule) or implicit (crossing an unspoken but understood boundary). Here are just some key types of boundary violations that can occur:

- Forming an intimate emotional connection with someone outside the relationship in a way that replaces or compromises the primary partnership (emotional-relational boundary violation).
- Crossing a line in physical closeness that violates the expectations of monogamy, even if no sexual intercourse occurs (physical boundary violation).
- Sharing deep personal thoughts, fears, or vulnerabilities with someone else that were previously reserved for the committed partner (emotional-relational boundary violation).
- Engaging in sexual acts with someone else without the knowledge or consent of the monogamous partner (sexual boundary violation).
- Having unprotected sex outside the relationship, potentially exposing the partner to sexually transmitted infections (sexual boundary violation).
- Lying about where one's time is spent or prioritizing the affair over quality time with the monogamous partner (time boundary violation).

Think of boundaries as what defines where *you* end and others begin. When that space isn't mindfully respected, even with the best intentions, boundary violations can occur, causing harm. A big part of this comes down to consent. Consent means having a shared understanding or agreement, where everyone involved knows what they're agreeing to and the possible outcomes.

Expressing our boundaries often means using different forms of consent. If your partner asks, "Hey, can we use your vibrator on you during sex tonight?", they're recognizing that the vibrator is yours (property boundary) and seeking your permission to use it on your body (physical and sexual boundary) for a length of your time together (time boundary). You then get to decide: yes, no, or maybe with some conditions.

Without consent, boundary violations happen. Of course, sometimes people unintentionally step over our boundaries. If you haven't made a boundary clear, it's hard for others to know it's even there. This is such an important thing to remember—whether you're at home, with friends, or at work. There's also a common tendency called the fundamental attribution error, which makes boundary conversations harder. It's that bias where, when we mess up, we tend to blame the circumstances. But when someone else messes up, we often assume it's because of who they are as a person. It's human nature, and it can make us quick to judge others. But if we can be more mindful of this, we can start to approach each situation with a bit more understanding. We can ask ourselves: is this person a genuine threat to me, or are they just someone who made a mistake and can learn from it?

EXERCISE: Reflection

- What are some of the boundaries that I have for each of these categories?
- What boundary categories have the most violations (e.g., sexual, communication)?
- Which kinds of boundaries do I have the most difficulty respecting for others? Which categories do those violations belong to?
- How have these boundary issues impacted me negatively?
- What are the main reasons why I want to have stronger (or more flexible) boundaries now?

Set and maintain healthy boundaries by talking about them

Now that you're becoming more aware of your boundaries, you're ready to start expressing them. The key is to stay mindful and be deliberate in how you communicate. This can be easier said than done in some situations, while in others, you might be pleasantly surprised at how naturally it comes. Many of us aren't used to speaking up for ourselves or letting others know what we need. We often hesitate to say "no" because we're afraid of upsetting or disappointing others. And when we put everyone else's needs ahead of our own, we lose touch with what we want and what really matters to us. This often leaves us feeling resentful, exhausted, unappreciated, and even mistreated.

EXERCISE: Boundary assessment

Use this checklist to identify how much your life is negatively affected by a lack of consistent boundaries.

- ☐ I'm afraid to say no and don't want to disappoint people.
- ☐ I don't speak up when I want something or when I am being mistreated.
- ☐ I frequently feel angry, resentful, or overwhelmed.
- ☐ I don't communicate my expectations to others.
- ☐ I feel physically or emotionally unsafe.
- ☐ I don't make time for self-care.
- ☐ I feel guilty when I set limits or do things for myself.
- ☐ I make commitments that I later regret.
- ☐ I'm frequently overscheduled, rushed, or tired.
- ☐ I do things out of obligation rather than because I want to.
- ☐ I don't spend enough quality time with people I care about.
- ☐ I don't have a strong sense of who I am and my values, interests, and goals.
- ☐ I'm tuned in to how other people feel, but don't always know how I feel.
- ☐ I accept blame for things I didn't do or couldn't control.
- ☐ I enable others to be irresponsible by doing things for them that they can do for themselves.
- ☐ I feel obligated to answer personal questions.
- ☐ I loan money or possessions to people who don't return them.
- ☐ People take advantage of me.
- ☐ My children don't respect limits and walk all over me.
- ☐ My children act entitled or spoiled.
- ☐ I feel burnt out at work.
- ☐ I spend a lot of time, energy, or money trying to fix or solve other people's problems.
- ☐ I act passive-aggressively instead of directly expressing my feelings and needs.
- ☐ I think I don't matter or aren't as important as others.
- ☐ I overshare personal information or get close to people before trust is established.
- ☐ I blame others for things I am responsible for.
- ☐ I harm others by not respecting their privacy, possessions, feelings, or bodies.

☐ I struggle with self-discipline (managing my money, time, eating, social media use, etc.).

EXERCISE: Reflection

- Have I ever thought that I don't have the right to set boundaries? That I don't deserve to be treated with respect? Or that I'm not worth the effort? If so, where do these beliefs come from?
- In what other ways has not having boundaries negatively affected me?
- How will boundaries improve my life? (Give some specific examples.)
- How will boundaries improve my relationships with others?
- How will boundaries improve my emotional and physical health?
- How will boundaries improve my sexual health?
- How will boundaries improve my self-esteem or relationship with myself?
- What has held me back from setting boundaries in the past?

AUTHOR'S NOTE: ON RIGID BOUNDARIES

To truly feel safe and secure, some boundaries need to be firm, and that's okay. These boundaries are usually about necessities, not just preferences. Take the rule of not attacking someone without reason— it's a basic principle that applies to everyone. But most boundaries aren't that universal. What feels strict to me might not even be a concern for someone else. For example, a neurotypical person might not need as much alone time as someone who is neurodiverse. And certain sexual positions might never feel comfortable for someone who has experienced trauma. We all have unique experiences, and those experiences shape our unique needs. That's just part of being human. And let's not forget, our boundaries also change over time depending on our relationships, the environment we're in, and where we are in our life journey.

EXERCISE: Reflection

- Did my childhood family have rigid or weak boundaries, or a mix of both?
- Were boundaries and rules consistent or inconsistent, flexible or inflexible, clear or confusing? What was that like for me as a child?
- What messages have I internalized about my right to healthy boundaries and the ownership of my individual needs?
- Generally speaking, are the majority of my boundaries rigid, flexible, or porous?
- Which of my boundaries are rigid right now? Are there any that need to be challenged in that regard? Are there any that need to be more rigid?
- Which of my boundaries are porous right now? Are there any that need to be challenged and strengthened into being flexible or even rigid?
- Do I have any boundaries that should remain porous? If so, how does that support, sustain, or serve me at this point in my life?
- What would my ideal boundary balance look like?
- How close to this ideal am I right now?
- What is something that is actively in my control that I can work on to move in the direction of my ideal?

INTIMATE RELATIONSHIPS SPECTRUM

Relationships exist on a spectrum, from healthy to unhealthy, with abuse at the far end. Relationship behaviors can generally be categorized as healthy, struggling, unhealthy, or abusive (Canadian Forces Morale & Welfare Services, n.d.). While a mix of behaviors is common, relationships should primarily lean toward the healthy side. Human connections are dynamic; they change and evolve as circumstances and stress levels shift. This means that couples often move back and forth between the "healthy" and "struggling" zones. Viewing relationships as a spectrum helps us understand both our own and our partners' behaviors more objectively. In a healthy relationship, both partners share in decision-making, while in an unhealthy one, one partner may try to exert power and control—sometimes subtly, sometimes overtly. In abusive relationships, this power dynamic becomes the primary characteristic. Even healthy relationships have their flaws, but what makes them work is the ability to openly discuss issues and work toward positive change.

For instance, when someone feels out of control, they might resort to unhealthy attempts at regaining power. While this doesn't excuse the behavior, recognizing that healthy and unhealthy reactions can coexist might make us more willing to address the issues rather than focus on blame. When relationship struggles start to veer into "unhealthy" territory, it often requires outside support, like therapy, to get back on track. And if abuse is present, the priority is always physical safety—seeking outside support is crucial. Relationships are fluid, and understanding where yours falls on the spectrum can help you take meaningful steps toward a healthier connection.

INTIMATE RELATIONSHIP SPECTRUM
HEALTHY
Relationship characteristics:

- Safe
- Trusting
- Secure
- Equality
- Respect
- Direct communication

STRUGGLING
Relationship characteristics:

- Uncertain
- Pressure
- Dishonesty
- Lack of communication
- Cold or distant

UNHEALTHY
Relationship characteristics:

- Insecure
- Hypervigilant
- Manipulation
- Isolation
- Indirect violence (breaking things, slamming doors)

ABUSIVE
Relationship characteristics:

- Unsafe
- Fearful
- Controlling
- Direct violence (physical, sexual)
- Belittling
- Name-calling

Unhealthy or abusive behaviors often involve power and control dynamics, though these dynamics aren't always easy to spot. One partner's actions might seem like a moment of rudeness at first, but if those actions consistently make the other partner feel bad about themselves, it could be a sign of a deeper problem. Over time, these behaviors can confirm the harmful belief that one person is "not enough" on their own and should submit to someone else.

Unhealthy behaviors can become abusive when they form a pattern. Even if it seems like just one incident, it's important to pay attention—these patterns often reveal a more systemic problem. The cycle of abuse is one way to understand how conflicts can escalate: things may calm down after a promise to change, only to escalate again later. This cycle can make it difficult to break free, but recognizing it is the first step to change.

No one deserves to be in an abusive or toxic relationship. There's no guaranteed way to know if a new romantic or platonic partner will end up being abusive or unhealthy, and even if there was, nothing would ever justify their abusive behavior. If someone ends up hurting you, it's not your fault—whether you missed the warning signs or chose to stay.

While it's helpful to be aware of red flags, like a history of abuse, threats, or physical force, it's often more empowering to focus on the positive qualities you want in a partner. Instead of always being on the lookout for what's wrong, think about the kind of love and connection you truly deserve. In an unhealthy relationship, there are only two paths—working on it to make it better or walking away. If you're unsure about your relationship, reaching out to friends, family, or a counselor can be a supportive way to get perspective and help. You deserve to feel safe, respected, and valued.

KINDNESS, EFFECTIVENESS, AND CONNECTEDNESS SKILLS

Positive relationship formation and maintenance are central tenets of Dialectical Behavior Therapy's interpersonal effectiveness skills. People who have consistently positive relationships in their lives tend to have these skills already ingrained. These abilities are useful for everyone, but they can be life-changing for people who have experienced trauma or who have attachment issues.

EXERCISE: Distorted beliefs about interpersonal relationships (Lynch, 2018b)

Check the boxes next to each myth that you believe is true or somewhat true.

- ☐ People are always secretly gossiping.
- ☐ There is a right and wrong way to interact with others.
- ☐ Feeling detached and alone is normal.
- ☐ Compliments are used to manipulate others.
- ☐ Being correct is more important than being liked.
- ☐ If I don't do it myself, it won't get done or be done properly.
- ☐ People can't be trusted.
- ☐ No one is capable of understanding me.
- ☐ Revealing my true feelings will lead to others using them against me.
- ☐ Relationships aren't meant to be fun.
- ☐ If I show vulnerability, others will take advantage of me.
- ☐ Love is fake, and romance is for fools.
- ☐ People are nice only when they want something.
- ☐ I am not like others.
- ☐ Keeping experiences to myself will improve relationships.
- ☐ In the long run, people will always let you down.
- ☐ Talking about inner feelings is a waste of time.
- ☐ Asking for help is a sign of weakness.
- ☐ No one can truly understand another person.
- ☐ I must sacrifice time and energy because others are incompetent.
- ☐ There is a right and a wrong way to interact with others.
- ☐ Giving someone an inch means they'll take a mile.
- ☐ Holding a grudge is necessary because people can't be trusted.
- ☐ Dependence is a sign of weakness.

☐ I should always smile, even when I'm miserable.
☐ It's best to walk away from conflict.
☐ People only care about themselves.

INTERPERSONAL EFFECTIVENESS SKILLS
Social safety

EXERCISES: Activating social safety (Lynch, 2018b)
Use the Big 3 + 1:

- Step 1: Take a deep breath.
- Step 2: Raise your eyebrows.
- Step 3: Engage a warm closed-mouth smile.
- (+ 1): Lean back in your chair (if you are sitting).

Open your body language:

- Instead of keeping your arms and hands close to your body, make broad, expansive gestures.
- Let your body relax and open up, signaling comfort and safety.

Move your facial muscles:

- When stressed, your facial muscles tend to tense up, making it harder to express yourself. To activate a sense of safety, consciously relax and move your facial muscles.
- Practice in front of a mirror, stretching and contracting different facial muscles. Make exaggerated expressions to train your brain to signal safety.
- Try raising and lowering your eyebrows, squinting, puckering your lips, stretching your mouth, and widening your eyes.
- Close your eyes tightly, tense your facial muscles, and relax them once you feel the peak of tension. Focus on identifying each muscle group in your face while doing this. Practice frequently throughout the day.

Breath:

- Slow and deepen your breath consciously, especially focusing on extended, slow exhalations.
- Inhale gently, and as you breathe out, aim to exhale for a longer duration than usual.
- Breathe into your belly rather than your chest.

Progressive muscle relaxation:

- Progressively tense and relax large muscle groups starting from your feet, then your legs, torso, arms, and neck, finally moving up to your face.
- Notice the release of tension after holding each muscle group tight for a few seconds.

Use touch:

- Touch soft objects such as pillows, stuffed animals, or pets to help calm your nervous system.
- Gently massage your face, neck, and scalp.
- Wrap yourself in blankets or towels to create a soothing "swaddling" effect.
- Experiment with placing a heavy object like a sandbag over your head and legs to observe how it feels.
- Cross your arms over your chest and give yourself a tight hug, rocking back and forth gently.
- Try rubbing your stomach in a clockwise motion.
- Place a hot water bottle (wrapped in a towel) over your stomach and lie down on the floor with cushions under your knees to feel its calming effects.
- Take a hot bath or use jets in a hot tub to massage your back and neck.
- Have a friend or partner massage your neck or feet, or give you a tight, comforting hug.

Chewing and eating food:

- Chewing helps activate the muscles associated with feelings of trust and safety. While anxiety may make it difficult to eat, chewing sends calming signals to your brain.

- Include foods that help you feel relaxed in your diet. Keep snacks, sugar-free gum, or protein bars handy to chew throughout the day.
- Chewing can act as a physical release for stress, so focus on moving your face and chewing when you feel tense.

Use hearing:

- When you're feeling stressed, listen to calming music or recordings of human voices, such as soothing podcasts or audiobooks.
- Avoid music that might make you feel anxious or agitated, and opt for sounds that help you feel at ease.

Use vision:

- Viewing images associated with warmth, comfort, or peace can help activate your social safety system. These might include photos of loved ones, pets, or places that bring you joy.
- When feeling anxious, look at these comforting images, take a few deep breaths, and observe the calming effect they have on your body and mind.

Establish new relationships or increasing intimacy in existing ones

The degree of intimacy in our relationships is directly correlated with our level of self-disclosure. We share our most vulnerable, deepest emotions and experiences in close relationships while we reveal less about ourselves in casual, surface-level relationships. To get to know new people and strengthen existing relationships, we can use the Match + 1 Intimacy Rating Scale. The concept of "Match + 1" refers to a straightforward rule: in order to form a close bond with another person, we must first reveal something about ourselves.

INTIMACY RATING SCALE (LYNCH, 2018B)

To develop more intimacy with another person, + 1 level. To reduce intimacy, if you feel insecure/unsafe, – 1 level. Re-evaluate regularly.

Level 1-2

- Talking about mundane, unemotional things like the weather, your commute, or how your food tastes.
- Expressing non-emotional opinions and comments about non-personal things such as restaurants, the color of clothing.

For example, "I love the veggie bowl at Moe's!"

Level 2-3

- Commenting on topics like politics, parenting, or philosophy *that don't involve emotion* and are based on personal values or goals.
- Making observations on topics that are considered acceptable by society, such as the environment, wildlife, entertainment, health, and social preferences.

For example, "I'm going to start volunteering at the library."

Level 5-6

- Expressing your innermost thoughts and opinions regarding your personal experiences.
- Revealing any potentially offensive judgments, preferences, or opinions.

For example, "I hate it when people don't use their turn signal!"

Level 7-8

- Discussing your relationship with another while expressing personal views and sentiments.
- Disclosing deeply personal information, such as the specifics of an unhappy marriage, and making judgments about it.
- Showing openness of expression, unrestrained laughter, or more direct eye contact.

For example, "I really enjoy spending time with you."

Level 9

- Expressing feelings of love or affection and a desire for greater intimacy.
- Telling tales of humiliating or embarrassing past behavior that would cause harm if it became public knowledge.
- Being open to disclosing your deepest insecurities and areas of weakness.

For example, "I want to see you more often."

Level 10

- Expressing a deep sense of love and caring.
- Discussing desire for a long-term relationship.
- Showing your true, underlying, and possibly previously unspoken vulnerabilities.
- Having a readiness to make significant personal sacrifices for the sake of the relationship.

For example, "I can't imagine my life without you."

EXERCISE: Match + 1 (Lynch, 2018b)

- Start by saying something friendly to the other person, like "Hi, how are you?"
- Then share a personal detail about your day, week, or life with the other person. For instance, you might say, "I just tried the new frappuccino at the coffee shop. It was so good!"
- Be mindful as you take in the other person's response.
- If you want to get to know someone better, you should disclose as much about yourself as the other person does (Match), and then reveal even more (Match + 1).
- Don't stop sharing personal information because of the other person's lack of immediate interest. Keep in mind that it takes time to get to know someone, and that the more you share, the more likely the other person is to share back.

- Match + 1 requires you to share something personal about yourself, not to pry into another person's life by asking them in-depth questions (though that is fine, too).

CASE STUDY: Maya

Maya, a 42-year-old woman, had always struggled to form deep connections due to past unhealthy relationships and a recent breakup. Seeking therapy, she hoped to overcome her emotional isolation and build more meaningful bonds. Her therapist emphasized the importance of vulnerability in relationships. Maya realized that her fear of vulnerability had caused her to push people away whenever a relationship began to feel too close. Through therapy, Maya learned to recognize her social signaling deficits—the unspoken cues that hindered deeper connection—and began practicing active listening, eye contact, and open body language. She also used the Match + 1 Intimacy Rating Scale, which encouraged her to gradually share more personal information and gauge the intimacy level of her relationships.

One day, Maya applied the Match + 1 exercise with a colleague, sharing a personal work challenge. The colleague responded with similar vulnerability, which helped Maya feel more comfortable and safe in expressing herself. As Maya became more comfortable with vulnerability and communication in her non sexual relationships, these skills naturally extended to her sexual relationships. She was able to openly discuss desires, boundaries, and emotional needs with her partners, which enhanced trust and created a deeper sexual connection. She learned to embrace vulnerability and communicate her needs effectively, leading to healthier, more fulfilling connections.

Reclaim It

Reclaim It

— CHAPTER 11 —

Let's Talk about Sex

GOALS

Learn about consent and sexual boundaries.

▶ Identify your sexual boundaries.
▶ Learn how to communicate with your partner(s) about sexual topics.

Overcontrolled focus: Check for rigid rules, social signaling, and bodily tension during conversations

Undercontrolled focus: Check for emotion-based reasoning or emotion-based reactions during conversations

SEX AND GENDER ROLES

Sex is often seen as a tricky and taboo subject. This makes it hard for many people to discuss openly. Many of us feel hesitant to talk about it for a variety of reasons. For example, women might internalize messages that tell them they should be submissive and avoid being sexually assertive or enjoying sex. On the other hand, men might feel pressure to always desire sex, initiate intimacy, and present themselves as confident and dominant. These expectations are rooted in outdated, unhealthy cultural norms about gender roles that simply don't reflect the complexity of real human experiences.

In traditional (heteronormative) narratives, it's often seen as the man's "responsibility" to make the first move, while the woman is expected to be coy or hesitant, only to eventually give in. These stereotypes paint an unrealistic and limiting picture of what sexual and emotional relationships should look like. In reality, people of all genders can initiate and actively participate in sex, and all of us, regardless of our gender, are capable of showing self-control and respecting boundaries.

These narratives are built on the idea of a sexual double standard—men are praised for enjoying sex, while women are shamed for the same behavior. But really, everyone deserves to experience pleasure without judgment. Whether we choose to have sex or not, it's a personal choice, and no one should feel ashamed or pressured about their sexuality. No matter your gender or sexual orientation, you have the right to engage in consensual sex with whomever you like and whenever it feels right for you.

SEXUAL COMMUNICATION

Sex involves more than just the physical; it's also about varying degrees of emotional connection. Communication is the key to creating that connection. Of course, talking about sex isn't always easy. We can feel vulnerable—maybe we're unsure of what to say, nervous about how we look, or hesitant to share our fantasies. But when we communicate openly and honestly, we set the stage for a more fulfilling experience. Better communication leads to better intimacy, better connection, and ultimately, better sex.

The importance of communication in bed

Expressing your needs isn't selfish—it's essential. When you communicate openly, you help ensure that everyone feels safe, understood, and satisfied. Sharing what you like (or don't like) during sex can make the experience better for both of you. Don't pretend to enjoy something just to make someone else happy—instead, describe what you want, and work together to make it happen. Advocate for your own pleasure, and remember that it's okay to ask for what feels good. If someone makes you feel bad for expressing your desires or doesn't respect your boundaries, that's a red flag. You deserve a partner who values your comfort and your pleasure, and it's perfectly okay to walk away from situations that make you feel disrespected.

Talking about sex can be intimidating, and many of us carry a lot of baggage that makes it feel awkward. Often, we don't disclose our fantasies right away, and that's understandable. But the longer we hold back, the harder it becomes to bring them up later. Open communication can make fantasies feel less daunting and more approachable—which means they're more likely to become a reality. The same goes for your partner: when they feel comfortable enough to share, you might discover you have more in common than you realized. And even if their desires are different, that's okay—together, you can find ways to make everyone happy.

Vulnerability is key to self-discovery, and being open about your desires helps bring them to life. If you're curious about trying something new, talking about it can help you understand what exactly draws you to it. And when you understand your desires, they become more real and authentic, giving you the freedom to act on them if you choose.

The benefits of communicating about sex go beyond the bedroom. Being able to talk openly with your partner fosters trust and strengthens the overall relationship. Sexual communication isn't just a one-time thing—it's an ongoing conversation that starts before, continues during, and goes on after the act itself.

Communicating about sex helps you to:

- express desire
- explore your fantasies
- learn about your partner's fantasies
- find common ground between your fantasies
- discover more about yourself
- make sex safer
- improve your overall communication and relationship
- lead to better, more fulfilling sex—and maybe even more of it!

EXERCISE: Reflection

- Do I feel comfortable talking about sex within my relationship(s)?
- Do I feel comfortable asking for what I want and need sexually?
- Did I have many/a few/no sexual partners before my current relationship(s)?
- Have I had any relationships that included satisfying sex?
- What made them satisfying?
- Have I had any relationships in which I was dissatisfied?
- What made them unsatisfactory?

Why is communication so hard?
Biological factors

Talking about sex can feel incredibly challenging, and part of that has to do with biology. For example, sexual attraction often comes out through non-verbal cues like blushing or getting an erection—things we can't always control but that speak volumes. Plus, alcohol or other substances can make it even tougher to communicate clearly. And let's face it, sometimes it's just easier to show intimacy through physical contact rather than putting those feelings into words.

Sociocultural factors

Our society and culture play a huge role in how we talk about sex. Media and sexually explicit content often shape our expectations, making it difficult to have open, realistic conversations. Gender and upbringing also influence how comfortable we feel expressing ourselves. On top of that, porn often gives a distorted picture of what sex is like (automatic with little conversation), which complicates how we think about our own experiences.

Most of us never received proper sex education, so we often lack even the most basic knowledge about our bodies and sexuality. Add to that the fact that talking about sex is often seen as taboo, and it's no wonder we struggle. We're conditioned to believe that we should just naturally "get" sex without much effort, and that makes it harder to admit when we need help or want something different. Cultural, religious, family, and peer influences also shape how we think about and discuss sexuality.

Psychological factors

There are also psychological barriers that make communication about sex difficult. Intense emotions can easily overwhelm our ability to express ourselves. Issues around power and control can turn discussions about sex into arguments about much bigger dynamics in the relationship. Gender norms, self-esteem, and personal insecurities all add layers of complexity.

Talking about our sexual needs and desires can be nerve-wracking because we open ourselves up to being judged or even rejected. And let's be real, sharing a fantasy or preference only to be met with disinterest can feel like a major blow. Sometimes we hold back because we don't want to hurt our partner's feelings, and other times it's our own anxieties around sex that get in the way. Remember, communication isn't only about what you say; it's equally about listening. Active listening creates a sense of mutual respect and understanding in sexual relationships. Now that we understand the importance of open communication, let's explore how assertiveness can help you express your desires confidently.

THE ROLE OF ASSERTIVENESS

Communication isn't just about what we say—it's also about how the other person hears it. For someone with an eating disorder, what they hear can sometimes be quite different from what was intended. For example, a well-meaning comment like, "You look so healthy!" might be meant as a compliment, but someone with an eating disorder might interpret it as "You're gaining weight." Their preconceived ideas about themselves can heavily influence how they perceive others' words.

Effective communication is essential, especially when it comes to boundaries and expressing emotions. Developing these skills is an important part of recovery for those with eating disorders. Many people with eating disorders struggle with asking for emotional support—sometimes their eating disorder becomes a way of expressing unmet needs or deeply repressed emotions, like anger, loneliness, or fear. It might also reflect a desire for more care, attention, or autonomy in their relationships.

That's why learning assertiveness is so crucial to the healing process. Being assertive means being able to express your thoughts and feelings in a way that is honest and clear, while still being considerate of others. It's about sharing your needs and letting others know how their actions affect you. Assertiveness is a skill that can be learned and practiced—and it's one that helps teach the people around you how to meet your emotional needs. Remember, others can't read your mind, so it's important to communicate directly and clearly. Finding the right balance between being assertive and not coming across as overly aggressive or passive can be challenging, but it's key to building healthier relationships. Let's dive deeper into different communication styles to explore how we can get there.

FOUR STYLES OF COMMUNICATION
Passive
Goals:

- Avoid conflict
- Please others
- Let others take control

Actions:

- Keep quiet; put myself down
- Apologize for self-expression
- Hide my disagreement
- Inconvenience myself

Looks:

- Making myself small

- Looking down
- Hunched over
- Avoiding eye contact
- Speaking softly

Emotions:

- Fear of rejection
- Helplessness and low self-esteem
- Frustration
- Resentment toward others who "use me"

Beliefs:

- My needs are less important than others
- I don't have as many rights as others
- My contributions are not as valuable as others

Assertive

Goals:

- Express myself
- Find an agreement
- Keep fair boundaries of mutual respect

Actions:

- Directly express needs, wants, feelings
- Expect others to be equally as open and honest
- Accept different opinions without dismissing them

Looks:

- Relaxed
- Comfortable body language
- Frequent eye contact without glaring

Emotions:

- Positive feelings about self
- Positive feelings about others

- Good self-esteem

Beliefs:

- My needs are equally as important as others' needs
- I have equal rights
- We both can make valuable contributions
- I am responsible for my behavior

Passive-aggressive

Goals:

- Get it my way, without taking any responsibility or having to assert myself

Actions:

- Deny personal responsibility
- Covert aggression
- Use sarcasm
- Agree to avoid discussion but look for ways to defect

Looks:

- Similar to passive

Emotions:

- Fear of rejection if being direct
- Resentful of other people's power and demands
- Fear of being controlled

Beliefs:

- My needs come first but I can't express that openly
- I am not responsible for my actions
- I am entitled to get it my own way, even if I made different commitments

Aggressive
Goals:

- Win at any cost
- Control others
- Always make sure others know who's in charge

Actions:

- Express myself over others
- Belittle or dismiss others
- Insult, ignore, or attack other opinions

Looks:

- Make myself large
- Look threatening
- Make penetrative eye contact
- Be loud

Emotions:

- Anger
- Powerful when winning over others
- Potentially remorseful afterwards for mistreating others

Beliefs:

- My needs are more important and justified than others' needs
- I have more rights than others
- My contributions are more valuable than others

EXERCISE: Reflection
Maybe you have an idea of which one you are, but if you take a deeper look and recall a few recent experiences and interactions, you could be surprised. What did you do? What were some of the urges you felt?

EFFECTIVE SEXUAL COMMUNICATION

One of the secrets to a fulfilling sex life is having open and honest conversations with your partner about what you need, want, and desire. This means keeping those lines of communication flowing. It's about being able to tell your partner exactly how you like to be touched or asking them for the kind of touch you're craving. And here's the thing: everyone is different. What worked well for a past partner might not be what your new partner enjoys. The good news is, all of this can be figured out by simply talking to each other.

What should we talk about?

Be ready to talk about everything—before, during, and after. Nothing is off the table. It's important to make sure you and your partner are on the same page about your views and expectations when it comes to sex, but sexual communication goes far beyond just that.

You must specifically discuss the following issues, as applicable:

- Sexual boundaries
- Relationship structure
- Frequency of sex
- Timing of sex
- Sexual positions
- Variety of sexual activities
- Sexual fantasies
- Use of pornography
- Differences in sexual desire
- Use of sex toys
- Masturbation
- Emotional safety
- Sexual needs
- Prophylactics
- Contraceptives
- The wedding night
- Human sexual response
- Sexual or love-making skills
- Pregnancy
- Sexually transmitted infections (STIs)
- Comfort with sexual intimacy
- Foreplay
- Initiation of sex
- Turning down sex
- Sexual experiences
- Preferences

MASTER LIST OF CONVERSATION STARTERS

- What does this sexual encounter mean to you?
- Is this casual or a relationship?
- Are you planning to be monogamous?
- Are you sleeping with other people?
- How do sex and intimacy differ, in your mind? What does it look like when they overlap?
- How do you personally define sex?
- What is your relationship orientation? What is your preferred relationship structure?
- Is marriage or engagement a prerequisite for you for sex?
- Do you have any prerequisites for sex?
- How often would you like to have sex?
- What is the "optimal" frequency for you to have sex? How often?
- If it were completely up to you, how many times a week would you want to have sex?
- How do you feel about how often we've been having sex?
- How do you feel about how long our sex sessions have been lasting?
- What are two sex positions that we haven't tried in a while that you'd like to bring back into rotation?
- What's your favorite position?
- How many sex positions do you think you've tried?
- What's the longest you think you could go without sex?
- Are there times you like to have sex more than other times?
- How would you describe your interest in sex?
- How do you masturbate?
- What do you think about when you masturbate?
- What does your masturbation practice involve?
- Is there anything about sex that feels inconvenient or anxiety-inducing to you?
- What turns you on?
- Where and how do you like to be touched?
- What are your sex safety preferences?
- What are some things that make you feel like getting sexy?
- What's something nonsexual that turns you on?
- What can I do to make our sex life better?

LET'S TALK ABOUT SEX

- How can I enhance our passion?
- What's the best thing about our sex life?
- What would you like to do more of in bed?
- What's the best method for me to inform you about the specific ways I prefer to be touched, pleased, and made love to?
- When was the last time you were STI-tested?
- What precautions have you taken to prevent STI transmission during sex?
- What STIs were you tested for?
- What were the results of those tests?
- What is your opinion on dirty talk?
- Would you ever go skinny dipping with me?
- Can I pull your hair?
- Do you like when I kiss you here?
- Would you ever want to make a sex tape with me?
- Where do you most like to be kissed?
- Can I observe you as you engage in masturbation?
- What do you say about me masturbating in front of you?
- What do you like to do during foreplay?
- What's your favorite type of foreplay?
- What's your favorite way for me to let you know I want to have sex?
- Are you feeling frisky tonight?
- What is something you've always wanted to try?
- What is one of your wildest sexual fantasies?
- Do you have any fetishes?
- Are there any kinds of sex you've never had but want to?
- Is there anything you'd regret not trying?
- What's something you've fantasized about but never tried?
- What sex act do you want to try that you never have?
- What are some of the sex acts your friends have talked about that you want to try?
- I'd love to learn more about any kinks or sex toys you've been interested in trying together—what are some of them?
- Have you ever been caught having sex?
- Have you ever had sex in a car?
- Tell me about the most unusual spot you've had sex.
- What is the longest you've ever gone without having sex?
- Have you ever had FaceTime sex?
- Have you ever shot a sex tape?

- What's your favorite part of my body?
- Think about all the times we've had sex. What are some of your favorites? What made those times special?
- Was sex discussed in your family growing up? What was the dialogue like?
- What part of your body are you most proud of?
- Have you had any memorable sexual dreams?
- What makes you feel safest in bed?
- How do you decide that someone is sexually compatible with you?
- What are your sexual non-negotiable needs?
- What's your favorite time to make love and why?
- Do you like to be spanked?
- Do you like to kiss during sex?
- Where do you most like to be kissed?
- What makes you most excited?
- Do you enjoy being teased?
- Which position do you prefer—top or bottom?
- What gets you in the mood the most?
- What turns you on the most during sex?
- Where's your favorite place to be touched?
- What time of day do you most enjoy having sex?
- Where is your favorite place to have sex?
- What are your hard nos?
- What are your favorite ways to give pleasure anally?
- What are your favorite ways to receive pleasure?
- When I touch you here, how do you feel?
- What's been your favorite moment from our sex life?
- How do you think our sex life will change through the years?
- How do you feel our sexualities differ from each other? How are we similar sexually?
- What bad sexual habits have we developed or could develop in our relationship which need to change?
- What kind of events/circumstances would lead you to cheat?
- What should we do if one day we wake up and still love each other but no longer want to have sex together?
- What are our sexual strengths and weaknesses as a pair?
- What aspects of your sexuality have you had to suppress in your previous relationships? What can I do to make you feel safe to express those with me?

- How can we communicate better with each other about our sexual needs?
- What would be some early warning signs that our sexual relationship is in trouble?

EXERCISE: Reflection
Think about the master list of conversation starters above.

- What is coming up for me right now?
- Anything surprising?
- Any topics that I've been more assertive with?
- Any topics that have been neglected?
- Has sexual communication been hard for me?
- If so, why do I think that is?

What's the best way to bring up sexual topics?
Talking about sex can be intimidating, but an approach that's playful, careful, and genuinely curious can go a long way. If you're eager to start a conversation, you could mention wanting to spice things up and ask your partner about their likes and dislikes. Consider using something like a "Yes, No, Maybe" list to explore boundaries and preferences together (see Chapter 12). It's a great way to discover where you both align.

Talking about sex before diving in helps to ensure that you're on the same page. But it doesn't mean you need to discuss it right away when meeting someone. Especially if you're exploring kinks or fetishes, boundaries, safe words, trust, and intimacy need to be established in advance to keep everyone comfortable and safe. Being with a partner who respects your limits is non-negotiable.

Over time, your sexual desires may change—new cravings, fantasies, or even the need for specific environments or toys might arise. A positive or even a negative experience can teach you more about what works for you. Since no one can read minds, expressing your evolving needs openly and clearly is crucial.

If talking about sex in person feels too intimidating at first, it's okay to start by texting about it. It's a neutral space where you can feel less pressure. However, sooner or later, it's important to switch to in-person conversations, even though it may feel awkward initially. These aren't one-off discussions; they're ongoing conversations that are always worthwhile. At its core, sexual communication is about love, connection, and genuine appreciation for your partner.

Start conversations about sex outside the bedroom

Bringing up sexual topics outside the bedroom can be helpful. Avoid talking about mishaps right after sex, as it might make your partner feel as if something went wrong that needs fixing. Plus, after sex, emotions run high and it's not always the best time for serious conversations. Instead, chat when you're both relaxed—over dinner or morning coffee, for example. It can be tough to tell your partner that you're not a fan of something they've been doing for a while, but the way you phrase it makes all the difference. Instead of saying, "Don't do it that way," try "I'd love it if you did it this way." It's more positive and constructive.

Try normalizing sexual discussions. If you and your partner can chat about steamy scenes from a show or celebrity gossip, it'll be easier to transition into deeper conversations about your own intimacy. Many people shy away from these discussions, but remember that your partner isn't a mind-reader.

It's essential to talk before getting intimate, especially when exploring new things. Knowing each other's fantasies, limits, and desires makes it easier to enjoy these moments spontaneously without having to repeat ground rules each time. But talking before sex doesn't just mean going over logistics—it's about sharing desires and building trust.

During sex, communication is just as vital. Consent is ongoing, and it's important to be aware of both verbal and non-verbal cues, especially when trying out bondage, discipline, sadism, and masochism (BDSM) or kink. Sometimes, we might hesitate to speak up during sex, fearing it will kill the mood or make things awkward. But most partners genuinely want to please each other, so gentle guidance can actually make the experience more enjoyable for both of you. It's all about being kind, patient, and specific.

CONSENT

Consent means freely giving permission for a specific sexual act. It's about bodily autonomy and ensuring that everyone involved feels safe and respected. Consent is never implied—it must be given explicitly. Silence, clothing choices, or past experiences don't equal consent. Consent is an ongoing conversation, and it's what creates a safe space for you to explore together. So, whether you're just beginning to explore new aspects of your sexual relationship or you're seasoned at navigating these discussions, remember to always be nice, patient, kind, and supportive. Keep talking, keep listening, and enjoy the journey together.

AUTHOR'S NOTE: ON RAPE MYTHS

Rape myths are harmful stereotypes and false beliefs about how people should behave, often used to blame survivors and excuse those who commit sexual assault. But let's be clear: consent can never be assumed or inferred based on someone's social behavior. It also can't be assumed from anything you did, or people think you did, in the moments, hours, days, or even long before the assault. Consent is always explicit, and it's important we all understand that.

Consent is feeling:

- confident
- safe
- respected
- informed
- self-determined
- comfortable
- enthusiastic
- empowered.

Consent is not being:

- forced
- afraid
- misled
- coerced
- unaware
- confused
- threatened
- pressured
- intimidated
- controlled
- intoxicated
- unconscious.

EXERCISE: Reflection

- What does healthy communication in a relationship look like to me?
- What would I like my sexual partner to do/say to make sure consent is ongoing?
- Why do I deserve to be in a healthy relationship and have a fun sex life?
- What are some signs of sexual coercion (e.g., they make you feel guilty for saying "no")?
- What would I advise a friend to do if they said their sexual partner was coercing them into sex?
- What are some situations where I feel uncomfortable saying "no" to people? How could I build my confidence to say "no"?

When it comes to consent, everyone involved in a sexual activity needs to make sure they're on the same page. You can't assume someone is okay with what's happening—you need to check in. For a sexual encounter to be truly consensual, all partners need to actively express their approval throughout. This can happen in different ways: verbally or non-verbally, as long as it's clear and enthusiastic.

You could ask your partner directly if they want to have sex, or look for signs in their body language or expressions—like an enthusiastic smile, laughter, eye contact, or eager touch. Remember, though, that body language should reinforce verbal consent, not replace it.

Consent is an ongoing conversation, and anyone can change their mind at any time. Just because someone said yes once, or has said yes before, doesn't mean they always will. Even if someone is initially excited about sex, they might change their mind—it means consent is no longer there. Your relationship status, past experiences, or even being undressed in bed with someone doesn't mean consent is automatic. Sex is never an obligation—it's a choice, and if it's not freely given, it's not consent.

For many, the concept of consent has been clouded by painful experiences like sexual abuse or emotional manipulation. If you've been conditioned to engage in sex without really having a choice, it can be challenging to reconnect with your own sense of agency. But trust me, it is possible. When you're ready to move toward a healthier, more mindful sexuality, it's important to first establish your own boundaries. You should be able to discuss what you and your partner want—and don't want—before having sex. If that conversation can't happen, it might be best to pause on having sex for now.

AUTHOR'S NOTE: ON ASSUMPTIONS

Making assumptions can be risky, especially when it's so easy to mis-read someone's body language or facial expressions. If you're not sure about the other person's consent, just ask. Remember, not hearing a "no" doesn't mean there's a "yes." Silence isn't consent. So, never make assumptions. If you're getting mixed signals, take that as a "no" and check in. It's always better to be sure.

AUTHOR'S NOTE: ON PHYSICAL AROUSAL RESPONSES

Arousal responses like wetness, erections, or even orgasm can sometimes happen during a rape or assault, and it's important to understand that these are automatic physical reactions. They are not something the survivor can control, and they definitely don't mean that they wanted, enjoyed, or consented to what happened.

EXERCISE: Reflection

- Is anything about consent surprising to me?
- What was I taught about consent?
- Is there information here about consent that contradicts what I was taught?
- Is there anything I hadn't thought of before?

How consent could be communicated

Here's what's on the menu: Let your partner know what you're comfortable with at the moment.

- "I'm not in the mood to have sex right now, but I'd love to kiss you."
- "I like cuddling you, but that's all I feel comfortable with today."
- "What I think would be really fun is if we... Do you want to give that a try tonight?"

- "Is it all right if I (explain in great detail what you plan to do to them) right now with you?"

Here are my boundaries: Talk about your boundaries before getting intimate. This might include the types of activities you're comfortable with (like penetration, oral, or specific kinds of touch) and how long you want the experience to last. This kind of discussion can feel easier once you've established trust and have had similar conversations before. It helps everyone know what's okay and what isn't, which makes for a safer, more enjoyable experience.

Here's what's on the table: Once you and your partner have built mutual respect, you might feel comfortable easing up on detailed consent discussions for every single touch. Instead, you can share what kinds of touches are always okay unless someone says otherwise. Over time, you might shift from explicitly saying "yes" to things to simply saying "no" if something isn't what you want. It's important to remember that reaching this stage takes time, patience, and a lot of trust.

Practice the language

Talking about consent can feel awkward at first—being honest and direct helps make things easier. You can even practice these conversations by yourself, maybe in front of a mirror. It might feel silly, but the more you practice, the easier it will get. Think about how you'd like to phrase things and when those conversations might happen. The goal is to make sure everyone knows what's okay and what isn't.

Remember, consent is dynamic. It means you're allowed to change your mind at any time, for any reason. If you're not comfortable, you never have to go along with something. If you need to stop, you don't owe anyone an explanation—it's always okay to just say "no."

Practice your "no"

Saying "no" can be hard, and it's completely normal to feel nervous or unsure about it. Practicing saying "no" in everyday situations can help make it easier when it comes to intimate moments. Whether it's declining a work request or setting a boundary with a friend, practice being firm but respectful. The more you get used to expressing your boundaries, the easier it will be in more challenging situations.

Remember, saying "no" is always your right, no matter who the other person is or what the situation may be. And if someone pushes past your boundaries, it's never your fault. Your comfort and safety are what matter most.

EXERCISE: Learn your "nos" worksheet
Jot down your answers to these questions in your notebook.

- What is your kindest, most loving and caring "no"?
- What might be a "no" that's still kind, but a bit more firm?
- What are some other "nos" that are even more firm?
- What is your final, most strong "no"?

Respecting your partner's boundaries

After talking about consent and sex, what comes next? It's crucial to make sure your partner feels safe and valued. This means respecting their boundaries and being mindful of any triggers they may have. To keep consent clear and make sex more enjoyable for both of you, find out what they want and enjoy. Listen to them without judgment and honor what they're comfortable with.

Respecting someone's boundaries isn't just about words—it's about how you make them feel. Don't hold it against them if they say "no" or need to pause. Don't make them feel guilty or interpret their needs as a personal rejection. When your partner says "no" or seems uneasy, pay attention and respect their wishes.

Consent is the foundation of healthy sexual relationships. It can be tough to hear "no" or "stop," especially if you care deeply about this person or really want things to keep going. It's natural to feel a sting, to think you've been rejected or you've failed. But these thoughts aren't necessarily true. Instead of getting stuck in that feeling, use mindfulness (see Chapter 6) and reframe cognitive distortions (Chapter 7) to move past those negative conclusions.

EXERCISE: Reflection

- Has there ever been a time that I interpreted my partner's boundaries as a rejection of me?
- Did it make me feel bad about myself or my body?

Triggers and safe words

A trigger is anything that sets off alarm bells in your body. It might come from a past bad experience or trauma, or just something that doesn't feel right to you. If you're comfortable, it can really help to talk about this with your partner. Safe words aren't just for stopping physical actions—they can be super helpful when emotional triggers come up too.

EXERCISE: Reflection

- What triggers am I aware of?
- How can these be avoided, if appropriate?
- What do I need my partner to do if they accidentally trigger me?
- How can I communicate these needs to my partner(s)?
- What are some safe words or signals I can use in the moment when I'm triggered?

CASE STUDY: Alex and Jamie

Alex and Jamie, a gay couple in their early thirties, had been together for two years. In the beginning, their sexual connection was effortless, but over time, Alex noticed that Jamie seemed withdrawn during intimacy. Jamie, on the other hand, felt overwhelmed by some of Alex's desires and didn't know how to express his discomfort. He feared disappointing Alex, and Alex didn't realize that the lack of communication was causing tension.

One evening, after a particularly strained encounter, Jamie decided to speak up. He told Alex, "I've been feeling a bit overwhelmed lately, and I think we need to talk about what works and what doesn't work for me." Alex was initially surprised but appreciated Jamie's honesty. He reassured Jamie that it wasn't a criticism, but an opportunity for them to align on their needs.

The couple used a "Yes, No, Maybe" list to establish clear sexual boundaries and began checking in with each other during intimacy. They made sure to communicate both verbally and non-verbally, ensuring ongoing consent. With time, Jamie felt more comfortable expressing his needs, and Alex became more attuned to his partner's comfort. Their sexual connection deepened, and their emotional bond strengthened. By prioritizing communication and consent, they were able to create a space where both felt safe, respected, and fulfilled.

— CHAPTER 12 —

Mindful Pleasure

GOALS

- ▶ Learn how to recognize your sexual wants and needs.
- ▶ Learn how to apply newly acquired mindfulness and communication skills to the exploration of sexual pleasure.

Overcontrolled focus: Be mindful of bodily tension, overthinking, and self-restraint during sexually intimate moments

Undercontrolled focus: Be mindful of impulsivity, disconnection from body, and emotion-based reactions to sexual intimacy

EXPLORATION

Pleasure is an essential part of being human. It's in our nature to find joy in the many sensations that stimulate our senses. But sometimes, our ability to enjoy pleasure gets tangled up in guilt, shame, or feelings of unworthiness—often due to our upbringing or difficult life experiences. These reactions are more common than you might think, but they can be transformed. In this chapter, we'll explore how consciously embracing pleasurable experiences can be a powerful form of self-care.

The key to recovery is becoming aware of your own body, feelings, and thoughts. By reconnecting with your inner experiences—your feelings and sensations—it's possible to move beyond suffering. We often believe that finding the right partner will magically solve our issues with intimacy. While a loving relationship can help, the truth is that the most important relationship we have is with ourselves. This relationship shapes how we experience intimacy and sexuality moving forward. To create the kind of intimacy you desire with others, you need to start by building a healthy relationship with your own pleasure.

If you're ready to explore sexual pleasure during your recovery, consider setting aside time for solo play. Masturbation can be an empowering form of self-care—a way to enjoy pleasure on your own terms, without the pressure of meeting someone else's expectations (or even your own self-judgment). For those who struggle with disordered eating, there can sometimes be impulsive or self-soothing sexual behaviors that don't feel quite right. There's nothing wrong with using sex to manage emotions on occasion, but if these habits start to feel that they're doing more harm than good, they could be pointing to deeper issues. Practicing mindfulness can help you tune in to your motivations (see Chapter 6). Feeling helpless to change unhealthy behaviors is common in eating disorders, but reminding yourself that you're taking steps to cope is a sign of strength. This proactive effort helps in finding healthier ways forward.

Sensuality is another vital part of recovery. This deep connection with our senses shapes how we view our bodies, and influences our body image. It's about paying attention to your body and reconnecting with your senses. For those recovering from eating disorders, it's important to (re)learn how to handle emotional experiences, including the vulnerability that comes from being open with others. Fear of pleasure and letting go can be heightened by feeling disconnected from your body, which disrupts your sensory experiences. Sensuality invites you to truly inhabit your body, to embrace it as a source of pride and pleasure—whether for yourself or with someone else. Reconnecting in this way is a beautiful way to heal and celebrate your body's abilities.

EXERCISE: Reflection

- What's coming up for me right now when I think about pleasure?
- What's coming up for me right now when I think about sensuality?
- How has my eating disorder impacted my relationship to pleasure?
- How has my eating disorder impacted my sensuality?

WHAT BRINGS YOU PLEASURE?
Sexual accelerators and brakes explained

Sexual desire and arousal aren't like flipping a light switch on or off. In the 2015 book *Come As You Are*, Dr. Emily Nagoski likens them to driving a car with both an accelerator and a brake pedal. The "accelerators" are the things that turn you on—what we call the Sexual Excitation System. These are all those little sensory inputs like touch, smell, taste, or sight that spark arousal. The accelerators are always running in the background, picking up on cues in your environment, even if you're not consciously aware of them.

On the other hand, there are "brakes"—the Sexual Inhibition System— which are all the things that put a damper on your arousal. Brakes play an important role by keeping us from being inappropriately aroused, for example when you're in the office or sitting down to dinner with your family. Just like the accelerators, the brakes are also always at work, scanning for anything that might make sex feel unsafe, uncomfortable, or just not appealing at that moment.

Understanding what presses on your accelerators and what slams on your brakes is key to better understanding your own desire. Your accelerators and brakes might be unique to you, and they can change over time or depending on the context. For example, something that turns you on one week might become a brake the next. Or perhaps not hearing from your partner all day puts a brake on your desire, while playful texts during the day act as an accelerator.

Getting in touch with your own accelerators and brakes can help you have more honest conversations with your partner about what you need. Sex is one of the most common issues couples face, and often, the challenge lies in having different levels of desire. If you're able to understand and communicate what affects your desire, you're in a better position to navigate these differences together.

Context matters

Beyond accelerators and brakes, our desire is also heavily influenced by context. Emotional context (like stress, love, and feelings of connection) and cultural context (societal expectations and norms) play huge roles in shaping our sexual experiences. For instance, when you're under stress, your brakes might be in overdrive, making it hard for any accelerator to get through. Or, the way you feel about your body—often influenced by media and societal beauty standards—can impact whether you're even open to feeling aroused.

Understanding the different contexts and how they interact with your accelerators and brakes can make it easier to get turned on or, at the very least, help you understand why desire might feel distant at times. Remember, human sexuality is complex, but that's what makes it beautiful. We're all unique, and there's no "normal" when it comes to how we experience desire—only what's right for us.

EXERCISE: Reflection

- Think of an example of a sexual encounter that went well. Try to recall as many details as you can. Why did you find it to be a good experience?
- Now consider a sexual encounter that went poorly. Try to recall as many details as you can. Why did it not go so well for you?

EXERCISE: Sexual accelerators and brakes identification worksheet
Consider the different areas below and write your answers in your notebook.
Common cues
Physical:

- Physical health
- Body hygiene
- Sensations in the body

My accelerators:

My brakes:

Mental:

- Mood
- Thoughts
- Memories
- Images
- Body image
- Anxiety
- Distraction
- Sexual worry

My accelerators:

My brakes:

Partner:

- Physical health
- Body hygiene
- Physical appearance
- Mental state

My accelerators:

My brakes:

Relationship:

- Trust
- Emotional safety
- Physical safety
- Clear boundaries
- Power dynamics
- Emotional connection
- Perceived desire
- Sexual frequency

My accelerators:

My brakes:

Setting:

- Privacy
- Safety
- Distance
- Lighting
- Distraction
- Comfort and confidence
- Stimuli (smell, touch, sound, taste, sight)

My accelerators:

My brakes:

Circumstances:

- Work stress
- Family stress
- Event or holiday stress
- Time of day
- Time of year

My accelerators:

My brakes:

Sexual or sensual actions:

- Imagination and visualization
- Sexual communication, language
- Sexual positions
- Erotica or fantasy shared
- Requests or adjustments made
- Body parts touched or not
- Oral sex or intercourse
- Toys and sensation enhancements

My accelerators:

My brakes:

Spontaneous vs responsive desire

Understanding the two main types of desire, spontaneous and responsive desire (Nagoski, 2015), can help you get a better sense of how your sexual desire works. We often think of desire as something that just happens—unplanned and uninhibited, like a spark out of nowhere. In the early stages of a relationship, you might feel those sudden, intense moments of attraction where you just can't keep your hands off each other. That's also the way movies and TV often portray desire: spontaneous, all-consuming, and totally natural.

If we let popular culture and porn shape our understanding of sexuality, it might seem as if spontaneous desire is the only "real" kind of desire. You know the scene: two people are overwhelmed by passion, clothes start flying off, and they have mind-blowing sex, just like that. If you asked most couples, though, they'd probably tell you that's not how things usually go. For some, spontaneous desire fits their experience—but for many, it doesn't. These portrayals can create a myth that everyone should feel the same intense, unprompted desire before having sex. But the truth is, desire doesn't always work like that.

Another misconception is that you need to feel desire before anything happens. In reality, responsive desire is often sparked after you've already started being intimate. Have you ever been feeling neutral about having sex but then decided to go for it, and found yourself really enjoying it once you got into it? That's what we mean by responsive desire. Responsive desire involves responding to the moment and letting the experience unfold. The key is to be open to that possibility, knowing that as arousal starts, your desire can follow. Sometimes, it's about gently taking your foot off the brakes and letting yourself lean into the moment.

If you're someone with spontaneous desire, you're easily aroused, think about sex often, and feel turned on even without a specific reason—your body leads the way. On the other hand, if you have a responsive desire, it might take more time to feel ready for sex. For you, desire often comes after the right context is set—when you're relaxed, the stress is low, and you feel mentally at ease. In this case, your mind sets the stage for your body to feel aroused.

Responsive desire is that growing spark that lights up when you're already in a sexual situation. It's when you might not have been actively thinking about sex, but after your partner gives you a lovely full-body massage, you realize you're in the mood. If you're more "sexy-minded," you might also consider relational, social, cultural, and situational factors in addition to just physical feelings of desire.

In the beginning of a relationship, even someone with responsive desire might experience a lot of spontaneous desire. Over time, as the new relationship energy fades and your body adjusts to those initial waves of feel-good hormones, that spontaneous desire often naturally settles. Recognizing this shift as a normal part of relationships can help you lean into responsive desire, which is still an exciting way to feel connected and enjoy sex.

Shifting from more spontaneous desire to more responsive desire can sometimes feel a bit unsettling, but it's entirely normal. Fluctuations in sexual desire don't mean there's anything wrong with you, your partner(s), or your connection. Many of us think of desire as something we either have or don't have, as if it's fixed or unpredictable. But desire is actually quite fluid—it changes with time, context, health, stress, and even partners. Knowing this can help you feel more grounded when your sexual desire changes.

Staying in touch with your own evolving desires—understanding what sparks them and how they ebb and flow—can be really empowering. And being able to share that understanding with your partner(s) is a great tool for navigating your sex life together.

TIPS FOR UTILIZING RESPONSIVE DESIRE

- *Refer to the list* of accelerators you compiled above in order to intentionally ignite your receptive desire.
- *Send your partner some flirty texts* or even engage in some dirty talk during the day. However, there will be no deep relationship discussions. The point is to relax, let your imagination run wild, and feel some anticipation building.
- *Rekindle the spark* you felt at the beginning of your relationship by flirting with your partner. Just have fun with it and tease them a little. Avoid discussing potential "brakes" like parenting, house tasks, or bills when you're together.
- *Engage in eye contact.* Amazingly, a lot of couples just stop giving each other their full attention. Make an effort to meet their eyes directly. The initial discomfort is worth the increased intensity.
- *Touch them as much as possible.* Touch the small of their back when you pass them, not constantly. Lean in and give them a kiss on the nape of their neck. Put their head on your lap and relax in front of the TV. Invite them in for a kiss. Ask them to touch you.
- *Schedule intimate time together.* Not necessarily for sex, though. It could be quality time, or even just cuddling. Desire can flourish in the relaxed atmosphere that is fostered by creating intimacy.

EXERCISE: Reflection

- In the past have I had more spontaneous or responsive desire? A mixture of both?
- Has it ever changed?
- Do I ever fluctuate between spontaneous and responsive desire?

WHAT IF I HAVE NO IDEA WHAT BRINGS ME PLEASURE?

If you're unsure about what brings you pleasure, start by spending some time with yourself—mindfully, without any pressure. This is a wonderful way to learn what feels good for you. Approach this journey with curiosity, almost like an adventure to discover your passions and pleasures. This can really help you feel more in tune with your body and more empowered when it comes to your own pleasure.

When you're with a partner, try to stay curious about how you're feeling. It's so important to prioritize your pleasure too! Even if you're feeling a little nervous, it's totally okay to express what you need, or even show them how you like to be touched. Trying out new things—whether on your own or with someone else—can sometimes feel awkward at first, and that's completely normal. It's the best way to start figuring out what you enjoy and what doesn't work for you. Remember, becoming comfortable talking about sexuality and feeling secure in your own sexual identity takes time. There's no rush, and there's no need to pressure yourself to have it all figured out.

Think of discovering your desires as an adventure. Practice makes pleasure! The more time you spend exploring, the more confident and interested you'll become. Enjoy the journey—it's all part of getting to know yourself better.

EXERCISE: Likes and dislikes
Use mindfulness and self-inquiry to check in with yourself:

- What turns me on? What turns me off?
- What types of touches or sexual activities make my body feel tense?
- What types of touches make me feel calm and relaxed?
- Where do I want to be touched and when? What kind of touch is okay and where?
- Is there anything that is never okay?
- What would I like to explore? What could that look like?
- Are there any kinks or fantasies I would like to try?
- What do I like about sex?
- How do I want to feel during sex?
- In what contexts do I feel the most at ease getting undressed in front of another person?
- In what ways does my partner's talk about my body make me feel uncomfortable?

- When it comes to physical contact, how can I determine what is sexual and what is merely affectionate for me?
- Are there words or actions that are acceptable in some contexts, or with some people, but not others?
- How much of a part, if any, do non-physical sexual activities have in my sex life (e.g., sexting, phone sex)?

EXERCISE: Yes, no, maybe worksheet

When you are alone, think about what you like about sex, your values around sex and relationships, your deal breakers, and things you might want to try. Write these down in your notebook. Add new items as you continue to explore your sexuality. See the list below for more ideas on what to include.

What would you put under each of the headings below? If you feel comfortable, you could share this list with your sexual partner.

Yes, please!!

Yes, I will try

No way

Maybe?

YES, NO, MAYBE IDEAS
General boundaries and comfort levels

- Talking openly about sex
- Using a safe word
- Discussing boundaries before sex
- Trying new activities spontaneously
- Watching erotic content together
- Engaging in aftercare

Types of touch and sensation (receiving or giving)

- Kissing (mouth, neck, body)
- Sensual massage
- Light scratching
- Biting
- Hair pulling
- Sensory play (blindfolds, ice, feathers)
- Temperature play (wax play, hot/cold objects)

Oral and manual activities (receiving or giving)

- Oral sex
- Mutual masturbation
- Rimming (anal oral sex)
- Using hands/fingers for stimulation
- Deep-throating

Intercourse and penetration (receiving or giving)

- Vaginal penetration
- Anal penetration
- Double penetration
- Using fingers or toys for penetration
- Wearing a strap-on

Kinks and power dynamics (receiving or giving)

- Light bondage (handcuffs, silk ties)
- Heavy bondage (ropes, restraints)
- Role-playing (teacher/student, doctor/patient, etc.)
- Sensory deprivation (blindfolds, earplugs)
- Spanking, paddling, flogging
- Domination/submission play
- Consensual non-consent (CNC)
- Voyeurism/exhibitionism

Toys and accessories (receiving or giving)

- Vibrators
- Dildos

- Butt plugs
- Cock rings
- Ben Wa balls/Kegel exercisers
- Nipple clamps
- Sex machines

Public and exhibitionist play

- Sex in a semi-public place
- Sex in front of a mirror
- Recording intimate activities (with consent)
- Attending a sex club or play party

Group and non-monogamous activities

- Watching others have sex
- Being watched while having sex
- Threesomes
- Group sex
- Swinging/swapping partners
- Consensual non-monogamy/polyamory

Fetishes and specialized interests

- Feet play
- Latex/leather outfits
- Pet play (kitten play, puppy play)
- Age play (daddy/mommy/little dynamics)
- Erotic hypnosis
- Objectification/humiliation play

Dirty talk and fantasy exploration

- Sexting
- Phone sex
- Watching or making adult films
- Reading or writing erotica
- Role-playing fantasies

Bodily fluids and edge play

- Cum play
- Watersports (urination play)
- Blood play
- Choking/breath play
- Electro-stimulation

Aftercare and emotional intimacy

- Cuddling after sex
- Discussing emotions after play
- Checking in about experiences
- Having non sexual intimacy (bathing together, massages)

CASE STUDY: Peach

Peach, a 48-year-old woman recovering from an eating disorder, has struggled with body image issues for most of her life. Her relationship with sex and intimacy has often been clouded by shame and self-criticism, stemming from both societal pressures and personal trauma. In therapy, Peach began to explore the concepts of mindful pleasure and sexual desire to reconnect with her body and her sense of sexual self.

Peach found it difficult to enjoy sexual intimacy, both with herself and her partner. Her history of using sex to cope with emotional stress left her feeling disconnected from her body, and she struggled with negative self-talk during intimate moments. Peach also experienced difficulty distinguishing between spontaneous and responsive desire, often feeling pressure to feel "turned on" in the way she believed was expected of her.

Through therapy, Peach learned to apply mindfulness to her body, thoughts, and emotions, starting with self-reflection exercises like identifying her sexual accelerators and brakes. She practiced mindfulness during solo play, focusing on her physical sensations without self-judgment. Over time, Peach explored how different types of touch, emotional safety, and communication affected her pleasure. She learned that her desire often followed after engaging emotionally with her partner, which fitted with her experience of responsive desire.

Peach also worked on improving her body image and self-worth by shifting her focus to the sensations of touch, smell, and sound, rather than how her body "looked." She began to identify and challenge the negative thoughts that hindered her sexual enjoyment, allowing herself to feel more present in intimate moments.

By integrating mindfulness and communication techniques into her sexual life, Peach experienced a significant shift in how she viewed herself and her sexuality. She reported feeling more in tune with her body, more confident during intimacy, and less likely to default to shame-based thinking. She found that approaching pleasure as an exploration, rather than a goal to achieve, allowed her to experience deeper intimacy, both with herself and her partner.

— CHAPTER 13 —

Embodied Sexuality, Embodied Self

GOALS

▶ Learn how to combine all the skills learned for enhanced pleasure and intimacy.
▶ Learn about the embodied self.

EMBODIED SEXUALITY

Embodiment is about experiencing and living in your body—it's a key part of who we are. It means feeling "at one" with your body, having agency and power within it, feeling free to take up space, and staying aware of your needs, wants, and rights. To be embodied is not just to see your body as an object but to fully experience yourself as a body. Sexual embodiment happens when you are connected to your whole self during intimacy—aware of your body, your desires, and how they connect. It's about being present, not judging yourself or treating your body like an object. Reclaiming the body as a source of freedom, joy, and connection requires consistent practice to help us stay grounded in our bodies.

Sexual embodiment means letting your senses, thoughts, feelings, and fantasies come alive. Disembodiment, on the other hand, happens when we get so lost in our thoughts or anxieties that we forget we even have a body. This can lead us to withdraw or become critical to protect ourselves. Staying present during sex is the heart of embodied sexuality—it's an art.

In our culture, there's a lot of emphasis on thinking and doing, while "being" gets overlooked. But being present helps keep us grounded, connected to ourselves, and in tune with others. Society pressures us to constantly produce and perform to feel valued, which can dull our natural capacity for sensuality, spontaneity, and connection.

We come into the world embodied, but we're taught to ignore our instincts in favor of who we "should" be. Over time, we shift from trusting our senses to relying on mental understandings of the world. Many of us prioritize intellect over feeling and mind over matter, which can disconnect us from our bodies and drain us emotionally. If we're not connected to our physical selves, our thoughts and emotions take over, and we miss out on the deep wisdom that lies within our bodies. Embracing embodiment means returning to your body's innate knowledge after being disconnected. It's about reconnecting and allowing yourself to feel fully alive again.

YOUR SEXUAL APPETITE AND YOUR FULL RECOVERY

Experiencing delicious food can feel a lot like the pleasure of intimacy. Just like exercise, sex helps release stress and flush out toxins. Orgasms—and other forms of pleasure—are powerful for our mental health, thanks to the hormones released during sex, which have natural antidepressant and calming effects. The same goes for touch, caresses, and the open expression of desire. When our sexual needs are met, it's easier to feel good about ourselves and develop a more positive relationship with our bodies.

Sex gives us a sense of security, making us more attuned to the desires we inspire in others. It also helps us feel at home in our bodies, fostering positive feelings about our physical selves. When approached with imagination and openness, sex can be a source of endless joy and intimacy. It invites us to savor the experience of being present in our bodies and sharing that with someone else. It's about discovering how trust, safety, and openness can pave the way to self-awareness and deeper connection.

Fully inhabiting our bodies means examining and letting go of the defenses that keep our sexual expression, desire, and presence bottled up. In intimate moments, thoughts like "I'm too fat" or "They're not attracted to me" can trigger defensive responses—fight, flight, or freeze. Practicing embodiment helps us step away from these learned reactions, giving us more independence from these coping mechanisms.

It's possible to find inner peace, let go of compulsions, and feel at ease in your body at any time. But learning to love and relate to your body, especially if you've experienced trauma and relied on eating disorders as a way to cope, can be a real challenge. Everything we've done so far contributes to this process. Giving ourselves permission to truly inhabit our bodies, to enjoy the sensations they create, to dare to seek pleasure, and to express our desires compassionately can help us reclaim our sexuality. We are rediscovering what it means to feel desirable and to desire, and allowing ourselves to experience that fully.

The journey is yours to define. Let go of what doesn't matter to you, and embrace what does. Try not to hold on to behaviors that make you feel bad, even if they seem "normal" to others. So many people, even when being intimate, feel shame, dissatisfaction, or endless self-criticism. Many engage in intimacy only under specific conditions—dim lighting, partial clothing, or the privacy of bedsheets—all in an effort to avoid feeling exposed. These patterns are common, but they're not inevitable. As you work through body acceptance, you have an opportunity to go beyond the typical experience; you're driven by a deeper motivation to address these challenges head on.

Self-objectification not only diminishes pleasure—it also keeps you trapped in a cycle of self-criticism and illness. Just because something is "normal" doesn't mean it's the best you can achieve. So let go of the messages from porn, adverts, social media, and even family. Push them away from your mirror, your bedroom, and your life. Cultivate a mindset of being fully present during intimacy by practicing it in your daily life. Challenge harsh self-judgments when you see yourself in the mirror. Remember that you have the power to give and receive the connection and pleasure you desire.

To be sexually embodied means not running away when things get scary or uncertain, but instead tuning in to what your body is telling you. It's recognizing that your body holds valuable knowledge and learning, so respect and listen to it. This also means practicing daily ways to connect with your physical self. Intimacy with another person is a powerful way to connect with your sexuality. Treat your body with the respect it deserves—after all, it's what allows you to experience the world in all its richness.

Being "embodied" during sex means being fully present with the sensations and pleasures of the experience. It's about awareness and responsiveness to your physical self. For those who've experienced trauma, though, being embodied can be especially difficult. Numbness might feel like a safe shield against discomfort, but it also blocks the joy of connection. Having a trauma-informed sex therapist by your side can be invaluable if you're struggling to feel safe during intimacy. Reaching out for help can make a huge difference in your journey toward greater embodiment.

It's completely understandable to feel disconnected if intimacy doesn't feel good, or if you feel pressured to engage. It's also okay if you don't want sex, or if your level of desire doesn't match your partner's. Desire naturally ebbs and flows, and sometimes it might seem as if everyone else is obsessed with sex—but that doesn't mean you have to be. Whatever you're feeling is valid, and you're not alone.

It takes practice and patience to get out of your own head and fully into your body, but it is possible. And remember, you don't need to force it. Embodiment isn't something to manage or control; it's something to explore and enjoy. One of the most beautiful things about this process is that it allows you to relax and let life unfold. You can let go of the pressure to figure everything out.

Just be in your body. At different times, we'll make different decisions about how to maintain connections, how to give and receive support, and how to express care. By the end of this journey, I hope you'll have a deeper understanding of what embodiment means and how it can support your healing, growth, and reconnection to your own inner wisdom. This journey is not about being perfect—it's about learning, exploring, and discovering what it means to truly be at home in yourself.

ESSENTIALS OF EMBODIED PRACTICE

Embodying yourself is really about taking a moment to tune in to your body and its sensations. Pause, take a deep breath, focus on your body, and gently ask yourself, "Hey, how are you doing?"

There are eight key elements of embodied practice that can help you reconnect with your mental and physical well-being, as well as boost your ability to experience sensual pleasure.

1. Embodied self-care
2. Embodied awareness
3. Embodied inquiry
4. Embodied intention
5. Embodied consent
6. Embodied action
7. Embodied inaction
8. Embodied pleasure

Embodied self-care

Self-care is all about recognizing and meeting our own needs—both physical and emotional—on a daily basis. It's also about making adjustments to our routines, relationships, and environments as needed. This could mean taking a moment to listen to your body before eating, noticing any cravings or sensations, and choosing food that feels nourishing. A big part of self-care is understanding what our bodies need, whether it's nourishment or intimacy. When we're in tune with our health, we can move away from extreme diets or overeating and instead focus on getting the right amount of nutrient-rich foods that make us feel our best. Before eating, we can pause for a moment to sense what our body truly craves.

Another great way to connect with your body is through regular body scans. A body scan is a mindfulness practice where you slowly bring your attention to different parts of the body, from head to toe, noticing sensations without judgment. Simply breathe, observe, and gently return your focus if your mind wanders. You might be surprised at how much more alive your body feels when you pay attention. When we're in tune, we can unlock more sensual pleasure by focusing on the parts of our bodies that feel good—even if we're dealing with pain or physical limitations. Movement can also help—either to energize us or to calm our nervous system.

If you want to improve your self-care, start small. Pick one new self-care practice that speaks to you and commit to it every day. Let it have some meaning for you. Consistent, small steps are much more powerful than big, sporadic efforts.

Pair with mindfulness and emotional regulation skills.

Embodied awareness

Pay attention to your thoughts and feelings, and notice how you protect yourself from harm—whether that harm is real or something you imagine. The more you increase your self-awareness, the more you'll start recognizing your mental and emotional triggers. Take the time to understand why you react the way you do, especially in your close relationships. Self-reflection can be incredibly helpful here. Make it a habit to check in with yourself regularly and ask, "How am I really feeling about this?" Try to break out of autopilot mode.

Being aware of your body's sensations is key—it helps you take a pause before reacting. Plus, there's a great bonus: you'll experience better sex. Staying connected with your body means you'll know more clearly what you do and don't want. You'll learn what turns you on and what makes you feel amazing.

Pair with mindfulness and cognitive distortion skills.

Embodied inquiry

If you're curious about what is happening around you or within yourself, it helps to make asking questions a habit. What do you need right now? How can you love yourself better? What do you want to experience, and how do you want to feel? These kinds of questions don't always have easy answers, but they're so important for living fully and embracing your sexuality.

To tap into the wisdom of your own body, take time to slow down, turn inward, and really notice what your body is telling you. Discover what kinds of touch feel good and how your body naturally wants to move. Use that insight to feed your desires and connect with your partner. When it comes to satisfying sexual experiences, it's often about both people feeling as if their needs are understood and cared for. While it's natural to want to please your partner, it's just as important to understand what you need from those experiences, too. Try to bring this kind of embodied curiosity into your everyday life. It can help you feel more connected, more alive, and more in tune with both yourself and others.

Pair with mindfulness, communication, self-inquiry, and emotional regulation skills. This element can be helpful for determining boundaries.

Embodied intention

Living an intentional life, or practicing embodied intention, means bringing a gentle but focused awareness to your actions and routines so they align with your goals. It's about asking yourself questions like, "How can I use my skills today?" or, "Is there something I can do this week, no matter how small, that moves me closer to my dreams?" These questions can help you understand what matters most to you and where you can get the biggest return on your energy and time.

When you have a goal and work toward it, you start to notice opportunities that you might have overlooked before. Living in alignment with your purpose can make life feel richer and more fulfilling. Of course, learning to do this takes time and effort—but it's worth it.

When you know what you want and why it matters, it's easier to find solutions that fit your needs. It also helps others understand you better. Acting in line with your true self opens the door to deeper conversations that build trust and lay the foundation for meaningful connections. By setting boundaries and being clear about what you need from others, you can enjoy more rewarding friendships and romantic relationships.

Pair with mindfulness, interpersonal effectiveness, and interpersonal connectedness skills.

Embodied consent

Without consent, there's no mindful sex, no good sex, and honestly, no sex at all. Consent is where it all begins. And not just any kind of consent—I'm talking about radical, embodied consent. Radical consent goes beyond verbal agreement; it involves being fully attuned to your body's responses and communicating your boundaries with clarity and respect. The kind of consent where your entire being gives a full-body, "Hell Yes!"—mind and body both completely on board. Using mindfulness techniques can help make sure that every sexual experience is fully agreed on. And honestly, consent isn't just about sex. It's about every aspect of our lives—respecting our own boundaries and those of others. It's about creating a life where we treat each other with care and integrity.

When we aim for this kind of full-body consent in ourselves and in our relationships, we inspire others to do the same. Consent stops being a hurdle and becomes part of who we are, how we connect, and how we move through the world. It's a beautiful way to live—a life rooted in respect and wholehearted "yeses."

Pair with mindfulness, communication, emotional expression, interpersonal effectiveness, and interpersonal connectedness skills.

Embodied action

When I say "embodied action," I'm talking about taking intentional steps that come from awareness and reflection. It's about more than just thinking things through—it's about truly feeling and acting on your choices in a meaningful way. Embodied action plays a crucial role in decision-making. Actions and choices are constantly shaping each other. When you act on a decision, that action, with all its real-life dynamics and challenges, affects how you move forward. The key is to stay mindful, to keep reflecting, and to decide if you need to take another step. It's also important to deal with your triggers. Learn to manage your emotions by gathering the support and resources you need. Instead of getting caught up in blame or shame, open up about your reactions in relationships. Pay attention to yourself, the people around you, and your environment. Ask questions, stay curious, and be open to learning and adapting as you go.

Pair with mindfulness, emotional regulation, emotional expression, interpersonal connectedness, and interpersonal effectiveness skills.

Embodied inaction

In today's world, rest often takes a back seat. We're pushed to always be on, to perform, engage, and stay constantly energized. It's easy to feel guilty for just thinking about taking a break because we've been taught to value non-stop progress and external measures of success. But the truth is, rest is not a luxury—it's essential. Remember, doing your best doesn't look the same every day. Some days, your best might mean powering through, and other days, it might mean slowing down. Our nervous systems can get overwhelmed by constant stress and stimulation, so giving yourself time to rest helps you reset, find balance, and stay healthy. When your body feels heavy or fatigued, take it as a sign to pause. It's okay to set down the tasks of the day and rest without guilt. Listen to your body. When it tells you to pause, honor that. Take a break, rest up, and let go of the guilt. You deserve it.

Pair with mindfulness, cognitive distortion, and emotional regulation skills.

Embodied pleasure

The human body is a landscape of sensations, full of experiences just waiting to be discovered. When I talk about "pleasure," I'm not just referring to sexual gratification—I'm talking about what excites us and brings us alive. Think of those moments when your skin tingles at a powerful piece of music or your heart opens to the beauty of a painting. These moments of awe are waves of pleasure that go beyond the physical; they are embodied experiences that shape how we move through the world.

The more we learn to be sensual with our environment, the more we can use the erotic to explore and fall in love with life—with our bodies, our surroundings, our passions, and each other. Pleasure isn't limited to one feeling; it's something we can mold and stretch to fit our needs. Our brains are wonderfully adaptable, allowing us to discover new sensations and deepen our experience of existing ones. When we train ourselves to seek out and savor pleasure, we become more attuned to sensation, making it easier to access joy in everyday life.

One way to enhance your experience of pleasure is to pay closer attention to your senses—what you see, hear, smell, taste, and touch. Look for opportunities to enjoy everyday pleasures: pick out soft fabrics that feel good against your skin, fill your space with fragrances that bring back good memories, surround yourself with beauty, take your time with food, and play your favorite music. Focus fully on these experiences, let yourself feel them deeply, and breathe in the bliss they bring.

Pleasure can be found in countless places. With practice, we can learn to enjoy almost any experience. The more we practice being present with our senses, the more we can tune in to the pleasurable sensations that exist all around us. Cultivating a pleasure-filled mindset takes time, but once we get there, life becomes a sensory adventure—a haven of joy that helps us manage stress and face challenges with more ease. Engaging in activities that bring you pleasure can be a powerful way to support your well-being. It becomes a tool to help you feel at home in your body and the world, especially in those moments that feel tough. Instead of a way to escape, pleasure becomes a way to be more present, connected, and alive.

Pair with mindfulness skills.

ASSESSMENT: EMBODIMENT

The purpose of this assessment is to help you evaluate your current level of embodied living and pinpoint areas for improvement. The assessment that follows is not meant to be all-inclusive, but rather to serve as a starting point for further thought. Add any other aspects of embodied living you find important. Make sure to evaluate how often and how well you are currently caring for yourself. Check in with yourself frequently.

Embodied self-care

- [ ] I drink at least six to eight cups of water per day.
- [ ] I eat regularly.
- [ ] I eat a variety of nutritious foods.
- [ ] I exercise at least a few times a week.
- [ ] I participate in organized sports, dance, or other physical activities.
- [ ] I do some other physical activities that are fun.
- [ ] I engage in a variety of self-care activities.
- [ ] I allow myself to fully experience and express my emotions without judgment.
- [ ] I get regular medical care for prevention.
- [ ] I get medical care when needed.
- [ ] I get sufficient rest/sleep.
- [ ] I take vacations.
- [ ] I go on day trips or short getaways.

Other:

Embodied awareness

- [ ] I have an awareness of my thoughts.
- [ ] I have an awareness of my feelings.
- [ ] I have an awareness of my attitudes, beliefs, and judgments.
- [ ] I have an awareness of my body.
- [ ] I practice yoga or another mind-body activity.
- [ ] I attend regular psychotherapy sessions.
- [ ] I write in a journal or diary.
- [ ] I read books that are unrelated to work, home, or family responsibilities.

☐ I employ my intelligence in new ways, such as by attending a historical museum, museum, aquarium, sporting event, or play.

Other:

Embodied inquiry

- I stay curious.
- I gratefully acknowledge the obstacles and hardships I have faced.
- I talk to myself in a supportive and consoling manner.
- I set aside time for introspection.
- I make time for general reflection.
- I acknowledge my failures and challenges as being part of the human experience.
- When I reflect on my professional or academic life, I have found significance and/or a sense of higher purpose.
- When I reflect on my own life, I am able to find a sense of significance and/or a higher purpose.

Other:

Embodied intention

- I plan my own self-care.
- I choose which of my thoughts and emotions will serve as the basis for my decisions, after careful reflection.
- I take stock of what's important to me and where it fits in my life.
- I prepare for my workouts by scheduling them in advance.
- I look for fresh approaches to self-care.
- I make time in my schedule to spend with loved ones.
- I seek out and complete stimulating projects.
- I identify soothing behaviors, things, people, relationships, and locations and actively seek them out.
- I actively seek out and engage in things that make me laugh.
- I keep my workload to a tolerable level.
- I make sure that no single day, or even segment of a day, is "too much" for me to handle.
- I maintain order in my workspace to help my work tasks.

- I try to keep my home as cozy and relaxing as possible.

Other:

Embodied consent

- I strike a balance between what's important to me and what other people want from me.
- I negotiate for my needs (benefits, pay raise).
- I explain my needs and boundaries to others.
- I respect and uphold my needs and boundaries.
- I aim for balance within my work-life and work day.
- I am sure that if I answered "no," the people in my life would respect my decision.
- I respect the needs and boundaries of others.

Other:

Embodied action

- I interact with others to unwind (e.g., connected with friends).
- I actively reduce the stress and tension in my life.
- I work on creative projects to unwind (e.g., draw, play instrument, creatively write, sing, organize).
- I engage in intellectual activities to decompress (e.g., read a book, write).
- I set up my workspace to be cozy and reassuring.
- I spend time with people whose company I appreciate.
- I keep in touch with significant individuals.
- I tell myself I'm awesome.
- I love and respect myself.
- I reread beloved books and watch favorite television episodes and movies.

Other:

Embodied inaction

- I take a break during the work day.
- I take time off when needed.
- I make quiet time to complete tasks.

- I say "no" to extra responsibilities sometimes.
- I make time away from my phone, tablet, computer, and video games.
- I make an effort to avoid taking charge or acting as the authority.
- I'm willing to be uncertain.
- I engage in activity when I lack authority or expertise.

Other:

Embodied pleasure

- I get massages.
- I wear clothes I like that feel good on my body.
- I enjoy listening to music, podcasts, radio programs, or forest sounds.
- I spend time with nature.
- I look for appealing visuals in movies, art, or nature.
- I am drawn to scents like those of lotions, flowers, candles, incense, and baking.
- I give myself time to engage in solo sexual activity.
- I give myself and my partner(s) time to engage in sexual activity together.
- I spend time with kind, considerate people.
- I sense the individuals in my life are there for me.

Other:

When you are done, look at your answers to see if there are any patterns.

- Are some parts of my life more important to me than others?
- Are there some parts of my life that I've neglected?
- Is there anything I'd like to do more of in my life?

EMBODIED SELF

Our body is the home of our mind, spirit, and soul. We are physical beings who experience the world through taste, touch, sight, sound, and smell, and I hope you've found gratitude for your physical self and your sexuality.

For many, this connection does not come easily. Especially for those who have experienced disordered eating, the relationship with the body can feel fraught, confusing, or even painful. When nourishment becomes a battleground, it's no surprise that pleasure, presence, and sexual connection can feel distant or unreachable.

Eating disorders often disconnect us from our own bodies. They teach us to override our hunger cues and mistrust our desires. This disconnection doesn't just affect how we feed ourselves. It affects how we touch, are touched, and allow ourselves to feel. Shame, rigidity, and fear can weave their way into our sexuality, muting desire or turning intimacy into a site of anxiety instead of joy.

And yet, I hope you've learned to value being present in your body. Our sexuality, when freed from judgment, brings us joy, intimacy, and connection. May we learn to savor every bit of it. And let us also hold space for the full range of emotions it stirs: guilt, sadness, trauma, anger, pain, and hurt. For those who are in recovery from eating disorders, these feelings can be especially intense. Body image struggles, past traumas, and the lingering effects of control or self-denial can all shape the sexual self in subtle and profound ways.

Celebrating the fullness of who we are means embracing the full spectrum of the human sexual experience—all of its deep pains and rich joys. The self is not just an abstract idea; it's something we live and feel. Our true nature is that of the embodied self—when we are present in our bodies, we can fully take in each moment, feeling every sensation as it comes. But for many in recovery, this presence must be relearned. Embodiment is not a switch we can flip; it's a practice of returning, again and again, to ourselves with compassion. Our bodies, once sites of shame or struggle, can become sacred places of truth, resilience, and pleasure.

Our bodies are made of interconnected systems, constantly communicating and working together in an intricate dance. But when we've spent years dissociating or controlling, that dance can become disjointed. We may lose touch with hunger, arousal, fatigue, and joy. Our journey toward full embodiment is ever-evolving, with moments of both disconnection and reconnection, especially as we heal.

Humans, like animals, have an innate ability to respond to threats. But we often stop ourselves from releasing the emotions and sensations that come with those experiences. This suppression is common in the development and maintenance of eating disorders. In an attempt to manage or control internal chaos, we often silence our body's signals, including sexual ones. And so, our capacity for pleasure and intimacy becomes stifled, buried under the weight of unprocessed pain. These unprocessed experiences affect our thoughts, behaviors, and beliefs, shaping how we see ourselves and the world around us. We cling to what fits our preconceived ideas and reject what doesn't, suppressing our embodied self in the process. This suppression affects us on a cellular level—we tense up, holding back from seeing or feeling things that we can't process. As a result, our bodies become less able to fulfill their purpose: to feel, to connect, to love, to enjoy.

In our day-to-day lives, we often find ourselves disconnected, not fully here, and missing out on the beauty of the present moment. We search for what's missing everywhere except where it actually is—within ourselves. The good news is that our bodies can also be a powerful source of healing, helping us reconnect with our embodied self. We just need to listen to what our body is telling us, let go of our stories, and accept life as it is. This journey toward embodying our true selves, especially after an eating disorder, is a continuous process of insight, healing, and growth. It is an invitation to feel more, not less. To reclaim pleasure. To rediscover desire. To come home.

Bibliography

Ackard, D., Kearney-Cooke, A., & Peterson, C. (2001). Effect of body self-image on women's sexual behaviors. *The International Journal of Eating Disorders*, 28, 422–429. https://doi.org/10.1002/1098-108X(200012)28:43.3.CO;2-T

Allen, J. P. & Miga, E. M. (2010). Attachment in adolescence: A move to the level of emotion regulation. *Journal of Social and Personal Relationships*, 27(2), 181–190.

Alleva, J. M., Sheeran, P., Webb, T. L., Martijn, C., & Miles, E. (2015). A meta-analytic review of stand-alone interventions to improve body image. *PLoS One*, 10, 9. https://doi.org/10.1371/journal.pone.0139177

American Psychiatric Association. (2013). *Diagnostic and Statistical Manual of Mental Disorders: DSM-5*. Washington, D.C: American Psychiatric Association. (under Alcohol Use Disorders)

Bardone-Cone, A. M., Harney, M. B., Maldonado, C. R., Lawson, M. A., *et al.* (2010). Defining recovery from an eating disorder: Conceptualization, validation, and examination of psychosocial functioning and psychiatric comorbidity. *Behaviour Research and Therapy*, 48(3), 194–202. https://doi.org/10.1016/j.brat.2009.11.001

Barker, M.J. (2018). *The Psychology of Sex*. London: Routledge and Psychology Press.

Barker, M.J. & Hancock, J. (2017). *Enjoy Sex (How, When and If You Want To): A Practical and Inclusive Guide*. London: Icon Books.

Behar, R., Arancibia, M., Sepúlveda, E., & Muga, A. (2016). Child Sexual Abuse as a Risk Factor in Eating Disorders. In N. Morton (ed.), *Eating Disorders* (pp.149–171). New York, NY: Nova Science.

Betz, D. E., Sabik, N. J., & Ramsey, L. R. (2019). Ideal comparisons: Body ideals harm women's body image through social comparison. *Body Image*, 29, 100–109. https://doi.org/10.1016.2019.03.004

Binik, Y. & Hall, K. (2014). *Principles and Practice of Sex Therapy*. New York, NY: Guilford Press.

Birnbaum, G. E., Reis, H. T., Mikulincer, M., Gillath, O., & Orpaz, A. (2006). When sex is more than just sex: Attachment orientations, sexual experience, and relationship quality. *Journal of Personality and Social Psychology*, 91, 929–943.

Bohane, L., Maguire, N., & Richardson, T. (2017). Resilients, overcontrollers and undercontrollers: A systematic review of the utility of a personality typology method in understanding adult mental health problems. *Clinical Psychology Review*, 57, 75–92. https://doi.org/10.1016/j.cpr.2017.07.005

Brennan, K. A., Clark, C. L., & Shaver, P. R. (1998). Self-Report Measurement of Adult Attachment: An Integrative Overview. In J. A. Simpson & W. S. Rholes (eds), *Attachment Theory and Close Relationships* (pp.46–76). New York, NY: Guilford Press.

Brewerton, T. D. (2007). Eating disorders, trauma, and comorbidity: Focus on PTSD. *Eating Disorders*, 15(4), 285–304.

Brotto, L. A. & Heiman, J. R. (2007). Mindfulness in sex therapy: Applications for women with sexual difficulties following gynecologic cancer. *Sexual and Relationship Therapy*, 22(1), 3–11. https://doi.org/10.1080/14681990601153298

Brooks, S. J., Rask-Andersen, M., Benedict, C., & Schiöth, H. B. (2012). A debate on current eating disorder diagnoses in light of neurobiological findings: Is it time for a spectrum model? *BMC Psychiatry*, 12, 76. https://doi.org/10.1186/1471-244X-12-76

Buelens, T., Luyckx, K., Verschueren, M., Schoevaerts, K., *et al.* (2020). Temperament and character traits of female eating disorder patients with(out) non-suicidal self-injury. *Journal of Clinical Medicine*, 9(4), 1207. https://doi.org/10.3390/jcm9041207

Burns, D. D. (1980). *Feeling Good: The New Mood Therapy*. New York, NY: The Penguin Group.

Burychka, D., Miragall, M., & Baños, R. M. (2021). Towards a comprehensive understanding of body image: Integrating positive body image, embodiment and self-compassion. *Psychologica Belgica*, 61(1), 248–261.

Byers, E. S. (2011). Beyond the birds and the bees and was it good for you? Thirty years of research on sexual communication. *Canadian Psychology/Psychologie Canadienne*, 52, 20.

Calogero, R. M., Tantleff-Dunn, S., & Thompson, J. K. (eds). (2011). Objectification Theory: An Introduction. In R. M. Calogero, S. Tantleff-Dunn, & J. K. Thompson (eds), *Self-Objectification in Women: Causes, Consequences, and Counteractions* (pp.3–21). Washington, DC: American Psychological Association. https://doi.org/10.1037/12304-001

Canadian Forces Morale & Welfare Services. (n.d.). Intimate Relationships Continuum and Chart. Retrieved July 8, 2025, from https://cfmws.ca/support-services/health-wellness/healthyrelationships/tip-sheets/intimate-relationships-continuum-and-chart

Cash, T. F. (2008). *The Body Image Workbook*. Oakland, CA: New Harbinger Publications.

Cash, T. F. & Smolak, L. (eds). (2011). *Body Image: A Handbook of Science, Practice, and Prevention* (2nd ed.). New York, NY: Guilford Press.

Cassin, S. E. & von Ranson, K. M. (2005). Personality and eating disorders: A decade in review. *Clinical Psychology Review*, 25(7), 895–916. https://doi.org/10.1016/j.cpr.2005.04.012

Castellini, G., Lelli, L., Ricca, V., & Maggi, M. (2016). Sexuality in eating disorders patients: Etiological factors, sexual dysfunction and identity issues. A systematic review. *Hormone Molecular Biology and Clinical Investigation*, 25(2), 71–90.

Chen, L. P., Murad, M. H., Paras, M. L., Colbenson, K. M., *et al.* (2010). Sexual abuse and lifetime diagnosis of psychiatric disorders: Systematic review and meta-analysis. *Mayo Clinic Proceedings*, 85(7), 618–629.

Clinebell, H. & Clinebell, C. H. (1970). *The Intimate Marriage*. New York, NY: Harper & Row.

Connors, M. E. & Morse, W. (1993). Sexual abuse and eating disorders: A review. *International Journal of Eating Disorders*, 13(1), 1–11.

Cook-Cottone, C. P. (2020). *Embodiment and the Treatment of Eating Disorders: The Body as a Resource in Recovery*. New York, NY: W. W. Norton & Company.

Cook-Cottone, C. P. & Guyker, W. M. (2018). The development and validation of the Mindful Self-Care Scale (MSCS): An assessment of practices that support positive embodiment. *Mindfulness*, 9(1), 161–175.

Cortés-García, L., Takkouche, B., Seoane, G., & Senra, C. (2019). Mediators linking insecure attachment to eating symptoms: A systematic review and meta-analysis. *PloS One*, 14(3), e0213099.

Cwynar-Horta, J. (2016). The commodification of the body positive movement on Instagram. *Stream: Interdisciplinary Journal of Communication*, 8(2), 36–56. https://doi.org/10.21810/strm.v8i2.203

Dalle Grave, R. & Calugi, S. (2020). *Cognitive Behavior Therapy for Adolescents with Eating Disorders*. New York, NY: Guilford Press.

Delvecchio, E., Di Riso, D., Salcuni, S., Lis, A., & George, C. (2014). Anorexia and attachment: Dysregulated defense and pathological mourning. *Frontiers in Psychology*, 5, 1218.

Don Morgan, C., Wederman, M. W., & Pryor, T. L. (1995). Sexual functioning and attitudes of eating-disordered women: A follow-up study. *Journal of Sex & Marital Therapy*, 21(2), 67–77.

Dunkley, C. R., Gorzalka, B. B., & Brotto, L. A. (2016). Disordered eating and sexual insecurities in young women. *Canadian Journal of Human Sexuality*, 25(2), 138–147. https://doi.org/10.3138/cjhs.252-A6

Dunkley, C. R., Gorzalka, B. B., & Brotto, L. A. (2020). Associations between sexual function and disordered eating among undergraduate women: An emphasis on sexual pain and distress. *Journal of Sex & Marital Therapy*, 46(1), 18–34. https://doi.org/10.1080/0092623X.2019.1626307

Dunkley, C. R., Svatko, Y., & Brotto, L. A. (2020). Eating disorders and sexual function reviewed: A trans-diagnostic, dimensional perspective. *Current Sexual Health Reports*, 12(1), 1–14. https://doi.org/10.1007/s11930-020-00236-w

Dunne, J. (2018). Mindfulness in anorexia nervosa: An integrated review of the literature. *Journal of the American Psychiatric Nurses Association*, 24(2), 109–117. https://doi.org/10.1177/1078390317711250

Duray-Parmentier, C., Nielens, N., Gourdin, M., & Janne, P. (2022). Eating disorders as an alternative to sexuality – how does eating disorders affect sexuality? *International Journal of Complementary and Alternative Medicine*, 15(1), 65–70. https://doi.org/10.15406/ijcam.2022.15.00591

Eddy, K. T., Novotny, C. M., & Westen, D. (2004). Sexuality, personality, and eating disorders. *Eating Disorders*, 12(3), 191–208. https://doi.org/10.1080/10640260490481410

Elliot, A. J. (2008). Approach and Avoidance Motivation. In A. J. Elliot (ed.), *Handbook of Approach and Avoidance Motivation* (pp.3–14). New York, NY: Psychology Press.

Erbil, N. (2013). The relationships between sexual function, body image, and body mass index among women. *Sexuality and Disability*, 31, 63–70. https://doi.org/10.1007/s11195-012-9258-4

Fairburn, C. G., Cooper, Z., Doll, H. A., & Welch, S. L. (1999). Risk factors for anorexia nervosa: Three integrated case-control comparisons. *Archives of General Psychiatry*, 56(5), 468–476.

Fairburn, C. G. & Harrison, P. J. (2003). Eating disorders. *The Lancet*, 361(9355), 407–416. https://doi.org/10.1016/S0140-6736(03)12378-1

Field, A. E., Camargo, C. A., Barr Taylor, C., Berkey, C. S., *et al.* (2001). Peer, parent, and media influences on the development of weight concerns and frequent dieting among preadolescent and adolescent girls and boys. *Pediatrics*, 107, 54–60. http://dx.doi.org/10.1542/peds.107.1.54

Fraley, R. C., Waller, N. G., & Brennan, K. A. (2000). An item-response theory analysis of self-report measures of adult attachment. *Journal of Personality and Social Psychology*, 78, 350–365.

Frederick, D. A., Gaganjyot, S., Morse, P. T., & Swami, V. (2016). Correlates of appearance and weight satisfaction in a U.S. national sample: Personality, attachment style, television viewing, self-esteem, and life satisfaction. *Body Image*, 17, 191–203. https://doi.org/10.1016/j.bodyim.2016.04.001

Gander, M., Sevecke, K., & Buchheim, A. (2015). Eating disorders in adolescence: Attachment issues from a developmental perspective. *Frontiers in Psychology*, 6, 1136.

Gewirtz-Meydan, A. & Lahav, Y. (2021). Childhood sexual abuse and sexual motivations: The role of dissociation. *Journal of Sex Research*, 58(9), 1151–1160. https://doi.org/10.1080/00224499.2020.1808564

Ghizzani, A. & Montomoli, M. (2000). Anorexia nervosa and sexuality in women: A review. *Journal of Sex Education and Therapy*, 25(1), 80–88. https://doi.org/10.1080/01614576.2000.11074332

Gilbert, K., Hall, K., & Codd, R. T. (2020). Radically open dialectical behavior therapy: Social signaling, transdiagnostic utility and current evidence. *Psychology Research and Behavior Management*, 13, 19–28. https://doi.org/10.2147/PRBM.S201848

Goldstein, A., Pukall, C. F., & Goldstein, I. (2011). *When Sex Hurts: A Woman's Guide to Banishing [sic] Sexual Pain*. Sydney: Read How You Want.

Haines, S. (2007). *Healing Sex: A Mind-Body Approach to Healing Sexual Trauma*. San Francisco, CA: Cleis.

Hall, K., Astrachan-Fletcher, E., & Simic, M. (2022). *The Radically Open DBT Workbook for Eating Disorders: From Overcontrol and Loneliness to Recovery and Connection*. Oakland, CA: New Harbinger Publications.

Halliwell, E. (2015). Future directions for positive body image research. *Body Image*, 14, 177–189. http://dx.doi.org/10.1016/j.bodyim.2015.03.003

Hambleton, A., Pepin, G., Le, A., Maloney, D., *et al.* (2022). Psychiatric and medical comorbidities of eating disorders: Findings from a rapid review of the literature. *Journal of Eating Disorders*, 10(1), 132. https://doi.org/10.1186/s40337-022-00654-2

Hardell, A. (2016). *The ABCs of LGBT+*. Miami, FL: Mango.

Harper, F. (2019a). *Unfuck Your Boundaries: Build Better Relationships Through Consent, Communication, and Expressing Your Needs*. Portland, OR: Microcosm Publishing.

Harper, F. (2019b). *Unfuck Your Intimacy: Using Science for Better Relationships, Sex, and Dating*. Portland, OR: Microcosm Publishing.

Hempel, R. J., Rushbrook, S. C., O'Mahen, H., & Lynch, T. R. (2018). How to Differentiate Overcontrol from Undercontrol: Findings from the RefraMED Study and Guidelines from Clinical Practice, 12.

Hempel, R. J., Vanderbleek, E., & Lynch, T. R. (2018). Radically open DBT: Targeting emotional loneliness in anorexia nervosa. *Eating Disorders*, 26(1), 92–104.

Hendrix, H. (1990). *Getting the Love You Want: A Guide for Couples*. New York, NY: Perennial Library.

Horesh, N., Sommerfeld, E., Wolf, M., Zubery, E., & Zalsman, G. (2015). Father-daughter relationship and the severity of eating disorders. *European Psychiatry*, 30(1), 114–120.

Homan, K. J., Sedlak, B. L., & Boyd, E. A. (2014). Gratitude buffers the adverse effect of viewing the thin ideal on body dissatisfaction. *Body Image*, 11(3), 245–250. https://doi.org/10.1016/j.bodyim.2014.03.005

Impett, E. A. & Peplau, L. A. (2002). Why some women consent to unwanted sex with a dating partner: Insights from attachment theory. *Psychology of Women Quarterly*, 26(4), 360–370.

Implett, E. A. & Peplau, L. A. (2003). Sexual compliance: Gender motivational and relationship perspectives. *The Journal of Sex Research*, 40(1), 87–100.

Isaksson, M., Ghaderi, A., Wolf-Arehult, M., & Ramklimt, M. (2021). Overcontrolled, undercontrolled, and resilient personality styles among patients with eating disorders. *Journal of Eating Disorders*, 9, 47. https://doi.org/10.1186/s40337-021-00400-0

Kang, Y., Zheng, L., & Zheng, Y. (2016). Sex and eating: Relationships based on wanting and liking. *Frontiers in Psychology*, 6, 2044. https://doi.org/10.3389/fpsyg.2015.02044

Kaplan, H. (1988). *The Illustrated Manual of Sex Therapy*. New York, NY: Routledge.

Keel, P. K. & Forney, K. J. (2013). Psychosocial risk factors for eating disorders. *International Journal of Eating Disorders*, 46(5), 433–439. https://doi.org/10.1002/eat.22094

Kelly, L. (1987). The Continuum of Sexual Violence. In J. Hanmer & M. Maynard (eds), *Women, Violence and Social Controls*. Atlantic Highlands, NJ: Humanities Press International.

Keogh, K., Booth, R., Baird, K., Gibson, J., *et al.* (2016). The Radical Openness Group: A controlled trial with 3-month follow-up. *Practice Innovations*, 1, 129–143. https://doi.org/10.1037/pri0000023

Kotera, Y. & Rhodes, C. (2019). Pathways to sex addiction: Relationships with adverse childhood experience, attachment, narcissism, self-compassion and motivation in a gender-balanced sample. *Sexual Addiction & Compulsivity*, 26(1/2), 54.

Krause, E. D., Mendelson, T., & Lynch, T. R. (in press). Childhood emotion invalidation and adult psychological distress: The mediating role of emotion inhibition. *Journal of Child Abuse & Neglect*.

Krause, E. D., Robins, C. J., & Lynch, T. R. (2000). A mediational model relating sociotropy, ambivalence over emotional expression and eating disorder symptoms. *Psychology of Women Quarterly*, 24, 328–335.

La Rocque, C. L. & Cioe, J. (2011). An evaluation of the relationship between body image and sexual avoidance. *Journal of Sex Research*, 48(4), 397–408. https://doi.org/10.1080/00224499.2010.499522

Levine, A. & Heller, R. (2011). *Attached: The New Science of Adult Attachment and How It Can Help You Find – and Keep – Love*. New York, NY: Penguin.

Levine, S. B., Risen, C. B., & Althof, S. E. (2016). *Handbook of Clinical Sexuality for Mental Health Professionals*. New York, NY: Routledge.

Levinson, C. A., Williams, B. M., & Christian, C. (2020). What are the emotions underlying feeling fat and fear of weight gain? *Journal of Affective Disorders*, 277, 146–152. https://doi.org/10.1016/j.jad.2020.08.012

Lew-Starowicz, M., Lewczuk, K., Nowakowska, I., Kraus, S., & Gola, M. (2020). Compulsive sexual behavior and dysregulation of emotion. *Sexual Medicine Reviews*, 8(2), 191–205. https://doi.org/10.1016/j.sxmr.2019.10.003

Linehan, M. M. (2014). DBT (R) *Skills Training Handouts and Worksheets* (2nd ed.). New York, NY: Guilford Publications.

Love, B. (1992). *Encyclopedia of Unusual Sex Practices*. New York, NY: Barricade Books.

Lynch, T. R. (2018a). *Radically Open Dialectical Behavior Therapy: Theory and Practice for Treating Disorders of Overcontrol*. Reno, NV: Context Press, an imprint of New Harbinger Publications.

Lynch, T. R. (2018b). *The Skills Training Manual for Radically Open Dialectical Behavior Therapy: A Clinician's Guide for Treating Disorders of Overcontrol*. Revo, NV: Context Press, an imprint of New Harbinger Publications.

Lynch, T. R., Gray, K. L., Hempel, R. J., Titley, M., Chen, E. Y., & O'Mahen, H. A. (2013). Radically open-dialectical behavior therapy for adult anorexia nervosa: Feasibility and outcomes from an inpatient program. *BMC Psychiatry*, 13, 293. https://doi.org/10.1186/1471-244X-13-293

Lynch, T. R., Hempel, R. J., Whalley, B., Byford, S., et al. (2020). Refractory depression – mechanisms and efficacy of radically open dialectical behaviour therapy (RefraMED): Findings of a randomised trial on benefits and harms. *The British Journal of Psychiatry*, 216(4), 204–212. https://doi.org/10.1192/bjp.2019.53

Lynch, T. R., Krause, E. D., Morse, J. Q., Mendelson, T., Crozier, J., & LaBar, K. S. (2001). Role of Emotion Suppression in Classical Fear Conditioning. In T. R. Lynch (Chair), Experiential Avoidance and Psychopathology: Recent Research and Methodological Developments. Symposium conducted at the Association for the Advancement of Behavior Therapy 35th Annual Convention, Philadelphia.

Lynch, T. R., Robins, C. J., Morse, J. Q., & Krause, E. D. (2001). A mediational model relating affect intensity, emotion inhibition, and psychological distress. *Behavior Therapy*, 32, 519–536.

Maltz, W. (2012). *The Sexual Healing Journey*. New York, NY: HarperCollins.

Mangweth-Matzek, B., Rupp, C. I., Hausmann, A., Kemmler, G., & Biebl, W. (2007). Menarche, puberty, and first sexual activities in eating-disordered patients as compared with a psychiatric and a nonpsychiatric control group. *International Journal of Eating Disorders*, 40(8), 705–710.

McCarthy, B. & McCarthy, E. (2003). *Rekindling Desire*. New York, NY: Brunner-Routledge.

McCrae, R. R., Costa, P. T., Jr., Ostendorf, F., Angleitner, A., et al. (2000). Nature over nurture: Temperament, personality, and life span development. *Journal of Personality and Social Psychology*, 78(1), 173–186. https://doi.org/10.1037/0022-3514.78.1.173

Meguerditchian, C., Samuelian-Massat, C., Valéro, R., Begu-Le Corroller, A., et al. (2009). The impact of weight normalization on quality of recovery in anorexia nervosa. *Journal of the American College of Nutrition*, 28(4), 397–404. https://doi.org/10.1080/07315724.2009.10718102

Mehak, A. & Racine, S. E. (2020). Understanding "feeling fat" and its underlying mechanisms: The importance of multimethod measurement. *The International Journal of Eating Disorders*, 53(9), 1400–1404. https://doi.org/10.1002/eat.23336

Menzel, J. E. & Levine, M. P. (2011). Embodying Experiences and the Promotion of Positive Body Image: The Example of Competitive Athletics. In R. M. Calogero, S. Tantleff-Dunn, & J. K. Thompson (eds), *Self-Objectification in Women: Causes, Consequences, and Counteractions* (pp.163–186). Washington, DC: American Psychological Association. https://doi.org/10.1037/12304-008

Metz, M. (2017). *Cognitive-Behavioral Therapy for Sexual Dysfunction*. Abingdon, UK: Routledge.

Mintz, L. B. (2017). *Becoming Cliterate: Why Orgasm Equality Matters—And How to Get It*. San Francisco, CA: HaperOne.

Morgan, J. F., Lacey, J. H., & Reid, F. (1999). Anorexia nervosa: Changes in sexuality during weight restoration. *Psychosomatic Medicine*, 61(4), 541–545.

Morin, J. (1996). *The Erotic Mind: Unlocking the Inner Sources of Passion and Fulfillment*. New York, NY: Harper Perennial.

Nagoski, E. (2015). *Come As You Are: The Surprising New Science that Will Transform Your Sex Life*. New York, NY: Simon & Schuster Paperbacks.

Nikodijevic, A., Buck, K., Fuller-Tyszkiewicz, M., de Paoli, T., & Krug, I. (2018). Body checking and body avoidance in eating disorders: Systematic review and meta-analysis. *European Eating Disorders Review: The Journal of the Eating Disorders Association*, 26(3), 159-185. https://doi.org/10.1002/erv.2585

Orzolek-Kronner, C. (2002). The effect of attachment theory in the development of eating disorders: Can symptoms be proximity-seeking? *Child and Adolescent Social Work Journal*, 19, 421-435. https://doi.org/10.1023/A:1021141612634

Paterson, R. J. (2000). *The Assertiveness Workbook: How to Express Your Ideas and Stand Up For Yourself at Work and in Relationships*. Oakland, CA: New Harbinger Publications.

Peplau, L. A., Frederick, D. A., Yee, C., Maisel, N., Lever, J., & Ghavami, N. (2009). Body image satisfaction in heterosexual, gay, and lesbian adults. *Archives of Sexual Behavior*, 38(5), 713-725.

Perel, E. (2007). *Mating in Captivity*. New York, NY: HarperCollins.

Pinheiro, A. P., Raney, T. J., Thornton, L. M., Fichter, M. M., *et al.* (2010). Sexual functioning in women with eating disorders. *International Journal of Eating Disorders*, 43(2), 123-129.

Porges, S. W. (2011). *The Polyvagal Theory: Neurophysiological Foundations of Emotions, Attachment, Communication, and Self-Regulation*. New York, NY: W. W. Norton & Company.

Powell, A. (2010). *Sex, Power and Consent: Youth Culture and the Unwritten Rules*. Melbourne, Australia: Cambridge University Press.

Price, C. J. & Hooven, C. (2018). Interoceptive awareness skills for emotion regulation: Theory and approach of Mindful Awareness in Body-Oriented Therapy (MABT). *Frontiers in Psychology*, 9, 798. https://doi.org/10.3389/fpsyg.2018.00798

Prochaska, J. O. & DiClemente, C. C. (1983). Stages and processes of self-change of smoking: Toward an integrative model of change. *Journal of Consulting and Clinical Psychology*, 51(3), 390-395. http://doi.org/10.1037/0022-006X.51.3.390

Pujols, Y., Meston, C. M., & Seal, B. N. (2010). The association between sexual satisfaction and body image in women. *The Journal of Sexual Medicine*, 7(2), 905-916. https://doi.org/10.1111/j.1743-6109.2009.01604

Rehman, U. S., Balan, D., Sutherland, S., & McNeil, J. (2019). Understanding barriers to sexual communication. *Journal of Social and Personal Relationships*, 36, 2605-2623.

Ringer, F. & McKinsey Crittenden, P. (2007). Eating disorders and attachment: The effects of hidden family processes on eating disorders. *European Eating Disorders Review*, 15(2), 119-130.

Rosenau, D. (1997). *A Celebration of Sex*. Nashville, TN: Thomas Nelson.

Ruscitti, C., Rufino, K., Goodwin, N., & Wagner, R. (2016). Difficulties in emotion regulation in patients with eating disorders. *Borderline Personality Disorder and Emotion Dysregulation*, 3, 3. https://doi.org/10.1186/s40479-016-0037-1

Safer, D., Telch, C., & Chen, E. (2017). *Dialectical Behavior Therapy for Binge Eating and Bulimia*. New York, NY: Guilford Press.

Safer, D., Adler, S., & Masson, P. (2018). *The DBT Solution for Emotional Eating: A Proven Program to Break the Cycle of Bingeing and Out-of-Control Eating*. New York, NY: Guilford Press.

Sansone, R. A. & Sansone, L. A. (2011). Sexual behavior in borderline personality: A review. *Innovations in Clinical Neuroscience*, 8(2), 14-18.

Satinsky, S., Reece, M., Dennis, B., Sanders, S., & Bardzell, S. (2012). An assessment of body appreciation and its relationship to sexual function in women. *Body Image*, 9(1), 137-144. https://doi.org/10.1016/j.bodyim.2011.09.007

Scheel, J. (2011). *When Food Is Family: A Loving Approach to Heal Eating Disorders*. Bedford, IN: Idyll Arbor.

Schoenmakers, E. C., van Tilburg, T. G., & Fokkema, T. (2015). Problem-focused and emotion-focused coping options and loneliness: how are they related? *European Journal of Ageing*, 12(2), 153-161. https://doi.org/10.1007/s10433-015-0336-1

Schreiber, R. E. & Veilleux, J. C. (2022). Perceived invalidation of emotion uniquely predicts affective distress: Implications for the role of interpersonal factors in emotional experience. *Personality and Individual Differences*, 184, 111191. https://doi.org/10.1016/j.paid.2021.111191

Segerstrom, S. C. & Smith, G. T. (2019). Personality and coping: Individual differences in responses to emotion. *Annual Review of Psychology*, 70(1), 651-671.

Shafran, R., Fairburn, C. G., Robinson, P., & Lask, B. (2004). Body checking and its avoidance in eating disorders. *The International Journal of Eating Disorders*, 35(1), 93-101. https://doi.org/10.1002/eat.10228

Shenk, C. E. & Fruzzetti, A. E. (2011). The impact of validating and invalidating responses on emotional reactivity. *Journal of Social and Clinical Psychology*, 30(2), 163-183. https://doi.org/10.1521/jscp.2011.30.2.163

Siegel, D. (2015). *The Developing Mind, Second Edition: How Relationships and the Brain Interact to Shape Who We Are.* New York, NY: Guilford Press.

Srivastava, S., Tamir, M., McGonigal, K. M., John, O. P., & Gross, J. J. (2009). The social costs of emotional suppression: A prospective study of the transition to college. *Journal of Personality and Social Psychology*, 96(4), 883–897. https://doi.org/10.1037/a0014755

Stice, E. & Bohon, C. (2012). Eating Disorders. In T. Beauchaine & S. Linshaw (eds), *Child and Adolescent Psychopathology* (2nd ed.). New York, NY: Wiley.

Tasca, G. A., Ritchie, K., & Balfour, L. (2011). Implications of attachment theory and research for the assessment and treatment of eating disorders. *Psychotherapy (Chic)*, 48(3), 249–259. https://doi.org/10.1037/a0022423

Tasca, G. A., Taylor, D., Ritchie, K., & Balfour, L. (2004). Attachment predicts treatment completion in an eating disorders partial hospital program among women with anorexia nervosa. *Journal of Personality Assessment*, 83(3), 201–212. https://doi.org/10.1207/s15327752jpa8303_04

Tiggemann, M., Hayden, S., Brown, Z., & Veldhuis, J. (2018). The effect of Instagram "likes" on women's social comparison and body dissatisfaction. *Body Image*, 26, 90–97. https://doi.org/10.1016/j.bodyim.2018.07.002

Tiggemann, M. & Kuring, J. K. (2004). The role of body objectification in disordered eating and depressed mood. *British Journal of Clinical Psychology*, 43, 299–311. https://doi.org/10.1348/0144665031752925

Tolman, D. L., Bowman, C. P., & Fahs, B. (2014). Sexuality and Embodiment. In D. L. Tolman, L. M. Diamond, J. A. Bauermeister, W. H. George, J. G. Pfaus, & L. M. Ward (eds), *APA Handbook of Sexuality and Psychology, Vol. 1. Person-Based Approaches* (pp.759–804). Washington, DC: American Psychological Association. https://doi.org/10.1037/14193-025

Tozzi, F., Sullivan, P. F., Fear, J. L., McKenzie, J., & Bulik, C. M. (2003). Causes and recovery in anorexia nervosa: The patient's perspective. *International Journal of Eating Disorders*, 33(2), 143–154.

Troscianko, E. (2009). The complicated relationship between anorexia and sex. *Psychology Today*. Retrieved January 13, 2022, from www.psychologytoday.com/us/blog/hunger-artist/201902/the-complicated-relationship-between-anorexia-and-sex

Vanderbleek, E. & Gilbert, K. (2018). Too much versus too little control: The etiology, conceptualization, and treatment implications of overcontrol and undercontrol. *The Behavior Therapist*, 41(3), 125–131.

Walker, D. C., White, E. K., & Srinivasan, V. J. (2018). A meta-analysis of the relationships between body checking, body image avoidance, body image dissatisfaction, mood, and disordered eating. *International Journal of Eating Disorders*, 51(8), 745–770. https://doi.org/10.1002/eat.22867

Weaver, A. & Byers, E. (2006). The relationships among body image, body mass index, exercise, and sexual functioning in heterosexual women. *Psychology of Women Quarterly*, 30, 333–339. https://doi.org/10.1111/j.1471-6402.2006.00308.x

Weiner, L. & Avery-Clark, C. (2017). *Sensate Focus in Sex Therapy: The Illustrated Manual.* New York, NY: Routledge.

Weinstein, A., Katz, L., Eberhardt, H., Cohen, K., & Lejoyeux, M. (2015). Sexual compulsion: Relationship with sex, attachment and sexual orientation. *Journal of Behavioral Addictions*, 4(1), 22.

Wiederman, M. W. (1996). Women, sex, and food: A review of research on eating disorders and sexuality. *Journal of Sex Research*, 33(4), 301–311.

Wildes, J. E., Marcus, M. D., Crosby, R. D., Ringham, R. M., et al. (2011). The clinical utility of personality subtypes in patients with anorexia nervosa. *Journal of Consulting and Clinical Psychology*, 79(5), 665–674. https://doi.org/10.1037/a0024597

Wincze, J. (2009). *Enhancing Sexuality: A Problem-Solving Approach to Treating Dysfunction (Therapist Guide).* Oxford, UK: Oxford University Press.

Woertman, L. & Van den Brink, F. (2012). Body image and female sexual functioning and behavior: A review. *Journal of Sex Research*, 49(2–3), 184–211.

Wonderlich, S. A., Crosby, R. D., Mitchell, J. E., Thompson, K. M., et al. (2001). Eating disturbance and sexual trauma in childhood and adulthood. *International Journal of Eating Disorders*, 30(4), 401–412.

Yean, C., Benau, E., Dakanalis, A., Hormes, J. M., Perone, J., & Timko, A. (2013). The relationship of sex and sexual orientation to self-esteem, body shape satisfaction, and eating disorder symptomatology. *Frontiers in Psychology*, 4, 887.

Zachrisson, H. & Kulbotten, G. (2006). Attachment in anorexia nervosa: An exploration of associations with eating disorder psychopathology and psychiatric symptoms. *Eating and Weight Disorders*, 11(4), 163–170.

Zapf, J. L., Greiner, J., & Carroll, J. (2008). Attachment styles and male sex addiction. *Sexual Addiction and Compulsivity*, 15(2), 158–175.

Further Reading

Couple focused

Discovering Your Couple Sexual Style: Sharing Desire, Pleasure, and Satisfaction by Emily McCarthy and Barry McCarthy

Enduring Desire: Your Guide to Lifelong Intimacy by Michael E. Metz and Barry W. McCarthy

The Return of Desire: A Guide to Rediscovering Your Sexual Passion by Gina Ogden

Transforming Sexual Narratives: A Relational Approach to Sex Therapy by Suzanne Iasenza

Sexual Awareness: Your Guide to Healthy Couple Sexuality by Barry McCarthy

Couple Sexuality After 60: Intimate, Pleasurable, and Satisfying by Emily McCarthy and Barry McCarthy

Mating in Captivity: Unlocking Erotic Intelligence by Esther Perel

Sex without Stress: A Couple's Guide to Overcoming Disappointment, Avoidance & Pressure by Jessa Zimmerman

Pleasure/Fantasy/Kink focused

Enjoy Sex: A Practical and Inclusive Guide by Dr. Meg-John Barker and Justin Hancock

Enhancing Sexuality: A Problem-Solving Approach to Treating Dysfunction by John Wincze

Tell Me What You Want: The Science of Sexual Desire and How It Can Help You Improve Your Sex Life by Justin Lehmiller

Consensual nonmonogamy focused

The Ethical Slut: A Practical Guide to Polyamory, Open Relationships, and Other Freedoms in Sex and Love by Janet W. Hardy and Dossie Easton

Polysecure: Attachment, Trauma and Consensual Nonmonogamy by Jessica Fern

Intimacy focused

Unf*ck Your Intimacy: Using Science for Better Relationships, Sex, and Dating by Faith G. Harper

Attached: The New Science of Adult Attachment and How It Can Help You Find – and Keep – Love by Amir Levine and Rachel Heller

Primarily vulva/vagina focused

Come As You Are: The Surprising New Science that Will Transform Your Sex Life by Emily Nagoski

Women's Anatomy of Arousal: Secret Maps to Buried Pleasure by Sheri Winston

When Sex Hurts: A Woman's Guide to Banishing Sexual Pain by Andrew Goldstein, Caroline Pukall, and Irwin Goldstein

Becoming Cliterate: Why Orgasm Equality Matters—and How to Get It by Dr. Laurie Mintz

Primarily penis/testicles focused

Coping with Premature Ejaculation: How to Overcome PE, Please Your Partner & Have Great Sex by Barry McCarthy and Michael E. Metz

Coping with Erectile Dysfunction: How to Regain Confidence and Enjoy Great Sex by Barry McCarthy and Michael E. Metz

Contemporary Male Sexuality: Confronting Myths and Promoting Change by Barry McCarthy and Emily McCarthy

The New Male Sexuality: The Truth About Men, Sex, and Pleasure by Bernie Zilbergeld

LGBTQIA+ focused

The ABC's of LGBT+: Gender Identity Book for Teens, Teen & Young Adult LGBT Issues by Ash Hardell

Queer Sex: A Trans and Non-Binary Guide to Intimacy, Pleasure, and Relationships by Juno Roche

Cracking the Erotic Code: Helping Gay Men Understand their Sexual Fantasies by Dr. Joe Kort

Trauma focused

The Body Keeps the Score: Brain, Mind, and Body in the Healing of Trauma by Bessel van der Kolk

Coping with Trauma-Related Dissociation: Skills Training for Patients and Therapists by Suzette Boon, Kathy Steele, and Onno van der Hart

Life, Reinvented: A Guide to Healing from Sexual Trauma for Survivors and Loved Ones by Erin Carpenter

Eating disorder focused

DBT Solution for Emotional Eating: A Proven Program to Break the Cycle of Bingeing and Out-of-Control Eating by Debra L. Safer, Sarah Adler, and Philip C. Masson

Dialectical Behavior Therapy for Binge Eating and Bulimia by Debra L. Safer, Christy F. Telch, and Eunice Y. Chen

Radically Open Behavior DBT Workbook for Eating Disorders: From Overcontrol and Loneliness to Recovery and Connection by Karyn D. Hall, Ellen Astrachan-Fletcher, and Mima Simic

When Food Is Family: A Loving Approach to Heal Eating Disorders by Judy Scheel

Life without ED: How One Woman Declared Independence from Her Eating Disorder and How You Can Too by Jenni Schaefer

Goodbye Ed, Hello Me: Recover from your Eating Disorder and Fall in Love with Life by Jenni Schaefer

Intuitive Eating: A Revolutionary Anti-Diet Approach by Evelyn Tribole and Elyse Resch